June 10 2006

through the eyes of wounded men

An Examination of the Interior Psychological Constructs of Men who Perpetrate Intimate Partner Violence

By

Herb Robinson, Ph. D.

authorHOUSE™

1663 LIBERTY DRIVE, SUITE 200
BLOOMINGTON, INDIANA 47403
(800) 839-8640
WWW.AUTHORHOUSE.COM

First published by AuthorHouse 08/23/05

ISBN: 1-4208-3456-8 (sc)
ISBN: 1-4208-3597-1 (dj)

Library of Congress Control Number: 2005901923

Printed in the United States of America
Bloomington, Indiana

This book is printed on acid-free paper.

OTHER WRITINGS BY HERB ROBINSON, Ph. D.

GONZAGA UNIVERSITY DOCTORAL PROGRAM IN LEADERSHIP STUDIES

RESPONSE OF COMMITTEE TO THE DISSERTATION

Dr. Shan Ferch, Ph.D. .... Chair of Committee

"Excellent, Exquisite, Great Scholarly Approach!" "Awesome!" "Beautiful!"

"The comments given to you [from the committee] regarding the exquisite and powerful writing you've done are very uncommon."

"It has been a great experience working with you."

"I admire the tenacity that is clearly a strength in you. You are a person of depth and richness."

"One of the best literature reviews I've read in my history in the Gonzaga Doctoral Program."

"It is uncommon for the committee to talk about publishing a document at the defense phase of the dissertation process."

Dr. Sandra Wilson, Ph. D. .... Committee Member

"Well written; what you have written is very, very good."

"Keep the review of the literature chapter, Chapter II, intact because it is publishable."

Dr. Nancy Isaacson, Ph. D. ....Committee Member

"Magnificent...........an honor to read"

"When I began reading I could hardly put it down. It provided some new insights for me."

"After reading Herb's dissertation, I looked at my husband differently and felt I understood him better."

"This deserves to be published."

"A significant, substantial work."

DEDICATION

This dissertation is dedicated to some of the most important people in my life. It is dedicated to Herbert Henry Robinson, II, my late father, from whom I always felt love and admiration. To Alberta Robinson, my mother, for her untiring care for me.

It is dedicated to my five children: Cheri Dean Henseth, David Robinson, Peri Elizabeth Layton, Tanda Rene Lunt, and Gaila Darie Robinson, and to their mother, the late Georgia Fairchild. My children have made the life I know possible by the quality of their presence in it.

It is also dedicated to a most special person who has always had as much or more excitement about the years of work toward this goal as I have. Jean Rabe has been a significant cheerleader and has encouraged me to keep surging ahead when fatigue was present. I am always inspired by her.

ACKNOWLEDGMENTS

I am eternally grateful to Dr. Shann Ferch for making this endeavor possible. He was always present and available. He did an outstanding service to this project by his clear technical guidance, from which I learned a lot. Far beyond that, and not to diminish the technical support, he helped keep the fire of enthusiasm burning by his skill in constantly calling attention to the positive aspects of my work, and with that as his strong lead-in he would say, "The rest of the changes are nuts and bolts stuff that I'm sure you can do."

I was overwhelmed by the time and energy Dr. Sandi Wilson poured into my paper. I was also sometimes overwhelmed by the task. She made many positive suggestions for my work and, while in the process of responding to her comments, new insights awakened within me as I worked to improve the document. Over many years of knowing her and attending her classes, I received a great deal of patient support and encouragement from her.

When I was going to attend my proposal defense in October 2001, I was on the elevator to go up to the second floor. The door was about a foot from closing and this woman's arm reached in and pushed the door open. Dr. Nancy Isaacson rushed in and hugged me and thanked me for the proposal I had written. She said, "I'll see you in a couple of minutes upstairs." As the door shut and the elevator moved to the second floor, I was deeply moved. Her guidance and comments were of inestimable value, and her personal care also helped keep the fire of enthusiasm burning.

PREFACE –
A PERSONAL NOTE

Ever since I was a little kid I didn't want to be me. I wanted to be like Billy Widdleton. I walked like Billy Widdleton walked; I talked like Billy Widdleton talked; and I even got the same kind of clothes he wore. 'Nen Billy Widdleton changed. Billy Widdleton didn't even like me. He began to hang around Corkey Sabinson. He walked like Corkey Sabinson, and he talked like Corkey Sabinson. 'Nen I found out that Corkey Sabinson walked and talked like Freddy Vandeman. So here I am walking and talking like Billy Widdletons' version of Corkey Sabinson's imitation of Freddy Vandeman. I then found out that Freddy Vandeman walked and talked, of all things, like that dopey Kenny Wellington. And that little pest, he walks and talks like me.

I was born in a little house in an apple orchard on Peschastin Creek near Wenatchee, Washington on May 31, 1933 in the geographical center of Washington State. My parents, Henry and Alberta Robinson, within a couple of years moved to Eastern Washington, where I grew up in Otis Orchards, Washington. We lived on a small farm and it was an important means of our survival. It was almost the total sphere of my knowledge and identity — that five-acre farm. We were very poor.

A person, I believe, does the greatest amount of learning in the first five years of life. I started school in the first grade at the Otis Orchards Grade School in the fall of 1939. They made me sit at a desk. They put a pencil in my hand and had me put marks on a piece of paper. The ability to put things on a paper with that pencil became a measurement of my knowledge, my grades, and consequently, my estimate of myself.

I still wanted to run, play, climb on things and do adventurous discovery, so I didn't do so well at putting things on that piece of paper. My first awareness of my relative mental prowess came when I ended up in the dummy reading group in the first grade. There were three reading groups. There were the smart kids who got to be in the smart-kids reading group called the "Shining Stars." There was another group, it was called the "Elves" reading group. The leftovers ended up in the dummy reading group. It was called the "Red Apple" group. Now I might have been dumb, but I wasn't stupid. I knew I was in the dumbest group.

Each group was taken to the front of the class, sat in little chairs, read their stories; the rest of us were given an assignment, but we listened to the stories being read in the front of the room. The shining stars read stories on ahead of the rest of us, tee-heed at the jokes, and left me behind. They read *Mother Pig's Joke*. Mother Pig had an apple tree in her yard and was going to make apple pies for everyone in the community. However, Billy Goat came by, wanted some apples right now, butted the tree, knocked down some apples, and ate them. When Mother Pig made all her pies, Billy Goat showed up for his pie too. His pie looked beautiful, crust and all, but when he bit into it that's all it was — crust — no apples. Tee-hee hee, Tee-hee hee, Tee-hee hee. Later the "Red Apple" group finally got their turn to read *Mother Pig's Joke*. The same stories, now boringly familiar, were not as funny. We still feigned a weak Tee-hee, however. I started to catch on. I became a dummy reading group person.

So I grew up on a little farm, we were poor, and I was in the dummy reading group. I became a poor dumb country boy. I was born in an apple orchard, I grew up in an apple orchard in Otis Orchards, Washington, Billy Goat ate Mother Pig's apples, I was in the Red Apple reading group, and I like apples — how's them apples. My mother did do some homework guidance for me. Reading was hard. My mind always drifted off to more pleasant things. My dad also listened to me read. I kept getting stuck on the word "the." I can remember a few books I read for mandatory book reports later in school. Some of those were: *Horses I've Known* and *Smokey* by Will James. I read about Lewis and Clark, and about American Indians before the white man came. Later I read some Zane Gray books. I didn't know until later in college that I had a mild form of dyslexia, which made reading a rigorous endeavor. My mother did make sure we had some music. She bought us tonettes and made us practice them. That led to my joining the Otis Orchards grade school band. Since I had learned on the tonette, I wanted to play clarinet. The clarinets were all checked out and the only instrument left was a trombone. I took it. I took lessons in high school, played band-accompanied solos in the winter and spring musical concerts, took superior rating for my trombone solos in Eastern Washington music competitions, and in 1951 received a four-year scholarship to Gonzaga University in music. I had no study skills, spent my time in the Hub drinking coffee and playing pool and lost the scholarship. I then joined the Marine Corps, where I played first trombone with the San Diego Marine Band and later with the Spokane Symphony.

I got low grades all through school. I spent my years in school at Otis Orchards on my academic back, looking up admiringly at my more intelligent classmates. I had to take bonehead (now it's called remedial)

English several times. And my experience of flunking out at Gonzaga University in my freshman year and loosing my scholarship confirmed my poor dumb country boy self-image. So even though I have gone to school most of my life, I can still hear the whispers of the "Red Apple" reading group.

I spent the rest of my life, like anorexic women who think they are fat, trying to compensate for being dumb. I studied theology, which led to a degree in 1959, at Baptist Bible College, Springfield, Missouri; philosophy, Greek, and psychology which led to a B.A. from Whitworth College in Spokane, Washington in 1968, and the humanities, art, literature, music, and philosophy that led to a Master of Arts in College Teaching degree from Eastern Washington University, Cheney Washington, in 1976. I even taught college for a few years. I taught five philosophy courses: Introduction to Philosophy, Philosophical Ethics, Philosophy of Religion, Traditional and Symbolic Logic, Music History and Art History — trying to feel less dumb. One time, I remember, two of my friends came to visit. They were schoolteachers. They were coming up the walk, I saw them out of the window and internally said, "I need to be careful of my English with those two teachers coming here." Then it hit me as if I'd been slow to catch on. "Why, *I* am a college teacher! What's wrong with me?"

This leads to this endeavor. When Gonzaga University opened their Leadership in Education Doctoral program in 1980, I rushed to apply. I progressed through the course work. With all the classes completed and my school loan to repay, I sent resumes around the world and got a call from Fairbanks, Alaska. I was hired over the phone and drove up the road to Fairbanks in December of 1985.

In Fairbanks, Alaska I became the director of the community program to treat men arrested for domestic violence. I conducted some four or five groups a week and directed the activities of four counselors. I met each week in a staff meeting with about 25 women workers in the women's shelter where my office was located. I also fulfilled a grant and conducted courses in the Fairbanks Correctional Center, an Alaska Prison. I also taught courses through the University of Alaska in Fairbanks. This work in Alaska began my therapy work in earnest with men who were abusive in their relationships. Later I did the same kind of work in Juneau, Alaska, taught through the University of Alaska Southeast, and worked in the Lemon Creek Prison, an Alaska maximum-security cross-cultural prison.

I had a dissertation topic in progress when I went to Alaska and wrote on it while there. Since I had spent some 25 years in the ministry, I wanted to study that field. The title of that dissertation was: *An Examination of the Distinctive Personality Challenges of Ministers: A View from the Perspective of Gestalt Therapy Theory* — some 400 pages of detailed documentation. I worked on it fairly consistently over a period of seven years. Since I was out of the continental United States and didn't stay in touch with Gonzaga University and since I didn't work through their doctoral process, the dissertation was rejected. Twice now I had flunked out at Gonzaga University. My poor dumb country boy consciousness once again rang in my ears.

I was discouraged and let the whole thing lie for a few years. In 1995, I again got the urge and reenrolled at Gonzaga University to try again to complete the process. So I took four core courses over again. It took a year for me to condense 200 pages to the 20-page candidacy paper by which I once again, for the second time, obtained candidacy. I began to write another dissertation, this time on a new subject, to understand the inner world of male behavior. I have worked toward this one for over seven years. Over the years people have asked me what my dissertation was about; when I told them, they would comment, "I would like to read that." So I have prepared this copy for sharing with special people.

I also think in this process I want to make a statement to that little saboteur self that sits on my shoulder and whispers in my ear and still sees me as a " poor dumb country boy." I am still trying to recover from the "Red Apple" reading group.

ABSTRACT

The purpose of this research was to explore the experiences of six men who had been arrested for intimate partner violence in order to discover the underlying factors that led to the violence.

A review of the literature examined the history of the masculinity stereotypes in Western Civilization. Recent research into refining the masculinity stereotype was examined. The perpetuation of the masculinity stereotype in the socialization of male children through the third year of life, the impact of the masculinity stereotype on abuse and murder of women, and an exploration of educational options for perpetrator training was discussed.

This study was a qualitative study. It employed a phenomenological approach to explore the interior consciousness of the research population. Since the researcher has spent many years treating perpetrators, a heuristic focus was also part of the study.

The stories of six men provided the findings of the underlying constructs of intimate partner violence: 1) implications from the practicing phase of child development (12-14 months); 2) implications from the rapprochement phase of child development (24-36 months); and 3) consequences of these two constructs: triggering mechanisms, response to triggering events, time in jail, family origins of the constructs, common male attitudes toward women, and an action plan for healing.

An educational design was recommended for treatment, employing experiential activities to engage and dissipate the underlying constructs that linger as roots of violence. A discussion of the general observations of the researcher was presented, with recommendations for further research.

FOREWORD

Writing a dissertation is a long-term grueling effort. I began thinking of my topic and working on this specific paper in 1995, some seven years ago now. In 1995, even though I had completed all of my course work for my degree, because there had been a lapse of time since I took my last classes, I had to take four core courses over again. Writing a dissertation is a joint endeavor that begins with course professors and then with dissertation committee members. When one is ready to begin the process one must select a committee. The committee consists of a chairperson and two committee persons who guide you through the process. Gonzaga University is unique, I think, in that from the beginning they help you get on a glide path toward graduation and walk with you through the many steps. That process involves selecting a topic and writing the first three chapters. The first chapter is the introduction to the study, the second chapter is the review of the literature, and the third chapter is the methodology being used for the study. Once one has progressed, a copy is submitted to the person's committee chair. In my case the chair of my committee read the document, read 10 pages or so, made corrections and passed it back with the comment to make these corrections throughout the rest of the paper. So I would take it home and work on it for some more months. I would make the changes and resubmit it. I would get it back to do the same again.

In January of 2000 I took my proposal seminar. I rewrote the paper and submitted it. In January 2001 I got it back with more corrections. I have a busy counseling practice so my main time to work on the paper was Sunday afternoons. I worked on it throughout 2001 until my committee chairperson felt it was ready to submit to the whole committee for the "Proposal Defense." Surprisingly, for me, I passed the defense. I was very grateful to my committee for their positive feedback that kept me inspired. It was now the task to write the final three chapters that dealt with the research data. I worked on that from October 2001 through January 2002 and resubmitted it. Each time I received comments from my professors, took the paper home for more revisions, and returned it for additional comments I call a "go-around." Thus far I have had probably 25 of those go-arounds.

When one is working with a committee of three people, one gets the benefit of three varying perspectives, which is very valuable. Each committee person has significant viewing points and makes important suggestions to strengthen the paper. In the process of making the document more readable, different committee members recommend portions of the original be enhanced, deleted, or changed. Consequently, the finished product is an outcome of varying mergings and synergies of all involved.

This document contains the original signed-off copy. It also contains small segments of the deleted material that, while approved by some committee members, were thought by others to impede the flow of the document, whereupon it was removed from the official version. There is no way to express enough gratitude to the committee for the significant hours they spent helping me refine this document. I am eternally grateful to them. I am also grateful for the important help I received from my proofreader Joannie Eppinga of the Eagle Eye Writing and Editing.

There is no way to mention all the significant people who have touched my life. One, however, was standing ahead of me on my path, and when I arrived he pointed me to so many broader insights, and taught me by his personal presence. When I met him I knew I was standing in the presence of someone who was farther on his journey than I was. I always return to the things he taught me. I quickly joined his classes, sat in his Gestalt Therapy training groups, and attended his numerous 72-hour weekend training events. He was not in the mainstream of academic institutions, nevertheless, I got opened to so much through him. I always return to the things he taught me. When one is ready a teacher appears. Thank you, Dr. John Roberts.

TABLE OF CONTENTS

CHAPTER I
INTRODUCTION

Intimate partner abuse is a problem of immense proportions (Ganley, Warshaw, & Salber, 1995). Early attempts to address the women abuse problem by women advocate groups focused on victim safety (Straus, 1998), but when that focus seemed inadequate, attention was directed toward understanding male behavior in an effort to stop the violence (Paymar, 1993). Pleck (1981) pioneered an exploration into existing definitions, re-examined traditional views of maleness, and suggested alternatives for defining male behavior (Buck, 1984; Pleck, 1985). Interest in a more critical approach for viewing male behavior resulted in a rapidly growing body of literature in the last 25 years (Pleck, 1981). A greater understanding of the causes of male violent behavior may provide better solutions to the intimate partner abuse problem. This inquiry sought to understand the internal experiences and the underlying constructs of men who abuse women; the similarities of experiences among these men; the socialization process that may underlie these behaviors; the negative consequences of abusive behaviors; and the process for prevention and change.

Violent men have been examined extensively (e.g., Dutton, 1995; Jacobson & Gottman, 1998). Much of the research has focused upon observing and categorizing the batterer using a quantitative approach (an exterior view). An alternative view may be helpful. One such view is an interior view, one that examines the internal perceived experiences of the abuser. Human interior realities have been designated in many ways: hierarchy of needs, Mallow (1978), ego states, Berne (1961), internal dimensions, Johnson (1991), holes, Perls (1969), shadows or archetypes, Jung (Adler, Fordham, & Read, 1953-1971), and in this study, constructs, Sanford (1961).

A construct, then, is an illusive internal experience that is usually expressed behaviorally. It is sometimes said of children that what they can't express verbally they act out. This is probably true of individuals of any age. Due to the difficulty many man have in expressing or differentiating feelings (Levant, 1997), attention given to their communications and behaviors may prove fruitful in understanding their interior world of constructs.

1

Men's studies, prompted by feminist scholarship, have laid the groundwork in the last 25 years for refining the definitions of masculine psychology (Levant, 1997; O'Neil, Good, & Holms, 1995; Pollack, 1990). Levant noted that feminist scholars in the last quarter century began to explore and develop an "authentic psychology of women" (p. 3); Levant further stated that women researchers reacted to the fact that this psychology was a discipline developed by men to treat women. Levant also noted that feminists challenged the concept that "theorists, researchers, and therapists enshrined the male as representative Homo sapiens to the detriment of women" (p. 3). Feminist researchers, by virtue of their work, helped promote the re-evaluation of this masculinity theory.

This study, similar to feminist gender research, may be viewed as a masculine gender research study. Some believe that the word "masculine" is so charged that the word and the concepts it represents should be eliminated (Stoltenberg, 1993). However, since there is a growing body of feminine research, there is also a growing body of research about males. Masculine research and the goals of masculinity awareness may have the same refining goals as feminine research, and the two may have followed similar paths.

For example, it seems that feminist research sought to clarify their intrinsic definitions and shake off any extrinsic long-held assumptions about women. Masculinity research is also seeking to discover intrinsic answers about the nature of men against a backdrop of centuries of assumptions (Pleck, 1995). Furthermore, Cahoon (1996) saw that the feminine stereotype refining endeavors fall into the broad philosophical context of postmodernity, as with post-constructionist, diversity, multiculturalism, and eco-feminism, in an attempt to "empower the previously disenfranchised" (p. 2). The post-modernity reconstruction was an attempt to set it apart from some of the rejected notions of modernity and its concrete assumptions. Likewise, masculinity research, according to Pleck's (1995) androgyny, is also seeking to wrench itself out of previous binding assumptions about manhood in an attempt to expand male psyche potentials to include aspects that have long been buried.

Consequently, theorists of what it means to be male began to explore "the specific strains, conflict, and pitfalls of the traditional male role's complex problematic construct, and the traumatic consequences of normative male upbringing" (Levant, 1997, p. 3). The outcome of those developmental years leaves many men in a predicament. Levant (1995) designated the predicament as a "complex problematic construct" (p. 3). An aspect of the male problematic construct suggests a strong male focus on maintaining a separate sense of identity and independence at the expense of relationships (Belcher & Pollock, 1993). This tendency of males stands out in bold relief when examined from the perspective of the female value sphere, namely that females tend to focus on a strong sense of interpersonal awareness and connectedness (Gilligan, 1982). Many males are found wanting and their "complex problematic construct" is seen as a limiting factor for interpersonal relationships in contemporary society (O'Neil et al. 1995, p. 3).

Moreover, Barns (1999), in his National Desk television presentation entitled "The War on Boys," cited several scholars (e.g. Gurian, 1999b, Sommers, 2000, and Pollack, 1998) regarding the relationship between male and female value spheres. They noted that a female value sphere, popularized by an American Association of University Women directed survey study in 1992, suggests that girls are being neglected and receiving an inferior education. Pollack stated that just the opposite is the case. Barn's synthesis noted that the normative value sphere for girls is now declared also to be a normative value sphere for boys. Pollack claimed that educational curricula in many schools are not designed for boys. Boys flourish in an environment that provides opportunity for spatial interactive kinesthetic movement. Boys are failing and dropping out at a significantly greater rate than girls. Consequently, active boys are causing too many problems and, according to Pollack and Gurian, are being drugged to bring their behavior into conformity with the female value sphere. "Approximately 3,000,000 kids are on Ritalin in the U.S. — 90 percent of them boys" (Gurian, 1999a, p. 4).

Contrary to the song "Why Can't a Woman Be More Like a Man?" from the musical "My Fair Lady," men are often being characterized as not measuring up to the female value sphere. Men are being measured, it seems, by the lack of certain qualities and not by the positive characteristics they possess (Wilber, 1996). Men, by virtue of the "complex problematic construct" (Levant, 1997, p. 3), are seen to be grappling with what it is they are supposed to be as their long-held masculine ideals are brought into question.

Many aspects of male behavior are portrayed as problematic (e.g.,Barns, 1999; Belcher & Pollack, 1993). O'Neil et al. (1995) noted some aspects of the problem as follows:

> Why are men so unhappy and seeking liberation in the men's movements? Why do men have so many problems with women in intimate and work relationships? Why do men experience emotional numbness and have difficulty expressing feelings — identifying and expressing

emotions? Why do men relate differently than women? Why do men have simultaneous dependence on and distance from female partners? How can we get men to change? Why do men work so much and die earlier than women? Why are men unable to feel and respond to emotions of others? Why do men tend to avoid domestic work and fathering roles? Why do men experience fear and shame of failure to "be a man"? Why do men have an exaggerated investment in work? Why do men disregard health risks? Why do men substitute unconnected lust for sexual intimacy? Why do men molest children, fear homosexuals, and become addicted or sexually dysfunctional? Why do men harass, rape, and batter women? Why do men predominate in the areas of substance abuse, homelessness, prison populations, violence, sex offenses, completed suicide, work till they drop, and in deaths preceding their spouses? (p. 164)

In enumerating male deficiencies, a fertile field of research into the causes becomes compelling. Consequently, Levant (1997) noted, "A cogent psychology of men has become, in fact, an urgent issue" (p. 3). A significant aspect of male psychology is the violence men perpetrate upon women. In the background to the problem, several broad issues are examined: the degree to which the abuse is happening, the attention the problem is receiving, some suggested solutions, attempts to define the perpetrators, and an examination of the field of study.

Background to the Problem

O'Neil et al. (1995) have noted several aspects of male violence; one of them was the phenomenon of male intimate partner violence. The focus of this study was upon this issue and the underlying internal psycho/physiological factors in men that result in the abuse of women. Sensitivity to intimate partner violence has heightened awareness of the problem, focused efforts to document its seriousness, and sounded a call for solutions (Ganley, 1995). Intimate male partners are responsible for half of all female homicide victims in the United States (Kellerman & Mercy, 1992). Crary (2000) referred to such homicide as "the grimmest oxymoron — intimate murder," because four women in United States are killed every day by their intimate partners. At least two million women are beaten each year by their male partners (Bachman & Saltzman, 1995;

Straus, Gelles, & Steinmetz, 1980). Women are several times more likely to need medical care after severe assaults and are much more likely to receive lasting psychological damage related to their abuse (Stets & Straus, 1990). The seriousness of male violence toward intimate partners prompts a drive toward deeper and more lasting answers.

A body of research, on a scale considered by Straus (1998) to be unprecedented, gives evidence of the attention this problem is receiving. Between 1974 and 1996, the Family Research Laboratory at the University of New Hampshire produced some 35 books and 300 articles on the topic. Ten new journals on the subject have also emerged since 1985, and a recent bibliographic compilation revealed 1,557 references on the subject (Straus, 1998). Along with research into the problem, attention regarding appropriate intervention is also seen as being important.

Crary's (2000) inquiry into domestic violence found that Michael Cohen, executive director of Maryland Network Against Intimate Partner Violence, proposed more space in women's shelters, more enlightened judges, more casework staff members, more financing of personnel, and better communication among agencies. Additionally, Crary stated that even though $1.4 billion has been poured into programs under the 1994 Federal Violence Against Women Act, more personnel were needed. Nevertheless, Bonnie Campbell of the U.S. Justice Department's Violence Against Women Office (in Crary) remarked that even with this expenditure and heightened awareness, it will take a long time, perhaps decades, to change societal attitudes.

Several states have made important efforts to effect the change of attitudes over the last ten years. For example, the Washington State Legislature directed the Department of Social and Health Services to formulate an Administrative Code (388:60) to direct the treatment and re-education programs for male perpetrators. These treatment programs exist in most major cities. Moreover, a recent study (Halpert, 1999) from the Washington State Governor's Intimate Partner Violence Action Group noted several recommendations: 1) boost penalties for violations of restraining orders; 2) provide more training for law enforcement; 3) authorize the Department of Social and Health Services to petition the court for intimate partner violence protection orders on behalf of, and with the consent of, vulnerable adults; 4) clarify the court's authority to order batterers to keep specified distances from victims and their children; 5) streamline reporting procedures; and 6) prohibit discrimination in housing for victims of domestic violence. Intimate partner violence is receiving widespread attention as key governmental agencies seek to address the problem.

Violence against women has been cited as the major health care problem in the United States, affecting more individuals and families than any other single health care problem (Hamberger, Saunders, & Hovey, 1992). Domestic violence and its consequences — child abuse and neglect, sibling violence, stranger violence, and the abuse of the elderly — not only destroys families, but also extends far beyond the primary home to other forms of social violence (Ganley et al., 1995). It is often carried like a disease from one generation to the next, infecting tomorrow's children (Hamberger et al.). The immense cost of the intimate partner violence problem is revealed in lost time at work, health care costs, thwarted child development, and judicial and prison costs (Ganley et. al.; Hamberger et al.).

An overview of the intimate partner violence literature reveals a focus on the following issues: 1) describing the issue (evolving a nomenclature, e.g. domestic violence, spousal abuse, woman battering, wife beaters, batterers, perpetrators, and intimate partner violators); 2) measuring the problem (intimate partner violence statistics); 3) protecting the victims of violence (the shelter movement); 4) psychological abuse; 5) developing a theory base of intimate partner violence; 6) punishing the perpetrators (the judicial system with jail, fines, and probation); and 7) developing extrinsic prevention methods (treatment programs) (Ganley, 1995; Gelles, 1993; Groetsch, 1997; Hart, 1992; Jacobson & Gottman, 1998; Jasinski & Williams, 1998; Jenkins & Davidson, 2001; Kakar, 2002; O'Leary & Maiuro, 2001; Paymar, 1993; Pence & Paymar, 1993; Sonkin, Martin, & Walker, 1985; Starr, 1983).

The individuals who perpetrate violence have been the focus of research in the later part of the twentieth century. Groetsch (1997) provided taxonomy of three categories of batterers: Category one, the least dangerous, the "remorseful batterer" (p. 11); Category two, "the sporadic batterer" (p. 67); and category three, the "serial batter" (p. 19). Groetsch further delineated six types of serial batterers: narcissistic, antisocial, borderline, histrionic, paranoid, and obsessive-compulsive; he also provided summaries of the psychological and behavioral characteristics of abusers. Moreover, Dutton (1995) discussed the psychopathic batter (a category similar to Groetsch's category three batterer), the over-controlled batterer, and the cyclical/emotionally volatile batter. Walker (2000a) provided a psychosocial taxonomy of batterers and reiterated the "power and control" thesis (p. 6). She affirmed the social learning theory origins of battering, among many other insights, and noted that batterers report that they came from a home with a "strict" wife-abusing "father" (p. 12).

Scientific studies of batterers involved the use of polygraph and other "psychophysiological recording devices" (Jacobson & Gottman, 1998, p. 20), which monitored the emotional levels of batterers in states of marital conflict. The outcome of the studies placed men into two categories. The first category was termed "cobras" to denote batterers whose heart rates lessened when acting out violence against their partners (p. 28). The second category used the concept of "pit bulls" to designate 1) men who became physically activated, high tension, heart racing, and so forth, when in marital conflict, and 2) men who were more emotionally dependent upon their partners (p. 28). Jacobson and Gottman outlined the territory of perpetrator characteristics. Other theorists have focused upon treatment and prevention of domestic violence. Hammer and Itzin (2000) focused on confronting the abuser and on a process for dealing with repeat offenders. Several studies focused on the nature, effectiveness, and evaluation of intervention treatment programs (Decker, 1999; Fall, Howard, & Ford, 1999; Feder, 1999; Roberts, 2002; Roleff, 2000; Said, 2001; Vincent & Jouriles, 2000; Wexler, 2000).

Karr-Morse and Wiley (1997) noted that violent potential is a fairly fixed phenomenon by the time a child is two years old; they stated that one in 20 male babies in their cribs would some day exchange the slats of their cribs for prisons bars. Subsequently, the etiology and longitudinal aspects of the problem become important, and the quality of the environment of the infant's home becomes a predictor of later violence (Karr-Morse & Wiley, 1997). Infants growing up in psychologically stressful environments are impacted by those environments. Stress hormones are activated in the brain that potentially set these individuals up for a life of guarded vigilance and a fight-or-flight consciousness. According to Perry (1997), fear and trauma in small children later manifest as anger and rage, and contribute to an individual's aggressiveness, impulsivity, and the possibility of violence. Consequently, an understanding of violence can be enriched by a broader examination of the experiences of the perpetrator. A prerequisite for this endeavor is a robust empathy for men (Levant & Pollack, 1995). The stress and pain of the male experience has taken on the nature of a crisis (Levant, 1992).

The valuable work of these researchers, especially the work of Jacobson and Gottman (1998), provided a describable range of categories. Much of the effort in the intimate partner violence field is extrinsic, focusing on defining the problem and formulating solution protocols, such as methods to control male violence. The extrinsic nature of violence control is demonstrated by focusing on better ways to apprehend, fine, imprison, punish, re-educate, manage, train, and control the perpetrator.

This attempt to bring external pressures for change upon the perpetrator is reflected in the work of the Washington State Governor's Intimate Partner Violence Action Group (Halpert, 1999) and numerous treatment manuals in use across the country (Sonkin et al., 1985; Paymar, 1993; Pence & Paymar, 1993). The question then becomes, do other approaches exist for dealing with male violence? For example, is there an intrinsic approach?

Statement of Purpose

The purpose of this study was to explore the experiences of males who are violent toward intimate female partners using a qualitative research method. More specifically, this study sought to describe the interior psychological realities, in this case constructs, that accompany male violent behavior toward intimate female partners. Interior psychological constructs are by definition not empirically verifiable, and are rooted in the physiology of the person. They are often indescribable physical experiences that are acted out and sometimes characterized by such later statements as, "I have no idea why I did that" or "Why I said that I'll never know. It just came out." It is often said of children and teenagers that they are "acting out." Whether a person is two years old or fifty-two years old, what cannot be verbalized is often "acted out." Attempts to describe these experiences are often overlaid with hierarchies of words that are not the experience but point to the experience. The broad range of words used to refer to those physiological (hence interior psychological) constructs may include: ecstatic, joyful, pleasant, calm, peaceful, disturbed, scared, hungry, depressed, sad, upset, angry, and furious. Due to the difficulty many men have in expressing feelings, the principles for dealing with internal constructs may be addressed by the tacit dimension of epistemology. The essence of the tacit dimension of epistemology involves the non-explicit. Some of the principles for dealing with the non-explicit, constructs in this case, involve an indirect approach involving illustration, paradigm, metaphor, example, and their mirroring effect in the explicit (Polanyi, 1966).

Furthermore, the examination of the abusive male experience is integrally related to a discovery of an underlying theory base. One's developing theory base about a problem directly affects how one sees it and what one does about it. If one's theory base is primarily derived from a quantitative method, an exterior view, looking at the subject population, then treatment methodologies may take the form of a more cognitive approach. However, if one's theory base is derived from a qualitative method that seeks to understand the individual's deep-rooted interior world, addressing the problem of intimate partner violence may take the form of experiential learning. The goal of this study was to understand the interior world of perpetrators, explore additional perspectives for viewing this population, explore similarities of their developmental history, or how they were socialized, and seek alternative treatment methodologies for addressing intimate partner violence.

This study employed a qualitative research methodology to gather data regarding the life experiences of six men who had been adjudicated for intimate partner violence. The six men were a purposefully selected sample because they provided the researcher with substantial and clearly articulated information for the study. The qualitative approach offers "depth, detail, and meaning at a very personal level of experience" (Patton, 1990, p. 18). Therefore, the information changes from being a "passing event, which exists only in its own moment of occurrence into an account, which exists in its inscriptions and can be re-consulted" (Geertz, 1973).

Subsumed in the qualitative research methodology is the phenomenological approach. Phenomenological inquiry seeks to understand the "individual and his stream of experiences" (Farber, 1966, p. 13), and "concentrates its investigations on descriptions of those essential structures that are inherent in consciousness" (Polkinghorne, 1989). The inner realities of the research population are the focus of the investigation, allowing everything to be "viewed from the point of view of one's own experiencing of them, and only insofar as they have meaning in and by one's experiences" (Farber, 1966, p. 14). Phenomenology, then, attempts to understand the flow of the participant's stream of consciousness captured in time as the participant experiences and interprets his or her world (Patton, 1990).

The study also was heuristic in nature in that I am a male therapist for male perpetrators who has had long-term, direct personal interaction with the clients (Moustakas, 1990). Though the present study focused on "liberating men," it is similar to feminist gender research in that feminist gender research is immersed, palpable, and critical (Loste, 2000; Nielsen, 1990). Feminist research is involved socially, and emotionally inclusive (Oakley, 1981). It is women centered, revisionist, and has a keen eye for gender inequalities (Kelly-Gadol, 1976; Nielsen, 1990).

Similarly, masculinity research was prompted by Pleck's (1995) destructuring the *Male Sex Role Identity Paradigm*, which he sought to modify with his *Sex Role Strain Paradigm* in order to expand the intrapsychic possibilities of maleness in what he called "androgyny." Feminist research sought to address society's presuppositions about women and their capabilities (Greer, 1979); masculinity research also wants to challenge societies' presentations of masculinity (Pleck). In this way, the process of each person individualizing his or her own uniqueness becomes the option for everyone regardless of historical gender assumptions.

I directed treatment programs for the research population for over 15 years. Consequently, I was immersed in the participative endeavor, reflected on the meaning behind the participants' experiences and words, accumulated a body of relevant data, and sat with their stuckness without words. As such, from a heuristic perspective, the experiences of the researcher became the template through which the data were filtered. The biases and counter-transference of the researcher were factors that had to be constantly scrutinized and dealt with. This heuristic method produced a merging of these data into thematic categories (Moustakas, 1990).

Significance of the Study

General characteristics of the research on male violence, some positive qualities of maleness, the impact of feminist researchers on the development of a male psychology, the male reaction to demands for new behavioral norms, and new insights into the nature of maleness and gender differences were considered.

The hurting of women by men is a long-standing problem, and many efforts are being employed to find solutions. Much attention to the problem is quantitative, extrinsic, observational, and anecdotal (Gelles & Loseke, 1993; Groetsch, 1997; Hart, 1992; Jacobson & Gottman, 1998; Jasinski & Williams, 1998; Pense & Paymar, 1993; Sonkin et al., 1985; Starr, 1983). The formulation of the problem precludes interventions employed for breaking the violence cycle (Paymar). This study sought to build upon the quantitative perspective by employing another approach – that of looking at the issue from the point of view of those doing the violence. The goal was to find a window into the violent male's internal consciousness in order to obtain a better understanding of his perception of maleness that gets expressed as violence.

Throughout the centuries, the ideology of what a man is supposed to be resulted in a cluster of prescriptions (Doyle, 1983; Mosse, 1996). Levant (1997) listed many positive male qualities. To be good men, males were told they "must become reliable providers, emotionally stoic, logical, solution-oriented, and aggressive" (p. 3). Levant's view may be summarized as follows: Men were taught to put their interests, wants, and needs aside in order to provide for their families. They were taught to endure stress, difficulties and pain to protect their wives and children. They were to be problem solvers. They were to persevere until the problem was solved, to use good sense, and to withstand adversity in the face of danger. They were to be goal oriented and innovative. They were never to give up. They were supposed to overcome defeat, and adjust to new situations. If they got knocked down, they were to get up and start again. They learned that doing for others was the way to show love and affection. Loyalty was also an important ideal. These values still pervade much of male consciousness (Levant, 1995, 1997). Nevertheless, questions about the importance of the traditional qualities of maleness are being raised.

Feminist researchers reacted to a culture that "enshrined the male as representative Homo sapiens" and developed a cogent female psychology (Levant, 1997, p. 3). Consequently, feminist research indirectly reflected upon masculine theories (Levant, 1995). That reflection made manifest many negative aspects of masculine behavior (O'Neil et al., 1995). The negative and missing aspects of maleness were often the focus, to the exclusion of many of the positive qualities of maleness, and in many quarters, masculinity has fallen into a state of derision (Levant, 1995). In fact, some male qualities such as being stoic, keeping a job, never letting them see you sweat, rationality, goal orientation, and competing are being discounted (Gurian, 1999b). Historical male value sphere behaviors are being supplanted in some institutions with female values such as sensitivity and interpersonal skills (Barns, 1999; Sommers, 2000; Tiger, 1999). The male gender role in many quarters is under attack (Pollack, 1990).

With the expansion of the female role, especially since women have been able to be financially independent, the role of the male provider has diminished in importance (Mosse, 1996). Many men still go to work to fulfill a long-held male provider role (Belcher & Pollock, 1993). Many men are now expected, however, to assume many of the homemaking tasks, which can often be tasks that reside outside of their sense of identity. Not only has the traditional male provider role diminished, but in addition many of the traditional male roles are no longer as vital (Levant, 1995). Many men are expected to exemplify elements of the female value sphere, such as commitment to relationships, nurturance of children, homemaking, empathizing, and communication at the affective level. The element Levant (1997) calls "emotional intelligence" (p. 14) is often missing for many men. Because of this unnatural fit, men are sometimes referred to as lacking important qualities of the female value sphere (Belcher & Pollack). Where does that assessment leave men in a society in which there seems to be less of natural fit and they perceive they are less valued and less vital?

According to Pollack (1999), highly individuated successful modern women, many of whom seek a full, deep and relational man, are often frustrated in finding partners with whom to share their lives. For many men, relating with more independent women brings to the surface their own emptiness and rootlessness. "Men are finding that their female colleagues, lovers, and wives are furious about men's subjugating, controlling, abusing, and defining women. Increasingly, women reject the traditional equation between one man and one woman in which there is a sign that means 'greater than' rather than 'equals'" (Belcher & Pollock, 1993, p. 2).

Consequently, men often suffer the terror of self-doubt and are often frozen by uncertainty (Kimmel, 1987; Pollack, 1999; Travis & Wade, 1984). "How do I be a man?" has become a burning question for many men (Levant, 1997, p. 4). Research and clinical experience alike have shown that many men do indeed manifest difficulties with commitment to relationships (Belcher & Pollack, 1993). They often experience a dysfunction in the expression of interpersonal openness (Pollack). Often, their proclivity for a style of emotional suppression, defensive autonomy, or self-sufficiency is under attack (Levant, 1997). Many do in fact struggle with the frustration of being expected to participate in mutual intimacy (Pollack, 1990). The "strong, silent pillar of the family has fallen from the shining ideal to an object of hostility and derision" (Levant, 1995, p. 3). Wilber (1996) summarized,

> It seems that . . . men are inherently insensitive slobs and testosterone mutants who "just don't get it." The message is, men should be more sensitive, more caring, more loving, and relational. What you call the male value sphere is everywhere under attack. The message is why can't a man be more like a woman? Yes, it's a certain amount of "turnabout is fair play." Used to be that women were defined as "deficient men," "penis envy" being the classic example. Now men are being defined as "deficient women" — defined by feminine characteristics that they lack, not by any positive attribute that they possess. (p. 3)

Many men are becoming aware of this problem and are trying to change. As they run straight into their limitations, the resultant pain is causing some to seek help. Kessler and McRae (1981) noted that from 1957 to 1976, symptoms of psychological unrest among men increased at three times the rate of those among women, causing men to seek counseling. The stress and pain of the male experience has been called "the masculine curse" (Lee, 1993, p. 152), and has taken on the nature of a crisis (Levant, 1995). Many men are seeking options for change and a growing body of masculinity research is looking for clues into the problem.

Scholars are now attempting to develop new insights into the male psyche (Pleck, 1995). What is the nature and seriousness of this male crisis that is attracting leading researchers? The response to this question has led some to seek a redefinition of the field. Such an attempt has taken on the scope of nothing less than the "reconstruction of masculinity" (Levant, 1995, p. 4; Pleck). That quest involves a scrutiny of long-held male beliefs (Levant, 1997), and the exploration into how any of those obsolete and dysfunctional ideas may be updated and reapplied to the current changing world (Pleck, 1995). According to Levant, a changing world calls for the development of fundamental skills that contribute to successful interpersonal involvement. Consequently, "A cogent psychology of men has become, in fact, an urgent issue" (Levant, 1997, p. 3).

Gilmore (1990) and Wilber (1996), by way of a parenthetical definition, suggested some distinctions regarding the concepts of "sex" and "gender." Gilmore studied many cultures and concluded that biological maleness (the sexual distinction) is a predestined phenomenon, while masculinity is a fragile, culturally constructed concept. Distinctions regarding "sex" are served by the terms "male" and "female"; distinctions regarding gender are made using the terms "masculine" and "feminine." The term "sex" is served by noting the biological differences between men and women are mostly universal, cross-cultural, and worldwide. "Males produce sperm, females produce ova, and females give birth and lactate, and so on" (Wilber, p. 1). Gender differences, masculine and feminine, are more culturally based and are changeable to some extent (Levant, 1997).

Biological sex differences are more basic and persistent, and they often leach into and color gender differences. Some have noted that females become women as the result of a chronological biological clock. "The idea that a man behaves in a certain way because he 'needs to prove his masculinity' has a powerful emotional resonance for many people. . . . By contrast, the analogous idea that women act to 'prove their femininity' would sound odd and alien" (Pleck, 1995, p. 27).

This writer sat as a counselor with men who because of impotence have stated, "I am no longer a man." Many men have stated, "I have to be a man about it," and "stand up and be a man." Such statements, it would seem, sound strange coming from a woman, and is it foreign for a woman to state that she "lost her womanhood." There seem, according to Pleck (1995), to be fewer standards or norms whereby a girl becomes a woman. However, strong sets of cultural norms often dictate what manhood is and what a man is supposed to be. The perceived lack of those cultural norms in a male's life portends a potential crisis and loss of manhood for many men (Belcher & Pollack, 1993). Manhood often involves a test that must be passed over and over again, leaving the impression that manhood is a delicate state arduously achieved and easily lost (Pollack, 1999).

In sum, the re-examination of gender theory, especially the research clarifying female gender theory, has heightened the quest for a theory of maleness. The masculinity value sphere, in many quarters, has fallen into a state of low esteem, and the female value sphere has become a template to which many men are expected to conform. Consequently, an extensive cataloguing of masculine flaws has led to greater inquiry into the nature of the male gender.

Overview of the Study

This chapter described the goal of the study, provided an overview of the current problems attributed to males, and introduced the issue of male violence toward women. The qualitative research methodology involving heuristic phenomenology was introduced. Chapter II presents an overview of the pertinent literature regarding masculinity history, masculinity theory, infant male development, and male power and control regarding women. Chapter III describes the research methodology. Chapter IV presents the participant data. Chapter V develops the analysis of the internal psychological constructs. Chapter VI covers the heuristic factor regarding the writer, and Chapter VII provides the summary, conclusions, and recommendations for further research.

CHAPTER II
REVIEW OF THE LITERATURE

The purpose of this study was to examine the internal male experiences that are expressed as intimate partner violence. The literature review examines four areas. First, the history of the masculinity stereotype in Western Civilization is considered. This chapter examines twenty-five centuries of instinctual human survival behavioral patterns, the trans-generational organismic imprinting of those normative male behavior standards, and the predictable sanctions for violations of the norms, even unto death. The fear-based imprints in the souls of our fathers and grandfathers throughout those centuries are explored, as they became a hypnotic subliminal prescription of what a man was supposed to be. It will be seen that those psychologically rooted prescriptive constructs were pervasive throughout history and persist to the present to the detriment of men. Second, this chapter explores the development of masculinity theory research in twentieth-century America. The historical masculinity stereotype still tends to dominate male identity, and the destructuring of the stereotype with an eye to develop a more accurate theory of maleness is examined. Third, current research is explored to reveal the way centuries-old prescriptions regarding maleness are perpetuated in male psychological development and socialization through the third year of life. And finally, this chapter reviews the insidious perpetuation of the masculinity stereotype as it is expressed in the abuse and murder of women with an eye toward power sharing in contemporary society. This chapter serves as a precursor to and grounding for the psychological constructs for the examination of male violence.

The History of the Masculinity
Stereotype in Western Civilization

Two teleological perspectives for viewing reality are suggested, based on Realism and Idealism. Realism is a view that reality is what can be verified by the senses (Thilly & Wood, 1957); *what you see is what you get!* Any attempt to read more into reality than can be verified by the senses is "a limbo of non-sense" (Thilly & Wood, 1957, p. 656); it is non-empirical, not sensorially verifiable. Idealism, on the other hand, affirms there is more to reality than the empirically verifiable. Idealism focuses upon what is called the "real world—a world of ideas, not the unreal and unimportant passing features of the visible world" (Stroll, 1971, p. 102). Consequently, the idealistic approach affirms that *there is more to life than meets the eye.* The view-lens for this discussion is in the idealistic realm in order to look for deeper meanings disguised in surface appearances.

Thales' search for a pervasive unifying principle in observed discrete patterns in a lunar eclipse launched an influential teleological ideal (Thilly & Wood, 1957). The discovery of natural cycles, basic regularities, pervasive patterns, and predictable outcomes or laws evident in the great realms of natural phenomena — from physics to biological life to human cognition to transcendent connections — affirms what Wilber (1995) calls the "'unity of science' – a coherent and unified world view . . . 'everything is connected to everything else'— the web of life as a scientific notion and not just religious conclusion" (pp.14-15, 26). Everything, all reality, is interconnected (Palmer, 1983; Whitehead, 1966).

Activity on the planet reveals remarkable patterns of "increasingly complex, sensitive, and responsive structures of being" (Wilber, 1981, p. 26), perceived as "a universal sequence of hierarchical levels of increasing consciousness" (Wilber, 1981, p. 7). It is also held by Wilber (1981) that whatever is pushing history is pushing it toward increasing spheres of integration, harmony, and complexity. Consequently, according to Wilber (1995), the universe has been conceptualized as follows:

> "Self-winding" and "self-organizing" systems are known as the sciences of complexity: General System Theory (Bertalanffy, Weiss), cybernetics (Wiener), nonequilibrium thermodynamics (Prigogine), cellular automata theory (von Neuman), catastrophe theory (Thome), autopoietic system theory (Maturana and Verela), dynamic systems theory (Shaw, Abraham), and chaos theories. (p. 14)

As such, researchers have viewed the scene of human history and have attempted to provide a comprehensive nomenclature.

History has been viewed through a variety of lenses: as stages, worldviews, historical epochs, and cultural epochs (Collingwood, 1965). As each epoch of history borrowed from and built upon the previous epoch, and each epoch, through new discoveries and scrutiny, differentiated, included, transcended, and excluded elements of the previous epoch. Mental maps of this self-winding, self-organizing reality complement each other. Jean Gebser, Pritirim Sorokin, Robert Bellah, Jurgen Habermas,

Michel Foucault, and Peter Berger, to name a few, have outlined the predominant "world views" of the various epochs of human development, and consolidated fairly clear viewing points of this interconnected "web of life" (Wilber, 1995, p. 15).

One of many perspectives on human historical origins, cosmogony, was put forth by Wilber (1981, 1996). He noted that from the big bang 15 billion years ago, to the hominidal awakening six million years ago, to the first emergence of foraging societies somewhere between a million and 400,000 years ago, and continuing to the present, the evidence argues for a sensible universe capable of comprehension. Wilber (1986) also noted that "Calculations done by scientists from Fred Hoyle to F. B. Salisbury consistently show that twelve billion years isn't even enough to produce a *single enzyme* by chance" (p. 26). Something is pushing, leading, and guiding the activity on the planet as it has moved "from simple insentient and lifeless atoms to vegetal life, and beyond vegetation to simple animal forms (protozoan, amphibian, reptilian), and then to higher animal forms (mammalian), with simple mental images and paleosymbols" (Wilber, 1981, p. 21). All of this inexorable activity set the stage for the first hominids "upon which human consciousness would [later] be built" (p. 21).

Each historical epoch contained several unique factors. For example, the economic/technological aspect of history involved: Foraging, Horticulture, Agrarian, Industrial, and Informational (Wilber, 1995). Others (Gebser, 1985; Habermas, 1979; Neumann, 1973) looked at each epoch from a prevailing worldview: i.e. archaic, magic, mythic, rational, and existential. Within each epoch several sub-factors have been considered:

1. economic production;
2. the dominant worldview;
3. modes of technology;
4. the moral outlook;
5. the legal codes or taboos; and
6. types of religion.

The mean level of human consciousness for each epoch was also investigated in terms of:

1) sense of space-time;
2) cognitive style;
3) self-identity;
4) drives or motivation;

5) defenses;
6) types of social oppression/repression;
7) types of personal pathology; and
8) degrees of death-seizure and death-denial (Wilber, 1995).

Researchers observed that there was a progression from physics (matter) to biology (life) to psychology (mind) to sociology, theology, and religion (spirit) (Laszlo, 1987). Laszlo further noted that there is an ever-progressing, ever-widening sphere of development from matter to life to mind to spirit. In sum, according to the aforementioned researchers, human history is dynamic — it is going somewhere — and it has done so in intelligibly observable patterns that involved the six epochs. One of the perspectives noted by Habermas (1979), the economic, will serve as the focalizing viewpoint for the discussion in this section.

These introductory remarks, then, serve as an orientation to the background and historical perspective from which the developing characteristics of the male gender stereotype will be explored. The male gender stereotype progresses in context with, and parallels, the development of female gender stereotypes. They are mentioned together of necessity. The relative status of men and women in each of these major historical stages of human development can be fairly well documented (Eisler, 1987).

This study, then, will employ the following broad designators in the review of the history of the masculinity stereotype in Western Civilization: Foraging; Horticulture; Agrarian; Industrial; and Informational. Sub-epochs will be also be noted in the Agrararian Epoch:

1. the heroic male (800 BC – 476 AD);
2. the otherworldly male (500 – 1000 AD);
3. the knightly male (1100 – 1500 AD);
4. the renaissance male (1500 – 1700 AD);
5. industrial — the bourgeoisie male (1700 AD – on); and,
6. in America,
   a. the aristocrat and his family (1630 - 1820),
   b. the common man and the suffragette (1630 - 1820),
   c. the he man and his compatriots (1861 - 1919), and
   d. partners at last (1920-on) (Pleck, 1980; Wilber, 1995).

Each of the epochs involved human activity. It is these activities that slowly identified characteristics that became customs and mores and evolved as the Masculinty Stereotypes (Pleck, 1980; Wilber, 1995).

Epoch One: Foraging

Hominids (Proto-Humans)

Homo erectus, a human ancestor, according to McNeill (1963) and Poirier (1974), lived about 1.6 million years ago in Africa. The species spread throughout the then known world. Probably because of their advanced survival skills, the early proto-humans were able to leave the subtropics. They had the ability to control fire and make fairly sophisticated tools. The *Homo erectus* was the stepping-stone to the modern human known as *Homo sapiens*. It is believed primitive humans crossed from Asia to North America on a land bridge that once linked Alaska with Asia (McNeill, 1963). Arieti (1967) and Piaget (1977) proposed that individual self-consciousness did not exist. Their theory proposed that hominids were psychologically imbedded in the natural environment with no powers of self-reflection, as are people today during the first year of human life.

Habermas (1979) noted that economic cooperation, though significant was not the key factor in the emergence of *Homo sapiens*. Theoretically, hominids (the adult males) were distinguished from the anthropoid apes by sustaining self-reproduction via social labor. They developed an economy involving the many elements of the cooperative hunt: 1) a proto-language, 2) development of a technology, 3) an economy, and 4) rules of distribution. Principles of cooperation and the rules of distribution were new innovations deriving from adult male hominids' functioning in egalitarian hunting bands.

Habermas (1979) noted, "The father role did not exist. They did not yet know a family structure" (p. 134). The male and female value spheres had already been differentiated into the societal cooperative hunt for men, and the nurturance of the young for women. It is important to observe that, even in archaic hominid societies, these two spheres were already beginning to be differentiated, and often sharply (Hunt, 1990). Females gathered and nurtured the young, men hunted, with no particular emphasis placed on either the male or female value sphere. These early sophisticated and mostly unconscious abilities were present in the hominids.

Hominids to Humans (about 1 million years ago)

It was the emerging concept of the family and the familialization of the male that elevated hominids, proto-humans, to humans (Habermas, 1979). An economy of cooperation for survival separated hominids from earlier primates. It "appears now that the evolutionary novelty that distinguishes Homo sapiens [from hominids] is not the economy but the family" (McCarthy, 1978; p. 238). The human family, according to Habermas, is marked by emergent characteristics that were found nowhere else in evolution. Humans broke up the social structure of a one-dimensional rank ordering adopted by an animal's assignment to one, and only one, status. A family-like relationship existed only between the mother and her young and between siblings. The idea of the father role was only beginning to emerge, and, therefore, the idea of the family was in the early developmental stages (Habermas).

Lenski (1970) reported that of the societies during this period, about 97% revealed this pattern of emerging male/female differentiation. Additionally, Lenski noted, the average number of these early foraging tribes was around 40 people, and the average life span was about 22.5 years. These small social groups were linked by tribal kinship and were sustained by pre-agriculture hunting and gathering. If evolution were to continue, a new integration was also needed. Because presumably the eight or nine months' pregnant female could not pursue game or contribute to her own survival very well, the integrating link was established by the novel emergence of the role of the father, with one foot in each sphere — the hunt and the hearth. The phenomenon of the human family "occurred only as the male was also assigned the role of father" (Habermas, 1979, p. 133). The two emerging value spheres of male and female could be linked. Habermas summarized this new development as follows:

> The mode of production of the socially organized hunt created a system problem that was resolved by the familialization of the male, that is, by the introduction of a kinship system based on exogamy. The male society of the hunting band became independent of the plant-gathering females and the young, both of whom remained behind during the hunting expeditions. With this differentiation, linked to the division of labor, there arose a new need for integration, namely, the need for a controlled exchange between the two subsystems. . . . But the hominids apparently had at their disposal only the pattern of status-dependent sexual relations. This pattern was not equal

to the new need for integration, the less so, the more the status order of the primates was further undermined by forces pushing in the direction of egalitarian relations within the hunting band. Only a family system based on marriage and regulated descent permitted the adult male member to link — via the father role — a status in the male system of the hunting band with a status in the female and child system, and thus 1) integrate functions of social labor with functions of nurture of the young, and, moreover, 2) coordinate functions of male hunting with those of female gathering. (pp. 135-136)

Maleness, it is seen, with its penchant for survival via pursuit of food, shelter, procreation, and the hormonal drive to exist, gave birth to the familial male of the species (McCarthy, 1978).

Epoch Two: The Horticultural Society (10,000 B.C. on)

Each epoch runs its course to its limit, ending in chaos, turmoil, and breakdown (Kuhn, 1970). Higher order solutions trigger and transcend the previous limits, but introduce new factors that lead to each successive epoch's demise and transformation. Differentiation, elimination, and inclusion inexorably push history. Older issues and perspectives are clarified and refined as new viewing lenses illuminate new and even more troubling problems (Wilber, 1996).

Wilber (1981) theorized that human consciousness evolved about six million years ago from the ancient hominid psychological embeddedness in nature to a more sophisticated conscious development. By virtue of a proto-language and a primitive technology, tools, division of labor, and distribution, a foraging society is purported to have emerged about one million to 400,000 years ago (McNeill, 1963). Then around 12,000 B.C., "Mankind was starting to wake up, and wake up very quickly, from its prehistoric slumber in subconscious Eden . . . . But what happened on this date . . . [was that] humankind discovered farming" (Wilber, p. 87). The mental leap that led to farming revealed the most significant development in human consciousness up to that time. To forgo immediate gratification, the simple present, and wait for the fruition (harvest) of one's labor (planting) marked a significant shift in consciousness (McNeill).

Because of this shift in consciousness, the hunting and gathering societies evolved into agricultural societies. Agriculture found expression in two different types of farming activities: the horticultural (using the hoe or digging stick) and the agrarian (using the heavier animal-drawn plow) (McNeill, 1963). Women were not well suited to chasing game, but they were able to use the hoe, even when pregnant. Wilber (1996) noted:

> A digging stick or simple hoe can be used quite easily by a pregnant woman, and thus mothers were as capable as fathers of doing horticulture. . . . In fact, women (the men still went off and hunted, of course) produced about 80 percent of the foodstuffs in these societies. Small surprise, then, that about one-third of these societies have female-only deities, and about one-third have male-and-female deities, and women's status in such societies was roughly equal with men's, although their roles were still, of course, sharply separated. (p. 48)

Consequently, societies with a horticultural element experienced a matrifocal dimension (Chavetz, 1984; Neilson, 1990). The concept of the female goddess and horticulture co-existed (Sanday, 1981). This correlation began roughly around 10,000 B.C. in both the East and West. "Where females work the field with a hoe, God is a Woman; where males work the field with a plow, God is a Man" (Wilber, 1996, p. 51).

Epoch Three: The Agrarian Society (4500 B.C. on)

The plow replaced the hoe, allowing larger areas to be cultivated; a concomittant shift in culture took place (Curwen, 1953). Agrarian societies began around 4500-2000 B.C., in both the East and West, and farming was the dominant mode of production until the Industrial Revolution. Even though the females played significant and meaningful roles in those early cultures (Chavetz, 1984; Martin & Voorhies, 1975), male activity became the primary means of survival. The miscarriage rate was much higher among women who participated in plowing and contributed to the shift from matrifocal to patrifocal societies as males dominated the productive sphere (Chavetz, 1984). The development of the patrifocal emphasis was probably the most appropriate response, due to the technological development of these societies. "This 'patriarchy' was a conscious co-creation of men and women in the face of largely brutal circumstances" (Wilber, 1996, p. 51). Thus, when men began to be the primary producers of food, the deity figures in these cultures switched from being female-oriented to being almost exclusively male-oriented. Agrarian societies, wherever they appear, have solely male deities (Sanday, 1981).

The development of farming resulted in the creation of a surplus and the subsequent potential for leisure and reflection. This freed a great number of individuals to pursue tasks other than food gathering. The subdivision of tasks and refinement of tools resulted in great increases in productivity and a differentiation in the individuals' roles (Hunt, 1990). The differentiation of roles was a functional outcome of the economic reality and expanded into hierarchical classes as surpluses accumulated. Since people were unable to carry large amounts of grain from place to place, it became necessary to use money or some medium of exchange. By 4500 B.C., the farming consciousness resulted in a massive expansion of cultural activities, cultural symbols, and cultural monuments exceeding in size and grandeur anything previous in history (McNeill, 1963). "For in the short span of a few thousand years, farming consciousness had spectacularly flowed into the magnificent city-state and theocracies of Egypt and Mesopotamia" (Wilber, 1983, p. 113).

Furthermore, McNeill (1963) noted that leisure and reflection allowed highly specialized classes to arise: men that could devote their time, not just to subsistence endeavors, but also to extended cultural endeavors. Mathematics was invented, writing was invented, as were metallurgy and specialized warfare. The first great military empires arose. Across the globe, beginning around 3000 B.C., came the Alexanders and Caesars and the Sargons and Kahns, rulers of massive empires that, paradoxically, began unifying disparate and contentious tribes into binding social orders. Along with these great agrarian cultures came the first sustained contemplative endeavors. It was a period that produced the great "axial sages:" Gautama Buddha, Lao Tzu, Parmenides, Socrates, Plato, Patanjali, Confucius, and the sages of the Upanishads (Jaspers, 1966).

In sum, the agrarian focus, with males as the primary agents of physical survival, combined with the refinement of techniques and tools, surplus, money, leisure, hierarchical classes, and contemplation, ultimately freed classes of men from production, while leaving women still largely tied to reproduction. The importance of the male role resulted in the perception of God as male, which led to a patriarchal society. Men talked to God and represented God, and women spoke to God through their husbands or male priests, which resulted in the ascendance of the male throughout much of the balance of human history (Wilber, 1996).

The Heroic Male (800 BC – 476 AD)

Surplus, money, and leisure liberated some individuals through wit, chance, or birth from the drudgery of labor (Hunt, 1990). Western culture began. The Greek thinkers searched for the universal, the one underlying unifying principle: the logos (Thilly & Wood, 1957). That search directed the focus of human consciousness above and beyond the mere physical world into the realm of Plato's ideal, the Good. The transcendent loci of human awareness, consequently, resulted in a view of the male as an ideal male being greater than the average man. The outcome was a belief in a vision of maleness termed the "heroic man" (Doyle, 1983).

The demographical hierarchies of earlier times permeated the cultures of the Greeks and Romans. Some 80% of the populations were slaves (Hunt, 1990). The heroic ideal male represented in the work of Homer and Virgil lived in a significantly masculine world, "a world inhabited by soldiers, adventurers, warriors, kings and Gods. Men were the 'doers,' the conquerors and rulers, of a threatening and barbaric world" (Doyle, 1983, p. 37). Women did not participate in such lofty positions, and were important only insofar as they served the needs of men. The women of epic times were not honored for their talents or abilities, but rather for their idealized physical beauty, charms, and dedication to men (Cantarella, 1987). According to Doyle, men were driven to war by the beauty of Helen of Troy. The father in ancient Greece was seen as the true parent of a child, and the mother was seen as a mere incubator. The phenomenon of patriarchy was well established in fifth-century B.C. Greek society. The epic male hero was first and foremost a fighter and a leader. Male ascendancy manifested as physical strength, power and skill in battle, and courage and loyalty toward all levels of society. "Essentially, the epic male role embodied the features of the warrior-ruler" (p. 27).

Classical Rome continued the ideal of the heroic male. Aeneas, in Virgil's Aeneid, traveled from Troy to Italy and founded the city of Rome. It was the male who was the pursuer that accomplished great feats, with the female of the Roman period a consort by his side or a victim of his endless pursuit (Gardner, 1986). Hunt (1990) noted that economic, political, and social limitations of Rome resulted in a weakened and vulnerable empire. Germanic and Slavic tribes invaded, the empire collapsed in the West, and the chiefs of the primitive tribes became the kings of emerging feudal states.

The Otherworldly Male (500 A.D. – 1000 A.D.)

Economically, the demise of the Western Roman Empire in 476 left Europe without laws and protection. This date, or 500 A.D., is considered the beginning of the Middle Ages. A feudal hierarchy, between the eighth and eleventh centuries, filled the void. Lords of manors protected serfs and peasants, who were protected by higher overlords, who in turn were protected by the king. A Christian paternalist ethic provided moral justification for the feudal agrarian economic system (Hunt, 1990). Plotinus and St. Augustine merged Plato's hierarchy of philosophical ideals, culminating in the transition of the Good into the concept of God in Christianity. The merging of Greek philosophy, Roman law, and then Christianity culminated in the course and development of Western civilization (Thilly & Wood, 1957).

The life and teachings of Christ, as interpreted by the early church fathers, infused new ideals into the classical epic ideal of masculinity. Self-renunciation, nonviolence, poverty, and service to others (Matthew 26:52, John 13:12-16) marked the advancement upon the epic ideal. The new ideal embodied a slowly changing view of patriarchy that took centuries in its development (Witherington, 1984). Early church fathers and the monastic tradition formulated the male/female gender ideals that permeated the Middle Ages (Buckley, 1986; Pagels, 1979).

The Platonic ideal of a cosmic heavenly blueprint or template of a hierarchical ladder of reality as an ever-increasingly complex refinement on which all particular entities were patterned, placed the primary viewing focus above and beyond earthly particulars (Thilly & Wood, 1957). Consequently, all things of the physical sphere were less valued, less desirable, less a point of focus, and sometimes even the embodiment of evil, which was to be avoided. Women and sex, the flesh, money, and most earthly things became a sin to be avoided, evidenced in the church fathers' belief in the causal link between sexuality and sin (Prusak, 1974). The ideal male, from a Christian perspective, was to renounce the world, the flesh, the temporal, and downplay all sexuality. The spiritual was the renunciation of all things on earth (Laeuchli, 1972). The hierarchy of Platonic idealism, of Christian spiritual principles, and of feudal economics furthered patriarchy. Saint Paul wrote, "For a man indeed ought not to cover his head, forasmuch, as he is the image and glory of God: but the woman is the glory of man. For the man is not of the woman; but the woman of the man. Neither was the man created for the woman: but the woman for the man" (1 Corinthians 11:7-9). These ideas continued to sanction patriarchy.

Men carried the image of God and the authority of God in all matters transcendent and secular. Not so with women, who were to be subject in all things to men. Eve and all of her gender were often portrayed by the early church fathers as the reason for the male's ills. Doyle (1983) noted,

"By virtue of their presumed insatiable sexual nature, women were cast as the embodiment of all that was evil. Following the earlier traditions of viewing women as the source of all evil (for example, the Hebrew's conception of Eve and the Greek's view of Pandora), the early church fathers portrayed women as the reason for men's and humanity's downfall and subsequent sinfulness" (p. 31). Pope Clement, an early church father, captured the anti-feminine sentiment by pronouncing, "Every woman should be overwhelmed with shame at the very thought that she is a woman" (Davis, 1972). The philosophical hierarchy of forms, the feudal hierarchy of agrarian management, and the gender hierarchy of patriarchy concomitantly progressed.

The Knightly Male (1100 A.D. – 1500 A.D.)

The feudal agrarian social order flourished and stabilized the society of Western Europe. The religious hierarchy of the Roman Church permeated earlier centuries; feudalism expanded authority to include the aristocracy and a military class. Towns, trade, and money accompanied the rise of the soldier, or knightly, class (Hunt, 1990). The ideal of the male gender was thus expanded further. The asexual, spiritual male became more of a sensual, chivalric, knightly male. Chivalry, a code of knightly behavior, was a feature of the High and later Middle Ages in Western Europe. From varied beginnings, it coalesced in the 12th century, flourished in the 13th, became decadent in the 14th and 15th, and merged into the Renaissance idea of the gentleman in the 16th century. The chivalric male was a fighter and a soldier. Physical strength enabled him to express his prowess in combat (Mosse, 1996). He was loyal to the king or lord, and devoted to the lady. Mosse stated,

> Courage and daring were some of the virtues that a man must possess; he was also supposed to be compassionate, loyal, and ennobled by the pure love of a woman. This ideal of chivalry was produced by feudal society in its decline, when the aristocracy clung to a code of honor as a symbol of its autonomy. As military officers, courtiers, and civil servants, the aristocracy now cultivated a code of honor linked on the one hand to the performance of duties, and, on the other, to trying to preserve self-respect and sense of caste. (p. 18)

The chivalric male was a rebirth of the Greco/Roman heroic male with some modifications.

The sensual aspect of the male and the lady became dominant. Women in the feudal period ascended ideological pedestals and were seen as the "lady" (Gold, 1985). They became stereotyped as Madonnas or temptresses and prostitutes (Dillenberger, 1985; Shahar, 1983). Women's idealized purity evoked honor and service from the male. The period of feudalism contributed to the dualistic view of woman as the Madonna or the whore, a view that has filtered down in various forms through the ages (Doyle, 1983). According to Doyle, the phenomenon of patriarchy continued to be important and grow in prominence with the practice of primogeniture, wherein the wealth of the father passed to the eldest son, bypassing siblings and the mother. Patriarchy grew as primogeniture affirmed and established the family lineage.

The Renaissance Male (1500 A.D. – 1700 A.D.)

Several economic factors led to the disintegration of the medieval feudal system. Hunt (1990) called attention to the fact that when the agrarian system shifted to a three-field system — spring and fall planting with land lying fallow every third year — production increased by 50% (White, 1962). Horses replaced the oxen, and transportation of goods and people augmented the distribution of commodities and growth in population centers. The population in Europe doubled between 1100 and 1300 (Miskimin, 1969). Cities and towns sprang up, with workers severing ties to the land and becoming specialized artisans and manufacturers. An increased rate of transportation resulted, along with increased interregional and long-distance trade and commerce (Hunt, 1990).

The idealism of Plato, Plotinus, and Augustine pervaded the Middle Ages. Attention was focused in the Heavenlies. With the rediscovery of Aristotelian thought known as "entelechy," the essence of a thing resided not in some heavenly blueprint but in the particular object. Another influential idea was William of Occam's "razor," a concept that emphasized the acceptability of logical verification of what could be verified by reason, and faith to understand other dimensions not verifiable by reason. Truth was severed into two camps (Thilly & Wood, 1957). Some truths could be verified logically, and the rest were sustained by faith. The acceptance of human deduction brought about a shift in focus. When people began thinking about the physical world rather than the heavenly, infinite subtle distinctions resulted. European man broke through the wall between man and nature that had resulted from scholasticism, and he began the exploration of the physical universe. This was not only the age of the rebirth of classicism; it was the birth of discovery and exploration. Men such as Gutenberg, Petrarch, De Gamman, Columbus, Cortez, da Vinci,

Michelangelo, Titian, Marco Polo, Copernicus (Wells, 1920), and those in the British Royal Society (Jones, 1961) revamped the understanding of the world. Man was no longer viewed as a passive pawn in a divine game, but became, with the new tools of induction and science, the master of the physical world (Thilly & Wood).

The ideal of the Renaissance male emerged in sixteenth-century England. The rich aristocracy and the serfs of feudalism broadened to include a growing middle class. The search for knowledge eclipsed the equestrian knight's search for glory and the lady's approval. A greater freedom of thought wrenched itself from the Roman church. The rebirth of the classical quest for knowledge emerged. "Men and some few women began to think for themselves about the wonders of the world and its mysteries" (Doyle, 1983, p. 33).

The Renaissance male ideal shifted greatly from the doer, powerful in battle, to the thinkers who engaged in refined rational and intellectual activities. Classical, or epic, man sought physical perfection; spiritual man was motivated toward an afterlife. However, Renaissance man sought intellectual liberation to explore the real world's subtleties (Doyle, 1983). The rebirth of classicism came to represent physical beauty, courage, moral restraint, and a strong will. Mosse (1996) noted that the masculinity stereotype was born out of the rise of the professional, bureaucratic, and commercial middle class. A key element of masculinity was the way a man of the period held himself. His reputation, standing, and dignity became equated with chivalry. "Courage and daring . . . [and being] compassionate, loyal, and ennobled by the pure love of a woman became the ideal of chivalry" (p. 18). Affronts to a man's dignity were played out through the ritual of dueling, which was practiced from the 1700s into the twentieth century (Mosse).

Patriarchy continued to be the norm for Western society during the Renaissance. Men still maintained power over women's lives, and women's lives were directed toward marriage or service through the convent (Labalme, 1980). Some earlier women, such as Hildegard of Bingen and Herrad of Landsberg, were even widely respected for their scholarly and scientific learning and writings, and achievement long thought proper only for males (Ferrante, 1980). The Renaissance male, then, a phenomenon of the middle class, focused attention more toward this world in his quest for physical beauty, intellectual discovery, and social status.

Epoch Four: The Industrial Revolution (1700 A.D. - on)

Beginning early with William of Occam (1280-1347) and the controversy over universals, a further paradigm shift in thinking started the movement that resulted in the Industrial Revolution and the Mechanical Revolution. According to Thilly and Wood (1957), from medieval times on, a Platonic ideal existed in the mental blueprint for reality. Occam entered the realist (universal ideas are the real measures)/nominalist (reality is expressed in the particular thing) debate on the side of the nominalists. Occam sought to divorce knowledge that could be verified from theology or faith. God must be accepted on the basis of faith, not proof (i.e. Anselm), because theological beliefs are not subject to demonstration. By opposing the scholastic attempts to prove Christian dogma and insisting that they be accepted on faith, he left the way open for all other problems to be dealt with through the empirical data of science. Universals, being superfluous, must therefore be eliminated from the interpretation of our experience. Consequently, the paradigm shift from accepting theological subjects through faith and applying logic and observation to everything else began the focus of mental directedness from the Heavenlies to the physical earth — hence the beginnings of science (Shahar, 1983). Acknowledging the century or two of lag-time for ideas to manifest in physical reality, the Industrial Revolution was on its way.

The Mechanical/Industrial Revolution

Hunt (1990) noted,

> Between 1700 and 1770 the foreign markets for English goods grew much faster than did England's domestic markets . . . . This rapidly increasing foreign demand for English manufacturers was the single most important cause of the most fundamental transformation of human life in history: the Industrial Revolution. (p. 37)

Mechanically, because of the exhaustion of the wood supply for ironworks and the replacement of wood by coal, a pumping engine to pump water out of coalmines was needed. Consequently, the machine-driven engine, locomotive and steam power, the application of electrical science, and the internal combustion engine all launched societies into the modern world (McNeill, 1963; Wells, 1920). The Mechanical Revolution and the Industrial Revolution advanced hand in hand. The Industrial Revolution built upon the Mechanical Revolution by replacing brawn with machine power, resulting in a division of labor which could mass-produce items on a much larger scale in the factory. In an early Victorian cotton mill, for example, the cheapness, uniformity, and, above all, the quantity of the product far exceeded that which could be produced by hand (Wells).

Changes were almost as radical in other traditional trades such as metallurgy and printing. The rise of new occupations such as engineering and railroading had driven the new technology deep into the fabric of British society by 1850 (McNeill, 1963). Significant cultural changes also had a profound impact upon the masculinity stereotype as it adapted to the historical changes. Within a century of industrialization, the emphasis on male physical strength was tempered and replaced with gender-neutral machines. The one main male gender measure, physical strength, became much less a delimiter of maleness. It is significant, therefore, that a women's movement on any sort of large scale emerged for the first time in history at this time. Mary Wollstonecraft's *A Vindication of the Rights of Women* was written in 1792; it was the first major feminist treatise anywhere in history (Wilber, 1996).

The Bourgeois Male (1700 A.D.– on)

By the eighteenth century a strong and powerful middle class had become well established in England. A new focus began to emerge for the males of this class. Money, status and prestige replaced the earlier goals of territorial conquest, spiritual fulfillment, and acquisition of knowledge. The middle class of urbanized Europe and England helped create the new bourgeois male ideal. As is suggested by the word "bourgeois," the derivation of which is French and means "a citizen of the town," the new man's goals were respectability and material success (Hunt, 1990). This man was driven to define himself by the achievement of the primary standard of male power: money. His main avenue to status and prestige was to succeed in business. "The entrepreneur, or business adventurer, was his model. To risk and then to succeed in business was the final proof of a man's worth" (Doyle, 1983, p. 36).

Mosse (1996) affirmed that the "masculinity stereotype" meant that being more clearly refined represented the way "men assert what they believe to be their manhood . . . and stood for a definite view of human nature and human action" (p. 4). The developing view of masculinity carried further the qualities of willpower, honor, and courage. It influenced significantly every aspect of cultural life, including naturalism, socialism, fascism, communism, national respectability, and war. Modern masculinity was based upon the view that the nature of a man's body — its beauty, symmetry, and poise — could be universalized into an ideal, beyond raw power, of manly beauty, virtue, and proper morals. All men were supposed to emulate the male ideal of masculinity in contrast to "immoral, weak, and servile men" (Mosse, 1996, p. 6).

Women of the eighteenth century, however, did not fare as well. They continued to be subjugated to men. "The ideal of the young virgin as a reward for the hardworking and successful male played a dominant role in eighteenth-century literature" (Doyle, 1983, p. 36).

The Male Gender Role Stereotype in North America

The male gender role in the United States also evolved as history's relentless pursuit continued. In just three and one-half centuries the evolving social climate effected several male gender transitions (Doyle, 1983). Elizabeth and Joseph Pleck (1980) wrote that the history of gender in North America is best conceived and divided into specific "periods that correspond to much broader and far-reaching changes in American politics and warfare and to new directions in economic, religious, and family life" (p. 6). Their chronology is as follows: agrarian patriarchy (1630-1820); the commercial age (1820-1860); the strenuous life (1861-1919); and compassionate providing (1920-1965). Consonant with the Plecks' (1980) four periods, Doyle's nomenclature will serve the present discussion.

The Aristocrat and His Family (1630-1820). New England, the Pilgrims, and the Puritan religion have an integral merging of origins and developments. The early religionists shaped the development and destiny of early America. It was these newcomers, with ingrained English religious traditions, who settled New England. The early English expeditions of 1583, 1585, and 1587 brought the first colonists (Good, 1964). Soon the Anglicans settled Jamestown in 1607, and the Pilgrims landed at Plymouth in 1620; the Puritans settled Massachusetts during the same period (Good). It was the members of the clergy and their followers, seeking religious freedom for themselves (Good), who planted the first settlements in the new land.

The Puritans saw themselves as vastly superior to the liberal majority of seventeenth-century England, because of their strict moral code and belief in a rigid patriarchy. The early New England clergymen were inculcated with English religious traditions (Callahan, 1960). The religious climate in the new land was developed from a major new emphasis on religion in England just prior to the settlement of New England (Callahan), influenced by Luther's "priesthood of all believers" and the desire to translate the Bible from Latin to the vernacular so schools could teach the word of God. The real sources of American inspiration must be understood from the perspective of the English Puritanism of the seventeenth century (Callahan;

Good, 1964). The Puritans especially disdained the "feminization" of English society that had come down from the earlier chivalric period. A core belief of Puritanism was that men were the spokespersons for God and were superior to women, and that women were to be subservient to men in all matters (Doyle, 1983).

Under English common law and Biblical principles, the man was head of the household, and as such he was the only one permitted to enter into contracts, to buy or sell land, and to represent the family in civil matters. The concept of primogeniture dictated that family assets passed to the eldest son. The father made all the important decisions in the family with regard to the children's education, career, and husbands for daughters. Consequently, women had few, if any, legal rights in the early colonies (Frey & Morton, 1986; Salmon, 1986).

Some principles of the bourgeois male, such as ownership of land and Pleck's (1987) agrarian patriarchy, lingered as important principles of male value. Land brought a man power, influence, and status. Landowners became a body known as the aristocracy, the rule of the *aristos*, or best. The aristocracy became synonymous with power, independence, self-confidence, intelligence, and individualism — the prevailing descriptive traits for masculinity.

Nevertheless, the aristocratic period waned with the American Revolution and the formation of the New Republic. Women took on a more important role in child rearing, children's education, and women's social concerns (Butterfield, Friedlander, & Kline, 1975; Kerber, 1974; Stewart, Winter, & Jones, 1975). The wheels were set in motion to bring about "the most fundamental transformation of human life in history: the Industrial Revolution" in the United States (Hunt, 1990, p. 37).

<u>The Common Man and the Suffragette (1820-1869).</u> A new social order began to emerge in the first half of the nineteenth century that abandoned the concept that a woman was an extension of the father and husband; in addition, some further distinctions were posited to each sex. This was called the doctrine of "separate spheres" (Cott, 1977). Women were granted their distinct sexual sphere and were permitted a greater range of activity. Males were seen in their sphere as aggressive and competitive by nature, and fit for political activities and economic venture (Doyle, 1983).

The ideal of the colonial period's male aristocrat was leveled to the ideal of the "common man." The common man was a businessman in Pleck's (1987) commercial age. A man was perceived as a person of common sense, a hard worker, and a keen negotiator in business (Gordon, 1980). The male ideal was expanding to include broader concepts such as the anarchic freedom of the uncivilized savage of the Old West (Smith, 1980). Women were still mostly assigned to the domesticity of the home (Jensen, 1986; Welter, 1966). Soon, however, women became involved in issues beyond the home, notably slavery through the abolition movement. This concern for slavery awakened women to their own plight (Hole & Levine, 1984).

Finally, by virtue of the Married Women's Property Acts 1839, women were liberated from male subjugation and could own property, receive pay for employment, sign contracts, and sue in court (Warbasse, 1987). Women extended their fight for equal rights and held the first feminist convention in Seneca Falls, New York, in 1848.

Multiple forces were at play that would further modify male identity. Males experienced erosion of their lofty patriarchal privileges. Women took a greater role in the home and society. The Union was at stake over the issue of states' rights, and men would focus on physical exertion and battle to bolster their diminished sense of masculinity.

The He-Man and his Compatriots (1861-1919). The period between 1860 and 1919, according to the Plecks (1980), was the period of the "strenuous life." The period began with the Civil War and ended with World War I. The changing times, with more female independence, left men to struggle with challenges to their masculinity. The tone of this period was set in a speech by Teddy Roosevelt before a men's group in Chicago:

> I wish to preach, not the doctrine of ignoble ease, but the doctrine of the strenuous life, the life of toil and effort, of labor and strife: to preach that highest form of success which comes, not to the man who desires mere easy peace, but to the man who does not shrink from danger, from hardship, or from bitter toil, and who out of these wins the splendid ultimate triumph. (Filene, 1986, p. 71)

The Industrial Revolution was in full swing. Great migrations of men from the farms to the cities were needed to stoke the furnaces of progress. With their declining sense of patriarchy (Kimmel, 1987), men began to create enclaves of gender-specific outlets. The fraternal system emerged; membership in fraternal lodges in the United States grew to an estimated 51 million members by 1901 (Pleck & Pleck, 1980). All-male saloons and clubs and male team sports such as football and baseball were born, as was the scouting movement; large numbers of males were also vicariously

33

living out some aspects of their manhood through the mock battles and the struggles on the field (Mosse, 1996).

Women also were expanding their roles into new areas. For example, between the years 1850 and 1870, the number of female factory workers jumped from 225,992 to 373,370 (Flexner, 1959). In addition to doing factory work, women were moving into other previously all-male occupations such as teaching, clerical work, and librarianship in increasing numbers (Garrison, 1974; Widdowson, 1984). The Seneca Falls feminist movement continued to grow as women from different backgrounds became more vocal in their demands for an end to the separate and unequal spheres that kept the sexes apart (Degler, 1980; Taylor, 1983).

The warfare and bloodshed of World War I marked another turning point for the masculinity stereotype. The he-man's strenuous life held sway for some 60 years. Women fought for their basic right — the right to vote. Such a change meant discomfort for many men, because they believed the suffragette movement meant additional changes in women's status, and that more would be sure to follow (Barker-Benfield, 1976; Donegan, 1985; Douglas, 1977). World War I rescued men from their waning status and reinforced their masculinity with an old model, that of the warrior-soldier.

<u>Partners at Last (1920-on).</u> World War I ended, and the Nineteenth Amendment gave women the right to vote. Social customs changed drastically with the flapper, the speak-easy, the Charleston, and freer sexual mores. As men and women spent more time in each other's company, the separate spheres began to merge into what the Plecks (1980) called "companionate providing." The burgeoning Industrial Revolution, technology, division of labor and specialization began to liberate men from seeing physical labor as their defining role. The Great Depression left a profound mark on the male psyche. The defining male role as breadwinner and provider vanished overnight. A man without a job lost status not only in his own eyes, but also in the eyes of his family (Komarovsky, 1940).

Another war, World War II, came to men's rescue. The age-old masculine attributes of courage, endurance, toughness, and "guts" were once again unfurled, and men found themselves getting to be "real men" again (Holmes, 1986). Women also rallied and went to the factories in great numbers. This development helped shatter the stereotype of women as the "weaker sex" (Anderson, 1981; Greenwald, 1980; Honey, 1984; Milkman, 1987).

Men returned from the war and, during the 1950s and 1960s, reasserted their superiority over women via their bread-winning ideals (Whyte, 1957). Women returned to their traditional roles in the families.

Social change raced headlong into the 1970s when ever-greater numbers of women left the homes to join the workforce. The sexual revolution left the traditional family an anachronism. The 1980s and 1990s brought more of the same. Single parent homes multiplied. Women excelled and men recoiled. Significant upheaval rocked the male psyche (Doyle, 1983; Mosse, 1996). The cultural shock of the gender role reversal is of such momentous proportions that Pollack (1999) states that the country is headed toward a gender Armageddon.

Epoch Five: The Informational Age

The inevitability of change can be so pervasive and extensive that the human mind staggers to grasp it (Houston, 1982). When Einstein published his theory of relativity in 1904, everything changed. Many are still living in nineteenth-century perspectives. In the nineteenth century, pictures had frames. Twentieth-century art piled stuff on frameless surfaces, and provided no more windows through which to look. Humankind lost a viewing point, an "Archimedean Point," from which to look at reality and has come to be one with the environment. The ideas of Einstein are yanking civilization into an unknown future. A global orientation is pervasive, while manufacturing is giving way to services and the management of information. Instant communication can threaten a person's job from anywhere on the planet. Change is pushing human history on a rapidly accelerating course (Houston).

Managing rapid change spun a new byword —"speed" (Toffler, 1994). Organizations and careers are flexing and reshaping constantly to manage the perpetual motion. Results include downsizing, restructuring, subcontracting, webbing, and networking. An organization must, like the cat, be able to adjust quickly and land on its feet, and to realign instantly (Toffler, 1994). Large (1994) noted:

> As recently as the 1960s, almost one-half of all workers in the industrialized countries were involved in making (or helping to make) things. By the year 2,000, however, no developed country will have more than one-sixth or one-eighth of its workforce in the traditional roles of making and moving goods. Already an estimated two-thirds of U.S. employees work in the services sector, and "knowledge" is becoming our more important "product." This calls for different organizations, as well as different kinds of workers. In 1991, for the first time ever, companies

35

> spent more money on computing and communications gear than the combined monies spent on industrial, mini, farm and construction equipment. This spending pattern offers hard proof that we have entered a new era. The Industrial Age has given way to the Information Age. (pp. 1-2)

Consequently, everyone is sharpening up. Individuals need to be on the cutting edges of their jobs, fields, or careers, and established clientele can be serviced from anywhere (Houston, 1982). Total commitment to one's chosen field of endeavor is essential. "You're in Paris, and you decide to use your American Express card. Getting credit approval involves a 46,000-mile journey over phones and computers. The job can be completed in 5 seconds" (Pritchett, 1994, p. 8). Old concepts of job security, tenure, and retirement programs are being replaced with uncertainty and ambiguity. The concept of "niche craft," wherein entrepreneurial individuals find needs and fill them, is becoming the norm. Pritchett observed,

> Less than half the workforce in the industrial world will be holding conventional full-time jobs in organizations by the beginning of the 21st century. Those full-timers or insiders will be the new minority. Every year more and more people will be self-employed. Many will work temporary or part-time, sometimes because that's the way they want it, sometimes because that's all that is available. (pp. 16-17)

One of the key factors of the Information Age is the acquisition and use of information. Possibly the concept of a university education will no longer be realistic. Perhaps there will be no "getting" of an education, since becoming educated may be considered a life-long process. The accumulated information of the last 5,000 years has been equaled in the last 30 (Toffler, 1994). A weekday edition of *The New York Times* contains more information than the average person was likely to come across in a lifetime in 17th century England (Pritchett, 1994). The available information doubles every five years (Wurman, 1994). Pritchett stated,

> ENIAC, commonly thought of as the first modern computer, was built in 1944. It took up more space than an 18-wheeler tractor-trailer and weighed more than 17 Chevrolet Cameos, and consumed 140,000 watts of electricity. ENIAC could execute up to 5,000 basic

arithmetic operations per second. One of today's popular microprocessors, the 486, is built on a tiny piece of silicon about the size of a dime. It weighs less than a packet of Sweet'N Low, and uses less than 2 watts of electricity. A 486 can execute up to 54,000,000 instructions per second. The cost of computing power drops roughly 30% every year, and microchips are doubling in performance power every 18 months. (p. 2)

Pritchett further noted, "Let's say you're going to a party, so you pull out some pocket change and buy a little greeting card that plays 'Happy Birthday' when it's opened. After the party, someone casually tosses the card into the trash, throwing away more computer power than existed in the entire world before 1950" (p. 27).

All of this has profound implications for the male gender stereotype. No longer are physical strength and physical speed necessary survival hunting skills. Women can sit at a computer and conduct business around the world. Physical strength is irrelevant. Change is rampant, and the speed of adaptability is essential, especially for members of the male gender. Many males are still stuck in the nineteenth-century patriarchal stereotype. Having explored the current research and the historical development of the masculinity stereotype, the contemporary research regarding current thinking about male development will now be examined.

The Development of Masculinity Research in Twentieth Century America

Early in twentieth century United States general interest in psychology and masculinity in particular launched an endeavor to understand maleness. That interest focused on the male sex role, alternatives to the male sex role, the socialization of males that led to limited communication skills, limited ability to communicate affect, and outcomes noted as action empathy, nonrelational sex, and somatization.

The Male Sex Role Identity Paradigm

Pleck (1981) wrote of "a set of ideas about sex roles, especially the male role, that has dominated the academic social sciences since the 1930s and more generally has shaped our culture's view" (p. 1). For 50 years (ca. 1930-80), research on masculinity was dominated by what Pleck (1981, 1995) called the "male sex role identity paradigm (MSRI)" (Pleck, 1995,

p. 1). According to Pleck (1981, 1995), the elements of the Male Sex Role Identity Paradigm have dominated our culture, and have been so closely absorbed into psychological thought that the paradigm became identified with psychological understanding of gender differences. The key elements of the paradigm were developed and tested in all-male samples; however, the theory is applicable to both sexes. Despite the fact that the theory is sufficiently general to include both sexes, the Male Sex Role Identity nomenclature was chosen. "With 'essentialist' philosophical roots, the assumption of an inherent, invariable masculine essence, this paradigm postulates an inner psychological need for a gender role identity. In fact, the development of personality depends, in this model, on the successful formation of such an identity" (Levant, 1997, p. 5).

The Male Sex Role Identity Paradigm puts forth the idea that a sex role identity is a primary factor in psychological development. Men were measured by their adoption of this paradigm for their identity. To "be a man" meant adopting the dicta of this paradigm, gender-specific values, behaviors, and socially prescribed attitudes (Levant, 1997). A man's sex role identity usually is derived from the model of the same-sex parent; however, this process of identification is difficult for the modern male because of "paternal absence, maternal over-protectiveness, the minimizing influence of the schools, and the general blurring of male and female roles that is occurring now in society" (Pleck, 1981, p. 3). The Male Sex Role Identity Paradigm purports that a man's failure to achieve secure male sex role identity results in "homosexuality . . . delinquency, violence, hostility toward women" (Pleck, p. 4).

Pleck (1981) summarized the propositions of the Male Sex Role Identity Paradigm as follows:

A. Developmental origins of Sex Role Identity
  1. Sex role identity is operationally defined by measures of psychological sex typing, conceptualized in terms of psychological masculinity and/or femininity dimensions.
  2. Sex role identity derives from identification modeling and, to a lesser extent, reinforcement and cognitive learning of sex-typed traits, especially among males.
B. Resultant failure of attaining Sex Role Identity development

3. The development of appropriate sex role identity is a risky, failure-prone process, especially for males.
4. Homosexuality reflects a disturbance of sex role identity.
5. Appropriate sex role identity is necessary for good psychological adjustment because of an inner psychological need for it.
6. Hyper-masculinity in males (exaggerated masculinity, often with negative social consequences) indicates insecurity in their sex role identities.

C. Problems faced by males in terms of Sex Role Identity
7. Problems of sex role identity account for men's negative attitudes and behaviors toward women.
8. Problems of sex role identity account for boys' difficulties in school performance and adjustment.
9. Black males are particularly vulnerable to sex role identity problems.
10. Male adolescent initiation rites are a response to problems of sex role identity.
11. Historical changes in the character of work and the organization of the family have made it more difficult for men to develop and maintain their sex role identities.

Propositions 1 and 2 concern the structure and developmental origins of sex role identity.

Propositions 3-6 focus on the results of failure in sex role identity development.

Propositions 7-11 interpret various problems faced by males in terms of sex role identity issues. Taken together, these eleven propositions constitute a comprehensive and consistent analysis—indeed, a worldview—of sex roles. (p. 7)

Early attention to masculinity, maleness, and emasculation was minimal. Articles entitled "The Effeminization of Men" appeared as early as 1893 (Dubbert, 1974). However, with his visit to the United States in 1908, Freud began to focus some attention on the sex role typing, or "character traits." Freud's early writings were general rather than specific. The first clear sex role identity statements seem to be those of Adler in his concept of masculine protest and the concept of the femininity complex in men (Boehm, 1932; Horney, 1932). Fenichel (1945) noted only two entries in his *The Psychoanalytic Theory of Neurosis* regarding sex typing and sex role identity (pp. 337, 506). So the Male Sex Role Identity Paradigm had its origins in the interaction between late nineteenth and twentieth-century social concerns about masculinity in the United States and the early stages of psychoanalytic thought.

Pleck (1981) stated that research into male gender stereotyping in the twentieth century, which led to the Male Sex Role Identity Paradigm, resulted from the development of American psychology's tradition of mental testing in the 1930s. The development of the early standardized intelligence tests provided a model for some of the first sex role identity theories. In the early 1930s the first masculinity/femininity sex role identity scales were presented as a single overall dimension of sex role personality identity (Pleck), a continuum, with male and female characteristics at opposite poles on the same dimension.

Beginning in the 1940s and continuing until the 1960s, the second major phase of sex role identity developed, based upon the induction of psychoanalytic theory into the understanding human behavior. The psychoanalytical concept of the unconscious was added, and sex role identity came to be viewed as a combination of the conscious and unconscious levels of the mind. Implications for masculine identity theory came from the belief that "masculine behavior in men might indicate overcompensation for an unconscious feminine identity" (Pleck, 1981, p. 8).

Sex role identity theorists, and especially male sex role identity theorists in the late 1960s, continued the differentiation/inclusion process in viewing individual masculinity and femininity as "two independent psychological dimensions rather than as opposite ends of the same dimension" (Pleck, 1981, p. 7). An individual's sexual identity came to be viewed as a composite of maleness, femaleness, and a combination of the two (androgyny). In sum, the theoretical development of masculinity theory has grown during the 1930s through the 1960s from having a simple component, to having multiple components, to consisting of a blend of components (Pleck).

Because of an innate psychological need to develop a sex role identity, the individual is preprogrammed to learn a traditional sex role as part of normal psychological development. Pleck (1981, 1995) noted that culturally defined sex roles do not arbitrarily restrict individuals' potential; on the contrary, they are necessary external structures without which individuals could not develop normally. From this perspective, individuals must be fitted to traditional roles, and the problem of traditional sex roles lies in the fact that so many people fail to fit them, rather than in the nature of the roles themselves. Nevertheless, since the historical Male Sex Role Identity Paradigm has permeated western thought so thoroughly, it is difficult to examine it objectively. Only recently has the paradigm been called into question. Levant (1992) confirmed that males are socialized by the principles they absorb from their parents, peers, and culture. He noted that until the late 1960s in the United States, the male sex role identity conformed to the traditional and stereotypical ideals. For male children of the post-war era, then, "being a man" meant conforming to seven basic tenets: 1) strict avoidance of anything feminine, 2) restricted emotions, 3) strength and aggression, 4) self-reliance, 5) pursuit of achievement and status, 6) disconnection of sex from intimacy, and 7) homophobia (p. 6).

The Male Sex Role Identity Paradigm was more applicable to the traditional code of masculinity regarding the standards of self-reliance and a limited emotional range earlier in the twentieth century than it is today (Pleck, 1982). It probably was useful in the austere and demanding conditions of the Industrial Revolution, the Great Depression, and two World Wars (Gilmore, 1990; Rotundo, 1993).

According to the Sex Role Identity Paradigm, the only way men and women can meet the supposedly inherent need for a sexual identity is to embrace the full set of gender-specific values, behaviors, and attitudes prescribed by society — their traditional gender roles. Failure to negotiate the process is thought to have serious consequences; for men, these include "homosexuality, hyper-masculinity, and negative attitudes toward women" (Levant, 1997, p. 5).

Levant (1997) outlined the lingering traditional male traits worth preserving as follows: having a willingness to work hard and sacrifice to provide for family, being able to withstand hardship and pain to protect others, showing affection through action (doing for others), having integrity and loyalty, showing persistence in solving difficult problems, and having the ability to take risks and stay calm in dangerous situations. Levant also noted male problem traits: 1) emotional numbness (difficulty in feeling, identifying, expressing emotions, and the inability to feel and respond to emotions of others), 2) overindulgence in anger and violence, 3) simultaneous dependence on and distance from female partners, 4) fear of and shame over failure to "be a man," 5) exaggerated investment in work, 6) disregard for health risks, and 7) substituting unconnected lust for sexual intimacy (p. 4).

Traditional male role assumptions continue to dominate the conventional wisdom. Research is a heady endeavor, the results of which may take decades to filter into conventional human consciousness. Data are accumulating that are likely to modify the male identity paradigm. "What researchers have confirmed, is that the gender role identity paradigm itself fails on two fronts: 1) in study after study on the development of boys, disconfirming data were ignored by investigators who would simply conclude that their hypotheses (consistent with the sex role identity paradigm) were upheld; and 2) the stereotyped gender roles that it promotes divide society along patriarchal lines" (Levant, 1997, p. 5). Pleck (1981) subsequently rejected the Male Sex Role Identity Paradigm.

The Sex Role Strain Paradigm

Pleck (1981) critically deconstructed so-called male sex role identity theories, creating in their stead the paradigm of sex role strain. In so doing, he highlighted the sometimes-devastating conflicts and stressors that gender stereotyping and ("macho") cultural expectations have created for men. Since that time, a number of feminist scholars have taken to task male phallocentric theories of human development, recasting the psychological understanding of women's growth from a relational, bonded perspective (Chodorow, 1978, 1989; Gilligan, 1982; Jordan, Kaplan, Miller, Stiver, & Surrey, 1991; Miller, 1976).

Where does that leave men? Boys and men have been left in the midst of the discredited, discarded shreds of biased, outmoded theory (Pollack, 1999). Pleck (1981) proposed, and subsequent researchers have thoroughly supported, the theory that men who embrace the male role identity paradigm are in a no-win situation. They suffer if they deviate from the norms prescribed by society, and they pay a significant price if they conform to them. According to Pleck, the gender role identity paradigm is harmful to men.

Contemporary sex roles are inherently contradictory, Pleck (1981) suggested, and are inevitably violated by a large number of men, with serious psychological and social consequences. Boys who are athletically inadequate, men who are unable to support their families, many males, who are insufficiently aggressive or display emotion too openly, are subject to the scorn of their peers and damage to their self-esteem.

But conforming to traditional sex norms exacts a price from the men themselves and from those around them (Levant, 1997; Pleck, 1981, 1995; Pollack, 1998). The relative disengagement from family life associated with the stereotypical male role has been linked to higher levels of psychological distress. Researchers then searched for an alternative model of sex role identity that might resolve these problems and proposed, among others, the androgynous conception. Androgyny has proved to be an important transitional concept in moving to a whole new way of viewing sex roles that has emerged in both the social sciences and society. Instead of seeing traditional sex roles as desirable and their internalization via sex role identity as the goal of psychological development, this new interpretation views these roles as limiting and constricting. This new interpretation of sex roles, the Sex (gender) Role Strain Paradigm (SRS), can be summed up in the following propositions:

1. Sex roles are operationally defined by sex role stereotypes and norms.
2. Sex roles are contradictory and inconsistent.
3. The proportion of individuals who violate sex roles is high.
4. Violating sex roles leads to social condemnation.
5. Violating sex roles leads to negative psychological consequences.
6. Actual or imagined violation of sex roles leads individuals to over-conform to them.
7. Violating sex roles has more severe consequences for males than females.
8. Certain characteristics prescribed by sex roles are psychologically dysfunctional.
9. Each sex experiences sex role strain in its paid work and family roles.
10. Historical change causes sex role strain. (Pleck, 1981, pp. 135-152)

Gilmore (1990) also noted that such tests of masculinity are very frightening for men, given that failing them can result in the loss of a sense of identity. This threat is so strong with the loss of the sense of identity, Gilmore continues, that the Fox Tribe of Iowa referred to its manhood ritual as an impossible goal to achieve. Yet Gilmore did not find what he imagined to be conventional wisdom, that women have been more nurturing and protective while men have been more disconnected and uncaring. He stated,

> One of my findings . . . is that manhood ideologies always
> include a criterion of selfless generosity even to the point
> of sacrifice. Again and again we find that "real" men are

43

> those who give more than they take; they serve others. Real men are generous, even to a fault. . . . Manhood therefore is also a nurturing concept, if we define that term as giving. (p. 229)

The central focus, then, of Pleck's (1981) work, is that research into sex roles can be summarized as contributing either to the Male Sex Role Identity Paradigm or the Male Sex Role Strain Paradigm. Pleck contended that the Male Sex Role Identity Paradigm is not a useful model for understanding sex roles. He noted that the basic template for identifying the Male Sex Role Identity Paradigm involves the following: "1) it uses terms such as insecure or inadequate; 2) it emphasizes the potentially psychologically harmful consequences of a man's relationship with his mother; and 3) it views homosexuality as the worst misfortune that can befall a man" (p. 7). While Pleck documented the dissonance between the Male Sex Role Identity Paradigm and the Sex Role Strain Paradigm, the Male Sex Role Identity Paradigm persists. Its tenets have pervaded the culture for so long and are so ingrained that it still finds expression in the culture. Many researchers continue to document its lingering antecedents in the male socialization process.

The Male Gender Role Socialization Process

One aspect of the male psyche still prevalent is the factor of male emotional limitations. The emotional illiteracy in many males is a learned phenomenon. Research into how male babies develop reveals that they are more emotionally reactive, more expressive, fussier, and more physically active than girl babies. They startle, cry, and become excited and distressed while girl babies are calmer (Haviland & Malatesta, 1981; Weinberg, 1992). Pollack (1998) noted, "Male infants are actually more emotionally expressive than female babies" (p. 11).

However, it is not long before this state of affairs changes. The male child experiences a significant trauma. He is pushed out of the loving pre-oedipal union before he has matured enough psychologically. The early pre-oedipal abandonment leaves the male child with deep longings for the lost attachment and with profound fears of abandonment. This traumatic experience persists and is played out in adult relationships (Pollack, 1990). Many men's lives are caught in the either/or stance between intimacy and identity. Pollack called this a dilemma and described it as males' tendency to defend their independence. The result of the pre-oedipal trauma is described by Levant (1997):

The early, emphatic separation from their mothers and the unavailability of their fathers are traumas whose reverberations are frequently lifelong, both in terms of relationship difficulties and psychic pain . . . [the result is evident in] the often-observed tendency of men to distance themselves in marriage: another is an excessive, and frequently unconscious, dependence on their wives. Because the traumatic rupture of the mother-bond and its prelapsarian tranquility are never mourned, men are liable to be driven by an unconscious belief that others are obligated to provide reparations for what was lost. The common manifestations of this "destructive entitlement" (Boszormenyi-Nagy & Ulrich, 1981) may range from selfishness to promiscuity to outright violence. (pp. 7-8)

Normative Male Alexithymia

Many men, due to the early male socialization trauma, have sublimated the earlier emotional realities to an internal subterranean cavern. They have been socialized out of the skills of emotional expression. "By the time boys reach elementary school much of their emotional expressiveness has been lost or has gone underground . . . little boys are made to feel ashamed of their feelings, guilty especially about feelings of weakness, vulnerability, fear, and despair" (Pollack, 1998, p. 11). Furthermore, according to Kindlon and Thompson (1999), "Boys, beginning at a young age, are systematically steered away from their emotional lives toward silence, solitude, and distrust" (p. xv). As adults, these men experience a significant sense of inferiority with regard to intimate relationships. They have strong feelings and physiological processes, but are unable to cognitively identify and report on them.

A term that has been coined for this condition is what Levant calls "alexithymia." Alexithymia originates from three Greek roots—*a,* no or not, *lex,* words, and *thymia,* feelings, no words for feelings. Levant (1997) noted, "People with alexithymia cannot put their feelings into words, and are often not even aware of them. Emotions may enter consciousness, if at all, as poorly differentiated and vaguely unpleasant physiological states" (p. 9). Males have deep and powerful feelings, and often find themselves unable to elucidate such feelings.

Sifneos (1967) first coined the term *alexithymia* in 1967 to describe symptoms he had observed in a group of men suffering from psychosomatic disorders. Krystal (1982) employed the term for the lack of ability to express feelings. Krystal described alexithymia as a psychological condition in which intrapsychic feelings are poorly monitored and poorly expressed. People with alexithymia have great difficulty describing their physiological experience. Among the other symptoms Sifneos and Krystal described are lack of flexible bodily movement; lack of awareness of physiological subtleties like shortness of breath, cold sweats, fast breathing, stone-cold staring and no facial expressions; and a general discomfort with physiological experience of feeling. "Most men balk at the suggestion that they have anything in common with these severely disturbed patients. But, in fact, these patients aren't as different from most men as one might think" (Levant, 1995, p. 52). Even though many men do not present with this kind of severity, the term has been modified to "normative male alexithymia" (Levant, 1997, p. 9) to accommodate the trauma- based "normative" state of males unable to deal with feelings.

The severity of the early socialization trauma manifests as severe physiological rigidity. Many men who have not finished the separation drama with their mothers spend their lives seeking "transitional or self-object relationships with mother substitutes" (Pollack, 1995, p. 42) in order to find a way back to that warm loving matrix. The unfinished business of the rapprochement phase waits for closure, which may never come.

Consequently, according to Levant (1997) and Pollack (1998), men may seek fantasy women in their longing for closeness, to heal and relieve the unspeakable premature traumatic separation. However, when the promise of that closeness becomes a reality, many men, due to subliminal organismic remembrances of earlier hurts, put up walls to put distance between themselves and their partners in order to protect themselves from re-living the early repressed pain, agony, and depression that are awakened by such a close encounter. A man may long for and pull in a female partner and simultaneously spend his time pushing her away. Such behavior is very crazy-making for the female partners (Levant, 1995; Pollack, 1990). It accounts for much of the experience couples face as they attempt to listen to and understand one another's "voices" (Gilligan, 1982). Additionally, numerous men are diagnosed with narcissistic personality disorders, which in psychoanalytic treatment must be brought into consciousness to address their symbolic re-enactment with current partners of the loving cocoon-like paradise from which they were dispelled (Model, 1976). Kohut (1977) also stated that in narcissistic patients, many of whom are men, it is the task of therapy to bring into awareness the skewed self-object transferences that are often played out in intimate relationships as unfinished separation experiences from childhood. The outcome is severe and life-long. Levant stated,

In the most basic sense, to live detached from one's emotions is to live isolated from oneself as well as from others — a condition that precludes true intimacy. In rendering them unable to avail themselves of a most effective way of coping with stress and turmoil — discussing their emotional reactions with an intimate friend or family member — the deficit leads many men to release their tensions through such pathological means as substance abuse and violent behavior. It predisposes them to stress-related illness and early death. And it excludes many men from the benefits of psychotherapy. . . . Like the more severe version identified by the researchers who first described it, normative male alexithymia is, in my view, a result of trauma, the prolonged insidious trauma of male gender role socialization. (p. 10)

The Impact of Alexithymia on Men's Lives

The outcome of the male socialization process precludes men from having many important human interpersonal skills. Their limited intra-personal experience or sense of what Wilber called "interiority" (1995, p. 255) is concomitant with their limited emotional relating skills. They lack the ability to acknowledge their own and their intimate partners' emotional reality. They experience a deficiency in interpersonal relating which prevents them from being able to experience vicariously their significant others' emotions and view the world from someone else's point of view (Selman, 1980).

Action Empathy
The female socialization process is different from that of males. Females remain in the maternal matrix, they receive more physical contact, and their peer-group play is interpersonal (Chodorow, 1978). Males, on the other hand, prompted to avoid "sissy stuff," compete, roughhouse physically, and become emotionally stoic. Males also are taught not to express their feelings, a lesson that is socialized through shame intra-psychically (Pollack, 1998). They develop what Levant (1997) called "action empathy." They can "psych" out a business prospect or a defense in a football game but cannot attend to their female partner's feelings (Brody & Hall, 1993; Eisenberg & Lennon, 1983; Hall, 1978; Levant, 1997). Historically, the struggle to survive has required that males be proactive, that they have action empathy. The typical scenario

in numerous counseling sessions, as well as living rooms, is as follows: A woman shares a problem with her domestic partner, seeking support, empathy, and understanding, and he does his action empathy thing and explains, explains, and explains and tells, tells, and tells her what she should do (Tannen, 1990). What men have difficulty with is emotional empathy, the ability to merely acknowledge and support their partner's emotional reality (Levant, 1997).

Anger

The traumatic rupture of the mother-bond results in an either/or trap for many men (Pollack, 1998). Many men are both desperately longing for the tranquility of pre-oedipal idyllic nurturing, and fending off any incoming loving warmth as a threat to their independence. The "early separation is so acutely hurtful to boys it can only be called a trauma — an emotional blow of damaging proportions" (p. 12). Expressing what they have been deprived of, empathy and warmth, is difficult, but men are permitted to express, and are good at expressing, anger and aggression. Men display anger and aggression much more often than women (Brody & Hall, 1993; Campbell, 1993). Anger and aggression are often more than physiological reactions to threat; they are also instruments of respect, dominance, and control (Campbell).

The acceptability of anger and aggression in the male socialization process permits males not only to express alarm, fear, or frustration with anger, but also to express feelings of vulnerability, such as fear, hurt, and shame, as anger; this process is sometimes described as a funneling of many emotions that all get expressed as anger (Keltikangas-Jarvinen, 1982; Long, 1987). Numbed by the pre-oedipal objectification schism, men have difficulty even in attending to interior emotional nuances: "They remain unaware of their anger until it erupts in outbursts of temper, which may have violent consequences" (Levant, 1997, p. 11).

Nonrelational Sex

Miller (1980) stated that the way individuals are treated and experience themselves as small children sets up a tendency to perpetuate that treatment for the rest of their lives. Given the objectification of the male child through emotional neglect, verbal abuse, shame, or physical abuse (Pollack, 1998), a boy's emotions do not disappear; they become truncated or retreat to some subterranean depth. "The relational rupture, this [separation] trauma, affects most boys — and most men — forever" (Pollack, p. 27). Negative feelings are often expressed as anger. Warmer, more positive and caring emotions are expressed through sex. For many men sex is a key means of experiencing closeness and expressing love. Levant (1997) observed,

> The boy's rigid pre-oedipal separation from his mother leaves him with the dichotomous choice of autonomy or dependence; feelings of caring and affection feel like a surrender of selfhood. The stereotypical notion that a "real man" is strong and self-sufficient taints with shame the simply human need for nourishing intimacy. (p. 12)

The mere experience of a warm, personal connection to another person runs up against strong intra-psychic barriers. The intra-psychic barriers are trace memories of the male's own early abandonment and objectification experience (Pollack, 1998). How can males now relate with females as mutual subjects with their adolescent hormonal urges if they received no or limited experience of emotional closeness in their lives? Their objectification results in regarding members of the female gender as sexual objects. As described by Zilbergeld (1992), sex for teenage boys has nothing to do with intimacy. It is detached from the rest of their lives and focused on the need to explore and prove themselves. This pattern seems to persist.

Objectified sex with a female object seems to be the reality of many men. Once a man has expressed his ultimate statement, "I love you," he has made what for some is the ultimate life and death statement. Shane (1973) illustrated this idea by describing a man who said, "I love you" as being terror- and panic-ridden. He has handed his life over to another person in that statement and waits for "his life" to be reciprocated by her. When it is not returned, he may be devastated. Sometimes it is possible for some men to express their love only in the heat of sexual passion — because only then are they authentically in contact with the depth of their feelings (Gray, 1996).

Somatization

Alexithymia, as an experience of numbness, pervades the male psychological reality (Levant, 1995). Somatization, from the Greek word *soma*, or body, is the process of internalizing emotions (Buck, 1984). Men experience bodily sensations; however, often their facial expressions don't show it. They experience emotions as tight muscles in their jaw, neck, and stomach that results in headaches, backaches, upset stomach, shortness of breath, and insomnia.

How does all of this happen? Small children are highly expressive, naturally playful, and un-selfconscious. When their activities are met with admiration, respect, appropriate guidance, and encouragement the child "blossoms like a rose" — an ongoing, gradual, and ever confident development. However, when those activities natural to living are met with attack or no contact, the absense of response, neglect, or abandonment, the child becomes confused, ashamed, and scared and withdraws from the previous spontaneity. The outcome is physiological discomfort, self-consciousness, or anxiety. These discomforts are avoided by a defensive, guarded, vigilant response to the environment. These chronic defenses become long-term patterns for coping. They take the form of muscle shields, ego boundaries, and armoring (Reich, 1949).

This armoring develops in one's life due to a non-nurturing environment, as a means of defending oneself from painful emotions. It results in the development of a persona. It affects a person's beliefs, attitudes, interpersonal relating styles, posture, muscle shape and tone, breathing patterns, and tensions in general. These patterns manifest as over reactive defensive mechanisms, anger, guilt, shame, and anxiety. They disrupt the graceful interactions with the environment, relationships, and one's capacity to experience one's own emotional realities.

These disruptions impact the contact boundary between a person and the environment (Perls, Herferline, & Goodman, 1951). The armoring process in males manifests as many negative interpersonal behaviors. According to Perls et. al (1951), these personality armors show up as conflicts in relationships, categorized as follows: 1) confluence — enmeshment or co-dependance where there is no clear demarcation between the self and the other person. 2) Introjection — swallowing "line, hook, and sinker" another's reality. In other words, a person thinks of a perception or a perspective as belonging to him or her, when it is really "out there." It is a false identification. 3) Projection — attributing to the outer world what is really only within the person. For example a person "makes up" what his or her partner is like and then treats the partner as if these beliefs about him or her are really that person. 4) Retroflection — turning everything that happens in the environment back on him or herself. It is when a person looks back at him or herself positively or negatively through the eyes of others. 5) Deflection — a turning aside, the avoidance of contact. These disruptions in the contact boundary between couples in relationships are then expressed in Gottman's (1994) divorce predictors: criticism, defensiveness, contempt, and stonewalling.

Taylor (1994) noted aspects of the nature of emotions:

1. They originate in the limbic system.
2. They then generate autonomic and endocrine activity. For example, consider the sympathetic arousal of the stress response, which includes increases in heart rate and blood pressure, and muscular tension.
3. The impact of emotion on the musculo-skeletal system may generate change in facial expression, posture, and movement, and may even trigger direct action, such as attack or flight.
4. Cognitive awareness of the emotion, the subjective experience of affect, is the fourth component. (p. 61)

The detachment trauma described by Bowlby (1973), arising from the breaking of the maternal bond and resulting in alexithymia, complements Taylor's feeling process. The feelings remain, possibly even more intently; they just are out of the conscious awareness of the person experiencing them. Pollack (1998) stated,

> Deep in the psyche of older boys and men lies the formative experience of a little boy struggling to maintain an early independent masculine sense of self. That little boy is not fending off too close a tie to mother, but rather is forever longing to return to her, and to the "holding" connection she once provided him, a connection he now feels he can never regain. (p. 27)

Many males experience love feelings, not as an intrinsic reality, but vicariously as the feelings are mirrored back to them from an intimate partner. Regrettably, the feelings are identified with the object: the intimate partner. Ongoing prescriptive responses by her are required to keep those feelings alive. Disapproval or criticism from the intimate partner often results in physiological pain and discomfort. So many women report "having to walk on eggshells to keep him happy." This is burdensome for the woman and she experiences the man as exercising power and control over her.

Even though the feelings are dealt with by "internalizing" (Buck, 1984), the muscle shield keeps them buried. While the stoic messages of "Keep a stiff upper lip" and "Never let them see you sweat" may ring in a man's ears, the physiological price is great. Feelings don't go away. They get stored in the physiological organs as tension, shortness of breath, a hanging-on bite in the jaw, a gut-level knot, and so forth, and result in chronic health problems, headache, backache, digestive upset, and insomnia among them. Over time, the physical toll of internalizing emotions very likely plays a role in the development of high blood pressure, heart disease, and other serious illnesses (Eisler & Skidmore, 1987; Ornish, 1990). Pollack (1995) described the current state of males:

> Most modern men continue to function emotionally much more like Robert Frost's neighbor in the poem "Mending Wall," who felt "Good fences make good neighbors." Men are often found walling themselves off from their own feeling states, fending off sadness and depression as well as empathic intimate relationships — especially with women — in ways that cause their significant others to feel a great deal of pain and consternation, and, I will argue, in ways that often tend to hurt and confuse the men themselves. Frost goes on to state, "before I built a wall I'd ask to know/what I was walling in or walling out." Indeed, that is the poignant and important question we must consider to understand why men so often find themselves in search of a type of sublime isolation, worshiping an idol of emotional stoicism — while continuing to yearn for connection and intimate fulfillment. (p. 33)

The stage is set for this masculine isolation at the age of two, the time of psychological birth in humans (Levant, 1997; Mahler, 1975). This is the period of separation-individuation (Pollack, 1995), the "crossover" (Levant, 1995, p. 32), the gender-specific dilemmas, the pre-oedipal rupture and trauma (Pollack), the broken bond and detachment (Bowlby, 1969) and the behavioral push out of the pre-oedipal union or "holding" connection with the mother (Chodorow, 1978; Pollack, 1995, 1998).

The lifelong consequence takes the shape of a defensive autonomy (Pollack, 1995), which results in what looks like a cold, unfeeling, narcissistic, nonrelational male (Pollack) and is manifested as the inability to identify and talk about physiological processes, otherwise known as normative male alexithymia. Normative male alexithymia is the male inability to identify and communicate physiological processes (feelings). With the disruption of the nesting of the male self in the physiology of the male — an experience of being soul-killed, disconnected, and unaware of the inner self — the long litany of masculine abuse follows. Many men often seek a woman to recreate the inner connections of the disconnected male psyche — and the male soma — to reconnect with his body and soul.

Men are often perceived as being emotionally illiterate, lacking the ability to be emotionally empathic. Consequently, anger is the primary emotion that is expressed. Sex becomes nonrelational activity in that it can be disconnected from love. This man buries and stores feelings within his body (somatization), only to have them surface later as anger, physical aggression, or physical illness.

Male Sex/Gender Development
Through the Third Year of Life

Researchers such as Blanck and Blanck (1974), Erikson (1963), Levant (1995, 1997), Lovinger (1976), Mahler (1975), Masterson (1981), Piaget (1977), Pollack (1990, 1998), Spitz (1965), and Werner (1940) have outlined many standards for optimal human development. When a critical mass of theory for optimizing human development exists and when those tenets are ignored, or missed, society becomes culpable. What are some of the current practices of male human development? How do those practices compare to current discoveries of optimal human development? What are outcomes of current male developmental treatment? In this section, treatment of the developing male child is examined; some comparisons are made to female developmental practices to explore the disparity between the two; and implications from male development are explored for an etiology of male violence toward women.

Conception and Pre-natal Development

From the start, according to Doyle (1983), male development is unique in its limitations compared to female development. Within the 28-day female cycle, an ovum merely waits. The ovum contains 23 chromosomes, 22 of which carry the unique genetic characteristics — one-half the genetic material necessary to develop human life. The 23rd chromosome is the gender-producing X chromosome.

A sperm from a male organism pursues the ovum. Significant distinctions become apparent at this point (Doyle, 1982). Male sperm, not the female ovum, determine the gender of the new life. Not all sperm are alike, however. There are basically four kinds. Some male sperm contain a 23rd X chromosome, a gymnosperm. When a gymnosperm unites with a female X chromosome, the result is a female human being. XX — "It's a girl!" Doyle further explains the gymnosperm has a round blunt head, a shorter, less active tail, and richer genetic material, and it functions better in an acidic environment. A second unique type of sperm contains a 23rd

53

Y chromosome: this is an androsperm. When united with a female X chromosome ovum, it produces a male human being. XY — "It's a boy!" The androsperm has a sharper head, a longer, more active tail, is faster moving, functions better in an alkaline environment, and is materially genetically deficient, inferior, and puny looking. However, the punier, deficient, Y, boy-producing chromosome, due to its greater mobility, fertilizes 50% more ova than does the girl-producing X chromosome. A ratio of 140 to 160 boy fetuses produced to about 100 girl fetuses is the result (Money & Tucker, 1975). However, according to Doyle, by the time of birth those extra 40 or 60 male fetuses spontaneously abort, resulting in about 105 male births to 100 female births. Moreover, two additional combinations are possible. Some male sperm contain both an X and a Y chromosome, which results in an XXY combination, known as the Klienfelder syndrome: a male person with a small penis and sterile testicles who is often mentally retarded. Additionally, some male sperm contain two Y-chromosomes, which result in an XYY combination. The result of this union is a kind of a superman, or at least a more aggressive male. Some male prisoners are of this type. From the outset, male development contains some limitations.

Doyle (1983) added that the XY chromosome union, "It's a boy," brings with it many problems. Males, unlike females, are noted to be susceptible to some 60 sex-linked diseases that diminish the quality of their lives and shorten their quantity in years (Montague, 1974). At conception, human prenatal development progresses through five stages. Embryo growth is rapid, accelerating to millions of cells in the first few weeks. For the first six-to-eight weeks the embryo is ambisexual; it has a general all-purpose sex gland that can develop into either testicles or ovaries. An H-Y antigen located in the Y chromosome causes the embryo to develop testicles by the third month, and the resultant testosterone does the rest. Hormonal sexual development is followed by organic sexual development, and finally by physical birth. Roger Sperry (1913-1994), the American neurologist who shared the 1981 Nobel Prize in physiology for his split-brain research, noted that from the 16th to the 26th week a chemical impacts the right hemisphere of the brains of male fetuses; retardation of the right hemisphere growth results. From this perspective males fare less well than females in pre-natal development.

Pre-birth Attitudes and Assumptions About the Male Fetus and Masculinity

Parental expectations upon learning the gender of the fetus affect both sexes. Historical traditions of maleness and femaleness influence the expectant couple's attitudes toward the coming child. Fifty years of documented research reveal that most couples, for several reasons, prefer male babies (Doyle, 1985; Winston, 1932). Even before birth, parental expectations are gender-specific. A Pygmalion phenomenon begins. Many pregnant women, when they find out the fetus is a male, believe more movement exists than there would be if it were a female. The belief is that boys are more physical and active, and girls are more gentle and passive. This is a foundational misperception that applies even in-utero (Florisha, 1978). Consequently, male pre-birth infants have an experience unlike that of female pre-birth infants. Males spend their first nine months of existence within the anatomy of their other-gender parent. Females begin their journey within the anatomy of the same-sex parent. The male fetus, from six months onward, is aware and reacting with an active emotional life to the physical and emotional environment within the mother (Karr-Morse & Wiley, 1999). Verny (1981) claimed he can

> see, hear, experience, taste and, on a primitive level, even learn in-utero (that is, in the uterus, before birth). Most importantly he can feel . . . what a child feels and perceives begins shaping his attitudes and expectations about himself . . . whether he . . . acts happy or sad, aggressive or meek, secure or anxiety-ridden . . . depends, in part, on the messages he gets about himself in the womb. The chief source of those shaping messages is the child's mother . . . [the] deep persistent patterns of feeling. Chronic anxiety or a wrenching ambivalence about motherhood can leave a deep scar on an unborn child's personality. On the other hand, such life-enhancing emotions as joy, elation and anticipation can contribute significantly to the emotional development of a healthy child. (pp. 13-14)

Verny's views are corroborated by Karr-Morse and Wiley (1999). They confirm the work of Janus (1997), stating that the pre-natal experiences imprint permanent impressions that become the foundations for the rest of one's life. What the mothers experience during the first nine months, the babies inject. Even before birth, therefore, the masculinity stereotype is becoming a part of the male infant's consciousness. The implication of such research is that with the emergence of a male infant at birth, a parental mind-set exists and is projected onto the child.

The Mother Wound: The Male Baby/Child (0 to 36 Months)

Parental projections onto a male baby begin a differentiation process. Immediately upon birth, "It's a boy!" or "It's a girl!" elicits parental projections. Historically boys were declared to be robust and strapping, and girls were declared to be petite and adorable. Rubin, Provenzano, and Lauria (1974) noted in an 18-item bipolar gender scale (e.g. strong/weak, active/passive, and noisy/quiet) that males were declared to be firmer, larger, better coordinated, more alert, stronger, and hardier. Parents of females, on the other hand, described their daughters as softer, smaller, prettier, and more delicate. Doyle (1983) noted,

> Fathers, more so than mothers, described their infants of either sex in more extreme ways. Surprisingly, in light of the different physical descriptions given by these parents, the infants of both sexes were not appreciably different in their average heights or weights, and Apgar scores, which are ratings of color, muscle tonicity, reflex irritability, and heart and respiratory rates assigned by the attending physician within ten minutes of birth. (p. 106)

Even before birth the long journey begins. Various stages of human development have been examined and presented. Wilber, Engler, and Brown (1986) sought to develop a synthesis of that research "that is developmental, structural, hierarchical, and systems-oriented, and that draws equally on Eastern and Western schools of thought" (p. 66). Each stage involves phase-temporary elements and trans-phase permanent elements.

The human developmental process passes through increasingly complex stages, with each stage involving the emergence of new structures, which in turn serve as operands for each new succeeding stage, while earlier outmoded structures that have served their purpose diminish and disappear. Each of the above researchers noted some five to nine chronological developmental stages. Mahler (1975), a leading researcher, presented the separation/differentiation stages thus: autistic stage (0-1 month); symbiotic stage (1-5 months); differentiation stage (5-9 months); practicing sub-stage (9-15 months); rapprochement sub-stage (15-24 months); and consolidation and object constancy stage (24-36 months).

Mahler's nomenclature (with some inclusions, as noted) will serve this presentation.

During the first year of human life the individual is negotiating the first developmental transition, consisting of the intuitive discovery of a separate sense of a physical self. Mis-negotiation of the primary phase (year one) of human life can result in a psychotic mental disorder (Wilber et al., Engler, 1986). Because most humans of both genders negotiate the broad developmental stages, attention will be given to the subtle aspects of the stages that are unique to male development, with some comparisons to female development.

The Autistic Phase (0-1 Month)

Emerging from within the mother, the infant remains for a time in a state of oneness with her and its surroundings (Kline, 1975). The baby has no sense of a personal self (Kaplan, 1978). For the first weeks of extra-uterine life the infant is basically a purely biological organism with reflexive, instinctual responses. The mother is not only the birth giver; she is the emotional/psychological cocoon out of which the infant begins its journey. It is the mother who, because she is the life-giver to the child, becomes the primary nurturing figure in the child's world (Brown, 1959). Mahler (1975) referred to this as a "closed monadic system" or a "primal undifferentiated matrix" (p. 41). It is similar to the "undifferentiated matrix" of Blanck and Blanck (1974, p. 28) and to Piaget's (1977) sensorimotor level (Wilber et al., 1986). The infant is dependent on the mother for its homeostasis, and is a mere unconscious recipient of the mother's care-giving style.

The Symbiotic Phase (1-5 Months)

The infant, from the second month through the fifth month, behaves and functions as though he and his mother were in a state of unconscious, boundaryless fusion. Mahler (1975) describes it as a "state of undifferentiation, of fusion with mother, in which the 'I' is not yet differentiated from the 'not-I' and in which the inside and the outside are only gradually coming to be sensed as different"(p. 44). At this stage, the infant behaves as if it cannot even clearly distinguish its existence from the mother's. It is a "delusion of a common boundary between two physically separate individuals" (p. 45).

The Separation — Individuation/Differentiation Sub-phase (5-9 Months)

From the fifth to the ninth month development is marked by the emergence of the infant from the fusion, symbiosis, or dual unity with the mother. Mahler (1975) called this "hatching": the infant's bodyself "hatches" or wakes up from its previous unconscious oneness with the mother. At this stage, "all normal infants take their first tentative steps toward breaking away, in a bodily sense, from their hitherto completely passive lap-babyhood. . . . There are definite signs that the baby begins to differentiate his own [body] from the mother's body" (p. 55). The infant begins to exist as a distinct bodyself but not as a distinct emotional self. The emotional self and the mother are still fused or merged.

Potential male developmental difficulties become realities at this developmental phase. Chodorow (1974) made some interesting observations regarding human gender identity. She stated that general and pervasive differences between male and female personalities and roles are attributable not to anatomically different genitalia but to "the fact that women, universally, are largely responsible for early child care" (pp. 43-44). The female child draws a markedly different sex/gender role personality identity from her early social environment than does the male child (Gilligan, 1982). Chodorow related that as a result, "in any given society, feminine personality comes to define itself in relation and connection to other people more than masculine personality does" (pp. 43-44).

From the beginning, male infants, when seen in the light of the best research on optimal human development, become the recipients of a long process of parental, family systems deprivation (Levant, 1995). Evolving out of this symbiotic union is different and more fraught with danger for males than it is for females (Chodorow, 1974). The male must negotiate a succession of separation phases from the primary nurturer — the other-sex mother. Goldberg (1976) stated, "The female [child] does not develop this kind of intense dependency on the male [opposite sex — father]. . . . The male was never her lifeline; she had no deep-rooted dependency on him for psychic nourishment. As a girl she was dependent on her mother and not her father" (p. 13). Not so with the male child; he has an identity with and a dependence on the opposite-sex parent. The attachment to and differentiation from the mother complicate his multi-stage developmental journey to manhood. Negotiating the various growth stages seems to be a process in which many males are prone to failure. The outcome of a male's advancing development will determine his success at negotiating out of this symbiotic oneness.

Kohut (1971, 1978) discussed his theory of the self-object. Kohut defined the self-object concepts in which another person is experienced as a part of one's self. Kohut (1971) stated, "Since all bliss and power now reside in the idealized object [mother], the child feels empty and powerless when he is separated from it and he attempts, therefore, to maintain a continuous union with it" (p. 37). The child's relationship with the mother-self-object carries lifelong consequences. The child benefits if, as Kohut stated, the mothers are "those [self/objects] who respond to and confirm the child's innate sense of vigor, greatness and perfection; and those to whom the child can look up and with whom he can merge as an image of calmness, infallibility, omnipotence" (Kohut & Wolf, 1978, p. 414).

Internal self-structures emerge from these developmentally phase-appropriate self-object relations. Inadequate or inappropriate self-object transference leaves the child missing significant developmental qualities. The obsessive fear of being abandoned by a significant partner that is experienced by some adult males may be understood from a "new framework for understanding and transforming the specific forms of dysfunction that emerge when optimal development goes awry" (Pollack, 1995, pp. 47-48). Men who have not negotiated successfully the individuation/separation drama with the mother often recapitulate that drama with the women in their adult lives.

Many of the developmental researchers employ conceptual terms to describe the phenomenon of each stage — ego, sensorimotor, undifferentiated matrix, and so forth. Ichazo (1991) suggests that, prior to or antecedent to conceptual descriptors, the human organism introjects and stores the developmental experiences in the various organic systems of the body. Ichazo offered his view of human developmental stages and of this stage of development in particular. Ichazo stated that "instincts and drives appear in our consciousness as [non] intellectual questions, because they are felt immediately . . . [as a] basic law of all life: that of simple survival . . . They are at the very basis of our psyche as instructions for living and surviving" (p. 95). Ichazo called this first stage *conservation.* He notes that the principle of conservation is established from the earliest primary human activity: eating, nursing, and later feeding ourselves (survival). Therefore, the maternal environment is the infant's world. "The conservation instinct is our basic instinct to feed ourselves in order to survive. It is the outcome of the needs of our alimentary tract, and the center is felt in the solar plexus at the top of the abdominal cavity" (p. 95). Therefore, all human ego functioning emerges from the maintenance of the stasis of the human organism. When all goes well there is a deep sense of trust, homeostasis, and well-being, a sense of being cared for.

Different infants innately have different needs; some are easily adaptable, while some are highly demanding and difficult. If a highly demanding child has a mother who is unable to be compatible with the child's needs, the unsuccessful match results in a feeling. This feeling is located in the alimentary canal, the solar plexus, and is called stress, emptiness, or abdominal discomfort. This feeling is not related solely to adequate physical nurturance; levels of emotional nurturance also impact it. The outcome, if all forms of nurturance are not present, is the developmental or survival fear that gets focalized in defensive anatomical structures, basically the stomach. When conservation is threatened, the result is greed, a deep hunger, a deep longing, a feeling that there is never enough, which becomes a self-structure capable of being re-ignited much later in life if a deep longing is unmet (Ichazo, 1991). Pathological consequences result: passive-aggressive or obsessive compulsive behavior, or personality disorders, or dysthymic disorders. The physiological structure of the body becomes the template for the psychological experience.

Pathology is imprinted in the *solar plexus* (Ichazo, 1991). Many men in treatment report that when confronted with abandonment by a significant other, they experience a tight knot in the gut, the shakes, high anxiety, and suicidal ideation, i.e. "abandonment depression" (Masterson, 1988, p. 79). Being abandoned is not just a historical phenomenon that happened years before; it is a lingering, ever-present physiological response to a present relationship trauma. It manifests as a gastrointestinal siege, experienced as a deep pain. The lesion of a male child's inability to negotiate this developmental phase persists throughout his life, as is described in Kohut (1971). Masterson's (1976, 1981, 1988, 1989) work in personality disorders provides training manuals for doing therapy intended to heal these early lingering traumas.

The process of negotiating these early stages is significant for male infants because of their heightened sensitivity to imprinting from the environment (Masterson, 1989). As the child begins to emerge from that fusion the first thing he faces is the mother — sometimes soothing, sometimes awesome and fearful. The mother becomes for this infant his whole world (Pope & Singer, 1978). Since this separation from the mother begins at five months, is more or less completed at 18 months, but is not fully resolved until 36 months, the figure of the mother dominates the emerging male consciousness. The infant's "delusion of a common boundary between two physically separate individuals" (Mahler, 1975, p. 45) gives way to the "first tentative steps toward breaking away, in a bodily sense, from the hitherto completely passive lap-babyhood" (p. 55). The transitional "lap-babyhood passive bodily sense" is left behind for the more permanent basic structure when the baby accomplishes "differentiation [of] his own [body] from the mother's body" (p. 86). In short, these stages belong primarily to the mother; as Kaplan (1978) says, the "mother is the one partner with whom the baby plays out the separation drama" (p. 118).

The father does not often enter the picture significantly. By all accounts, "this is an intense relationship — basic, awe-inspiring, fundamental, and consequence-laden" (Wilber, 1983, p. 119).

The emotional state of this infant male is not like that of his sisters. Haviland and Malatesta (1981), in a review of data in twelve different studies of male and female infants, noted the following:

> Constitutional differences in young male and female infants are clearly in evidence. Boys have a tendency to cry sooner and at a higher frequency than girls. In general, they are more irritable, less soothable, and have a higher intensity of crying during the first year. They also startle more readily, show more lability of state, with a more rapid buildup of tension and quicker peak of excitement than females. Girls are known to be soothable and more readily consoled. The above findings seem to indicate that boys are more emotionally labile and become distressed more easily than females, at least during infancy. (p. 196)

Weinberg also noted, in a 1992 study of six-month-olds, that male babies express more of their affective experiences than girl babies. Six-month-old boys, Weinberg reported, continued to exhibit significantly expressions of emotions such as fear, happiness and frustration; their verbal expressions are more positive, they exhibit more discomfort by being fussy and crying, and they make more gestures toward their mother than do girl babies. This finding led her to conclude that boys early on react more and are more social than girls. Male infants, then, are more absorbent, fragile, responsive to the environment, and socially adaptive than female infants. Later on, boys change; such externalized sensitivity largely ceases to exist. Haviland and Malatesta (1981) pointed out that it is here at this early stage that the human male becomes the recipient of the structure's punishment.

Levant (1995) noted that even though males begin life with a high degree of surface emotionality, which is the foundation of later "emotional self-awareness" and "emotional empathy," this natural emotionality "gets squelched so early and so thoroughly that they later have trouble believing it was ever part of their make-up at all. And the fact that all but one of these studies were based on observations of infants who were only days old strongly suggests that these differences are innate" (pp. 31-32). This crossover in emotional expression lingers throughout the male life and has a dampening effect on later male/female relationships.

When a group of mothers were told they were playing with a nine-month old male, they offered him a toy train to play with. When they were told the child was a girl, the mothers offered a doll. What gender label a child is assigned does, then, seem to influence the ways adults act toward the child (Delk, Madden, Livingston, & Ryan, 1986; Sidorowicz & Lunney, 1980; Will, Self, & Datab, 1976). Silverman (1987) noted that the higher degree of sensitivity of male infants and the mothers' resultant minimized stimulation results in a "less stable state system . . . (which) leads to decreased social interaction . . . [because] the animated face of the mother is highly arousing . . . and may over-stimulate the male infant, given his less stable state system . . . This then produces diminished social interchange between mother and infant, and, as does not happen with female infants, provides increasing separation with mothers and sons" (p. 328). It seems then that, according to these studies, the difference between female and male babies is that girl infants are generally calmer, less irritable, and more alert than boy infants (Haviland & Malatesta, 1981). Boy infants are fussier and more easily agitated, gesture more, get angry more easily and have their feelings closer to the surface than females.

Consequently, girls bond more readily with their mothers than do boys. They make better audiences for their mothers than do boys (Levant, 1995). Girls are better at receiving and responding to the mothers' emotional cues, and they develop their emotional empathy better than boys. Male infants experience a different reality. Rather than enliven the male infant's already labile expressiveness, mothers are more likely, according to Haviland and Malatesta (1981), to make a special effort to keep their sons contented. According to Levant, the male infant, "unable to distinguish between himself and his mother during his first months of life . . . feels his emotionality being dampened and enfolds this feeling into his sense of self: he is a being who holds his emotions in check" (p. 34). These mother/son interactions that occur at a few months of age are seemingly insignificant, but they go to the core of a male's identity (Pollack, 1998)

The Practicing Sub-phase (9-15 Months)

This stage marks the peak of the child's grandiose-exhibitionistic narcissistic relationship with the world. In Mahler's (1975) words, the practicing sub-phase is "the junior toddler's oyster":

Libidinal cathexis shifts substantially into the service of
the rapidly growing autonomous ego and its functions,
and the child seems intoxicated with his own faculties and
with the greatness of his own world. Narcissism is at its
peak! He is exhilarated by his own abilities, continually
delighted with the discoveries he makes in his expanding
world, and quasi-enamored with the world and his own
grandeur and omnipotence. (p. 71)

Furthermore, as development progresses, according to Blanck and
Blanck (1979), the person continues to expand his awareness as additional
aspects of the environment are absorbed into his world. However, the
self/object, inner/outer are still a single unit. Mahler (1975) affirmed
the primacy of the mother as either a positive or negative force for the
developing infant in learning "to differentiate between a 'pleasurable/
good' quality and a 'painful/bad' quality of experience" (p. 43). Mahler
additionally affirmed, "The roots of infantile psychosis are to be sought
in the second half of the first year and in the second year of life. This
time span came to be recognized as the 'separation-individuation phase'
of development" (p. x). Wilber (1981) concurred:

Now as the child emerges from the . . . [mother] and
develops a rudimentary body-self set apart from the. .
. . Mother, it also becomes vulnerable. Since there is
now self, there is now other, and "wherever there is other
there is fear." Fear of extinction, overthrow, dissolution,
Thanatos [death], and all centered on the figure of the
Great Mother. The relationship of the body-self to the
Great Mother is thus a relationship of being to non-being,
life vs. death; it is existential, not circumstantial. The
Great Mother, then, is both the Great Nourisher, the Great
Protector, and the Great Destroyer, the Great Devourer,
what (Sullivan, 1953) would call the Good Mother and the
Bad Mother. (pp. 118-119)

A longitudinal study conducted by Goldberg and Lewis (1969)
observed 32 males and 32 females and their mothers in free-play activities
and in a frustration-producing situation. Their outcomes revealed that at
13 months girls were more dependent, clung more, were less exploratory,
and were quieter. The boys, on the other hand, were more independent,
vigorous, exploratory, and active. The researchers placed a barrier
between the children and their mothers. Girls often stood at the barrier

and cried; boys often tried to circumvent the barrier (Brooks & Lewis, 1974; Jacklin, Maccoby, & Dick, 1973). At the early age of 13 months, boys and girls expressed striking gender differences (Wasserman & Lewis, 1985). Significant in this regard, Goldberg and Lewis (1969) found a link in the different genders' behaviors. They noted that mothers touched, talked to, and handled their daughters significantly more than they did their sons (Doyle, 1985; Katz, 1986). Also, when a male child reached the 13th month the attention he received from his father increased. Fathers began interacting with their sons a great deal more when the son began to walk (Lamb, 1981). Fathers were concerned that their sons would grow up to be men. "When we started walking our dads made sure we started walking like men" (Levant, 1995. p. 34).

Ichazo (1991) notes that at Mahler's Practicing sub-phase "the natural instinct for associating oneself in a community with other human beings is a basic principle of survival" (p. 95). The key element in the larger community is the father, as he becomes more involved. From now on in the child's development the father may spend more time with the child and "rescue" the child from the mother matrix by taking the child into new realms where the mother is not present. Ichazo (1991) called this phase *Relations*, the paternal field:

> We are basically related to our environment, even more directly than with our skin, by our lungs and the alveoli, which are in immediate contact with the air and through it our environment. Our emotions are the outcome of how well we cover our relations with other people. The instinctual innate question of this instinct is "With whom am I?" The answer to this question, "Am I with a friend or a foe?" will trigger the primary emotions of like and dislike. This emotional center of attention will develop an ego interested in our human relations, how we appear to others, and how others appear to us. (p. 95)

The principle of relations, according to Ichazo (1991), comes into play when the human develops an identity separate enough to begin to distinguish between self and the other. Often the father is helpful at this stage, for the father comes and takes the child away from the undifferentiated matrix and helps the child differentiate as an individual. Being with another is a significant experience. Is that person safe? Do they love me? How do I feel them in my physiological affect? If they are safe and loving I feel both hearts — theirs and mine. They will not hurt me. Without that security one can become totally disconnected, instinctual, and innately isolated and alone, feeling scared, anxious, and unknown. The father wound is a deep wound. If a man couldn't relate well with his father, he cannot relate well with himself, and he cannot relate well with a woman.

This ego image, according to Ichazo, is always developing a self-system image based upon its role in the social context. When all goes well, an internal sense of well-being is experienced; when not, it naturally develops into the "poison of hate" (p. 96). "It is the outcome of the needs of our circulatory system, composed of the heart, lungs, arteries, veins, and kidneys, and it is centered and felt in the cardio-pulmonary plexus at the center of the thoracic cavity" (p. 95). The father relationship results in what Ichazo calls the Relation Instinct and, significantly, is mirrored in the cardio-pulmonary physiology of the child and, later, the adult. Inadequate negotiation of the Relation Instinct developmental phase later may be evidenced in premature heart attacks, for example.

The Psychological Birth of the Emotional Self (15-36 Months)

Mahler (1975) stated that the "psychological birth of the human infant" (p. xi), pertinent to the rapprochement phase (15-24 months), involves a major differentiation of the self/object unit. A separate and distinct emotional self is attempting to emerge and to differentiate from its previous symbiotic union. "The biological birth of the human infant and the psychological birth of the individual are not coincident in time. The former is a dramatic, observable, and well-circumscribed event, the latter a slowly unfolding intrapsychic process" (p. 3). Mahler described the subtle changes in infant behavior that indicate a degree of outer directedness, and she characterized the fruition of that process as "hatching" (p. 53).

Separating and differentiating from the mother at this phase, a boy "will play out the drama of becoming a separate and unique self with this one human partner [the mother] and no other person" (Kaplan, 1978, p. 118). This is a "consequence laden" transition (Wilber, 1983). This period is characterized as an experience of great loss for the male child (Pollack, 1992). The small child leaves behind the grandiose, narcissistic "the world is my oyster" practicing phase for the potentially trauma-fraught rapprochement phase. A heightened sense of separation from mother portends a heightened separation anxiety and abandonment depression. The small child must slowly grow out of the delusion of his own grandeur. "Because there is now a separate self, there is now a separate other; the world is no longer its oyster. Researchers are fond of saying that at this stage, paradise has been lost" (Wilber et al., 1986, p. 88).

The developmental trauma for boys is becoming a growing concern (Pollack 1995). Female children often emerge within the mother's cocoon of comfort and protection and progress developmentally, in kind, with the primary nurturing source (Chodorow, 1978). Pollack pointed out the sense of "loss associated with the boy's definition of his own identity and core gender self, an experiential process that requires separation from the most cherished, admired, and loved object in his life [his mother]" (p. 40). Girl siblings can remain connected to the mother as this "broken maternal connection or disidentification" (p. 40) occurs for the boy. Often the father is emotionally unable to provide an alternative nurturing figure for his son's lost mother.

Negotiating this separation/individuation phase, according to Chodorow (1978), most likely is not only a moving away to exciting outside interests by the son; the mother is consciously or unconsciously participating in the distancing of her son from the close loving environment. It is not a passive, allowing release on the part of the mother:

> Girls tend to remain part of the dyadic primary mother-child relationship itself . . . and in an attachment characterized by primary identification and the fusion of identification and object choice. By contrast, mothers experience their sons as a male opposite. Boys are more likely to have been pushed out of the preoedipal relationship, and to have had to curtail their primary love and sense of emphatic tie with their mother. A boy has engaged, and been required to engage, in a more emphatic individualization and a more defensive firming of experienced ego boundaries. . . . The earliest mode of individuation, the primary construction of the ego and its inner object-world, the earliest conflicts and the earliest unconscious definitions of self, the earliest threats to individuation, and the earliest anxieties which call up defenses, all differ for boys and girls because of differences in the character of the early mother-child relationship for each. (pp. 166-167)

Reciprocally, a son's male core gender identity develops away from his mother. The disidentification is outer-directed from the mother to the son. She disidentifies from him in what Pollack (1995) called a "*behavioral push*' out of the nest [the psychological safe cocoon]" (p. 41). The cuddly little boy of the practicing phase becomes the tantrum thrower of the rapprochement phase. Mother has lost her loving little baby. This premature behavioral push out of the maternal nurturing cocoon can be a significant trauma and a lifelong loss for the male child.

Pollack (1998) stated that the behavioral push out of the nurturing holding environment constitutes a significant separation trauma. He declared that this is "one of the earliest and most acute developmental experiences [for] boys" (p. 40). The separation trauma can result in a hardening, a narrowing, and a de-limiting of the male's emotions — articularly their soft, vulnerable, and empathic sides. This trauma of separation manifests in many ways: 1) boys end up with rocky and shaky self-esteem; 2) they become unhappy and disaffected; 3) they become clinically depressed; 4) they sometimes develop psychosomatic diseases like vomiting and long crying spells; 5) they seek recognition by acting out and are sometimes diagnosed as being hyperactive or as having attention deficit disorders; and 6) they also, years later, "as men unconsciously long for connection with mother and the nurturing 'holding' environment she once provided" (p. 38). "This relational rupture, this trauma, profoundly affects the psychology of most boys — and of most men — forever" (p. 27). Pollack further stated,

> That little boy is not fending off too close a tie to mother, but rather is forever longing to return to her, and to the "holding" connection she once provided him, a connection he feels he can never regain. If a boy had been allowed to separate at his own pace, that longing and sadness would not be there, or would be much less. (p. 27)

The child at this stage is doing two things, among many others. 1) He must go away from the mother. If adequate space is provided, the child will run away from the mother. As the child runs away, the stress begins to show on the mother. She wants to run after the child to make sure that he is safe. The child will run away for some distance until he or she reaches the end of an invisible psychological tether. If one could look closely into the child's eyes, fear and excitement would be seen. 2) Then the child will stop, turn around, and make visual contact with the mother. Then he will race back into her arms. When the child races back to the mother's arms, he is refueled. The child must be allowed to do both, go away and return. Masterson (1988) noted the following: "The child needs emotional 'supplies' for the emerging self and will keep returning to the mother to receive them" (p. 31). In the practicing phase the child races off and the mother comes and swoops him up — it is a delightful game. In the rapprochement phase it ceases to be a game. "In fact the new concern doesn't seem like practice at all. It is serious business. It can be seen on the child's face — [the child] looks worried, hurt, fretful, sometimes even panicky" (Bowlby, 1969, p. 31).

The loss for males with regard to the outward behavioral push is different from that of females, due to the fact the mothers tend to see their daughters as more like themselves, wherefore daughters remain in the loving holding cocoon. Condorow (1978) stated that this is not so with boys, because mothers experience their sons as male opposites. Boys therefore are pushed out and are sometimes prematurely cut off from their primary love source and experience a broken bond with their mothers. "We may be seeing a developmental basis for a gender-specific vulnerability to traumatic abrogation of the early holding environment, an impingement in boys' development — a normative life-cycle loss — that may, later in life, leave many adult men at risk for fears of intimate connection. This traumatic experience of abandonment occurs so early in the life course that the shameful memory of the loss is likely to be deeply repressed" (Pollack, 1995, p. 41).

Freud drew from the Oedipus myth to note a later stage in human development—the Oedipus phase. However, the pre-Oedipus phenomenon also is cited as a significant developmental transition. Sophocles' Oedipus was betrayed and abandoned to die by both his mother and father. Pollack (1995) suggested that the pre-oedipal experience of young men is one of feeling or unconsciously experiencing a sense of having been abandoned, betrayed, or hurtfully separated. "Like Oedipus," he says, "most men may have no conscious memory of this earlier trauma, though their vulnerabilities (especially to shame) in adult life may be the evidence of the unhealed wound" (p. 43).

Probably the key work on the child's separation from the mother is the work of Bowlby (1969), in his *Attachment and Loss* in three volumes: *Attachment* (Vol. I) (1969); *Separation* (Vol. II) (1973); and *Loss* (Vol. III) (1980). Bowlby (1969) stated, "From time immemorial mothers and poets have been alive to the distress caused to a child by loss of its mother; but it is only in the last fifty years that, by fits and starts, science has awoken to it" (p. 24). Bowlby documented the research and studies of the effect of the loss of a mother on the child. He then stated that the child goes through three phases: "Protest, Despair, and Detachment" (1969, p. 27). The consequence is such that when the mother is reintroduced to the child,

> it can be seen that all is not well, for there is a striking
> absence of the behavior characteristic of the strong

attachment normal at this age. So far from greeting the
mother he may seem hardly to know her; so far from
clinging to her he may remain remote and apathetic;
instead of tears there is a listless turning away. He seems
to have lost all interest in her. (p. 28)

The premature and unwanted separation of, in this case, the male child
from the mother, has profound effects on the child. Bowlby (1980) further
noted that when the separation occurs, the behavior of the child is one of

protest and of urgent effort to recover his lost mother.
He will often cry loudly, shake his cot, throw himself
about, and look eagerly towards any sight or sound which
might prove to be his missing mother. This may [be
accompanied] with ups and downs [and] continue for as
long as a week or more. Throughout it the child seems
buoyed up in his efforts by the hope and expectation that
his mother will return. Sooner or later, however, despair
sets in. The longing for mother's return does not diminish,
but the hope of its being realized fades. Ultimately the
restless noisy demands cease: he becomes apathetic and
withdrawn, and despairs broken only perhaps by an
intermittent and monotonous wail. He is in a state of
unutterable misery. (p. 9)

The detachment phase experienced in childhood becomes a set of deeply
ingrained structures. According to Bowlby (1980), "defensive processes
once set in motion are apt to stabilize and persist" (p. 21).

Bowlby's three-volume work is consistent with the extensive research
in the field that indicates great harm comes from the separation of a
child from its mother. The separation trauma, once experienced, is often
lifelong. Pollack (1992) noted that boys feel

the need to defend against urges toward affiliation and
intimacy because of the repressed trauma of shameful
and premature separation. Having experienced a sense
of hurt in the real connection to their mothers (as a
result of her societally constructed role to make gender
differentiation clear) and the subsequent loss of finding
no equally salient alternative in their fathers, many boys,
and later men, are left at risk for empathic disruptions in
their affiliative connections, doomed to search endlessly

> . . . and yet fend women off because of their fear of
> retraumatization. (p. 41)

It is at this stage of development that grave psychological consequences
are likely to result if the child's needs are not met (Mahler, 1975). The
birth of the emotional self and the misnavigation of this phase may result
in the development of personality disorders (Masterson, 1988, p. vii).
*The Diagnostic and Statistical Manual of the American Psychological
Association, IV* (1994) categorizes personality disorders in three clusters,
as follows: Cluster A: Paranoid, Schizoid, Schizotypal; Cluster B:
Antisocial, Borderline, Histrionic, Narcissistic; and Cluster C: Avoidant,
Dependent, Obsessive-Compulsive, not otherwise specified (pp. 275-286).
Masterson (1988) examined the personality disorders and categorized
them into three significant forms: Borderline, Narcissistic, and Schizoid.
He explained,

> These behavior patterns — officially called "personality
> disorders" — are not only increasingly prevalent among
> people seeking professional help today, but also reflect
> major psychological themes in American culture at large;
> fear of abandonment, emphasis on the self to the exclusion
> of others, difficulties in intimacy and creativity and with
> assertion of the real self. (p. vii)

Similarly, Wilber et al. (1986) noted the following regarding his theory of
the Spectrum of Consciousness:

> The spectrum of consciousness is also a spectrum
> of (possible) pathology. If consciousness develops
> through a series of stages, a developmental "lesion" at
> a particular stage could manifest itself as a particular
> type of psychopathology, and an understanding of the
> developmental nature of consciousness — its structures,
> stages, and dynamics — would prove indispensable to
> both diagnosis and treatment. (p. 66)

Moreover, it is the misnavigation of the rapprochement phase of human
development that appears to lead toward the personality disorders. When
the concept of loss is mentioned, the natural response might be, loss of
what? The loss must be compared to some standard — a lesser loss, or
a process of development that affords the male child a greater degree
of human optimizing potential. That standard of comparison is often

considered the superior way girls are raised in relation to the way boys are raised.

Chodorow (1974, 1978, 1989) affirmed that the differences are not so much related to genetic sex differences but to the fact that mothers universally are responsible for childcare. Mothers tend to speak with their daughters in more emotional terms than with their sons (Dunn, Bretherton, & Munn, 1987; Fivush, 1989). They tend to relate to sadness with girls, and communicate about anger with boys (Fivush, 1989). By school age, boys begin to expect negative reactions from their parents if they express much sadness. Little girls, however, receive more acceptance for expressing sadness (Fuchs & Thelen, 1988). Pollack (1995) noted that mothers were slower to use the word "angry" with girls, while they used it more often with their boys. The father role, on the other hand, is also significant in the "gender-bifurcated socialization of the expression of emotion" (p. 46). Fathers use more emotional-impact words with daughters (Gleason & Greif, 1983; Schell & Gleason, 1989). They engage in more "negative teasing or aggressive verbal jostling with their sons than with their daughters" (p. 46).

Little girls, on the contrary, do not have to traverse such a consequence-laden developmental journey. They are like their mothers. Traditionally they watch their mothers put on Band-aids, wipe noses, set the table, and take care of others, and they blossom within the nurturing cocoon of mother's presence. This can mean that

> girls emerge from this period with a basis for "empathy" built into their primary definition of self in a way that boys do not. . . . Girls emerge with a stronger basis for experiencing another's needs or feelings as one's own (or of thinking that one is so experiencing another's needs and feelings). Furthermore, girls do not define themselves in terms of the denial of pre-oedipal relational modes to the same extent, as do boys, therefore, regression to these modes tends not to feel as much a basic threat to their ego. From very early, then, because they are parented by a person of the same gender . . . girls come to experience themselves as less differentiated than boys, as more continuous with and related to the external object-world, and as differently oriented to their inner object-world as well. (Chodorow, 1978, p. 167)

Female personalities find greater ease in relating and connecting [equaling] than the male personality does (Pollack, 1995). Due to the mother's parenting style, the "interpersonal dynamics of gender identity formation are different for boys and girls, and is pretty much fixed by age three" (Gilligan, 1982, p. 7). Because little girls tend to remain in the bonded relationship with the mother their

> identity relationship takes place in a context of ongoing relationship. Mothers tend to experience their daughters as more like, and continuous with, themselves. Correspondingly, girls, in identifying themselves as female, experience themselves as like their mothers, thus fusing the experience of attachment with the process of identity formation. Consequently, male development entails a) more emphatic individuation and b) more defensive firming of experienced ego boundaries. For boys, but not girls, issues of differentiation have become intertwined with sexual issues. (Chodrow, 1978, pp. 150-167)

For girls, due to the integration of, identification with, and relational attachment to the mother, the separation/individuation process is muted. In order for boys to individuate, on the other hand, they must separate and distance intra-psychically and interpersonally from the mother. "Achieving and maintaining this separation may require more of a defensive hardening of the self and ego boundaries of little boys, and later of adult males, on both a conscious and an unconscious level" (Pollack, 1995, p. 39).

Males experience relationships and issues of dependency differently from females. For boys and men, separation and individuation are critically tied to gender identity, because separation from the mother is essential for the development of masculinity. Becoming a woman is not defined as the achievement of separation from the mother. A girl can individuate and remain attached. Male gender identity is often characterized by separation and fear of intimacy, and femininity is often marked by attachment and fear of separation. "Thus males tend to have difficulty with relationships, while females tend to have problems with individuation" (Gilligan, 1982, p. 9).

Pollack (1995) noted that, years later, in a man's consciousness, is the residue of his boyhood's experience of being caught between his dependency on his mother and his search for a clear sense of self. He needs to separate and become an individualized person, and yet he is being pushed out before he is emotionally ready; "he is . . . struggling with the very real loss of an earlier afflictive oneness — which can never be regained" (p. 40). As a consequence, males are constantly looking for the idealized lost mother of the practicing phase, and they tend to rework their early fractured separation attempt with the women currently in their lives. According to Pollack, they are "more vulnerable to traumatic and premature actual separations-disruptions that may later be experienced by the child as a loss or abandonment," which results in a "problematic course toward affiliation and intimacy because of the repressed trauma of shameful and premature separation" (pp. 41-42).

Men are often viewed as being shallow and emotionally aloof. However, the converse is often true. Basically, the shallowness is a defense device to protect a man's vulnerability. "Once the unconscious defense is penetrated by a woman he becomes profoundly attached to the point of deep and almost total dependency" (Goldberg, 1976, p.12). Numerous men have stated in this author's presence, "I thought I would die. I never will let myself get that close again. I will never do that again." Such dependency may have been the reality of the male's earliest existence. In-utero he is totally dependent. At birth his survival is in his mother's hands. She is the one who bathes him, suckles him, clothes him, feeds him, protects him, wipes him, and comforts him. In all aspects of his life, she sustains his survival. Unlike his sister who has no such dependency on the opposite-gender parent, the mother is his lifeline. "Many adult men, once they begin to establish a primary relationship with a woman, begin to abandon almost all of their other relationships. The dependency becomes increasingly intense and the crisis, if and when she does leave him, is often life-shattering" (Goldberg, pp. 12-13).

Many men struggle throughout their lives to individualize in context with women. When men don't adequately complete their separation drama from the mother, they often continue the separation/individualization drama with the women in their lives. If a man does not develop an independent self, he is often looking for another matrix in which to imbed himself, and the outcome is co-dependence. Pollack (1995) wrote, "Yet he is also struggling with the very real loss of an earlier affiliative oneness — which can never be regained, within this model, without a threat to masculine identity" (p. 40). As a consequence, males may be more vulnerable to traumatic and premature actual separation — disruptions that may later be experienced by the child as a loss or abandonment — than females are. Pollack noted, "Boys, then, have not only a more problematic course toward identity . . . . This is a loss that ensued with their mothers and was probably unassuaged when their fathers proved unable to assume an alternative nurturant role" (p. 42).

The different nurturing styles for boys and girls will often lead males and females to develop in different directions. The sense of maleness in men differs from the sense of femaleness in women. Consequently, masculinity (or maleness) sometimes becomes more conflictual and more problematic than femaleness. Chodrow (1978) stated,

> Underlying, or built into, core male gender identity is an early, non-verbal, unconscious and almost somatic sense of primary oneness with the mother, an underlying sense of femaleness that continually, usually unnoticeably but sometimes consistently challenges and undermines the sense of maleness. Thus, because of the primary oneness and identification with his mother, a primary femaleness, a boy and man's core gender identity . . . is an issue. (p. 109)

As a result, boys and men work to break away and eschew directives from women while at the same time longing for emotional unity.

Pleck (1981) described his concept of gender role strain, in which men cannot carry the heavy load of trying to live up to such idealized and inhuman masculine standards. The ramifications of such an impossible ideal and the limitations of developmental training often result in the inability of men to identify, express, and describe their feeling states. This is especially true for feelings of warmth, caring, sadness, and pain. Many men lack the ability to link words with feelings. They experience significant depths of feelings; the feelings, however, are often not accessible verbally (Levant 1995). So for many men feelings are experienced as a vague, felt sense; they are unable to verbalize and convey them in a clear, articulated, emotional message to a loved one (Pollack, 1995). Anger, on the other hand, is the one expression of feeling universally permissible for males. Through anger, boys and men are able to express their vulnerability and powerlessness as a means of protection, distancing, and safety. Again, "The way I was treated as a small child is the way I treat myself the rest of my life" (Miller, 1984). The temper tantrum of the 2½-year-old boy goes on forever.

Not only is anger a common consort for males, it is a means of finding safety. According to Pollack (1995), a man "would be obsessionally concerned with maintaining an independent self" (p. 47). This polarized dichotomy of longing for closeness and persisting in independent autonomy sometimes appears to be similar to a narcissistic personality disorder.

It would seem then that many a man would resist any sense of dependency, especially on anyone who would remind him of his early childhood dependency, for example a mother figure. Even though the longing is deep for an idealized object, concomitant with that longing is the long memory of the earlier childhood tie that was disrupted. For this man, and for significant female partners, a profound confusion exists in the form of "come close—don't leave me" in conjunction with "don't get too close, smother me, or tell me what to do." The stress continues; sometimes it is called "the war between the sexes" (Robinson, 1959; Travis & Wade, 1984).

In sum, the rapprochement phase of human development, Mahler's (1975) "psychological birth of the human infant" phase, is a risk-laden transition. This is especially true for males. The male child may experience significant losses in his psychological potential due to limitations in the nurturing style directly related to his separation drama from his mother. Little boys have received a "behavioral push" out of the nurturing matrix; they are "pushed out" before they are psychologically prepared for the separation. They experience the traumatic "abrogation of the early holding environment," an "impingement" in their development, a "normative life-cycle loss" of the nurturing cocoon of their mothers. They have tasted the Promised Land in the practicing phase, and in the bifurcation of the rapprochement phase they are left with the ghost of the once priceless love-bond, left to search for the return of the restful cocoon, a return that, for many, never comes. In my clinical practice, this was evident in the gut-sobs of a 50-year-old man who, recently rejected by his lover, stated that he wanted to just go back and be rocked on his mother's lap.

The Consolidation and Emotional Object Constancy (24-36 Months)

This final sub-phase is Mahler's (1975) consolidation of the separation-individuation process, and involves the attainment of the emotional self-object constancy (24-36 months). It involves the integration of the self and object representations, and the integration of part-self images into a whole-self representation (which includes both "good" and "bad" aspects of the self). And even though the child is differentiating from the "other," the child's mind/body representation is not yet totally differentiated. A mind/body fusion remains. It is at the later oedipal stage that this differentiation will be accomplished within the separate organism.

Ichazo (1991) linked this developmental state to the physiological dynamic of the individual. At this level individuals learn to dance with the environment. Ichazo called this the "Adaptation Instinct." The adaptation instinct is the outcome of the constant need to adapt to the natural environment, and also is necessary for adapting to the social environment, because this is a basic need of survival. The idea of the link between the body (soma) and the soul (psyche) is one of the most ancient concepts, and the description and correlation as an outcome of a specific "body system" is key to the analysis of Ichazo.

Ichazo (1991) further noted that the child has incorporated the solidity and integration from the mother (the gastrointestinal sphere); he has experienced the journey away from her with the father (the cardiovascular sphere); now he absorbs the environmental relationship somewhere between the two, asking himself how and where he fits into the mother-father relationship. The physiological template in the person involves the central nervous system, composed of the encephalon, the spinal cord, and the peripheral nerves, and it is felt in the center, in the cranial cavity.

Also involved is what Ichazo (1991) calls the Practical Ego, one's problem-solving ability. If, out of the integration of the earlier stages, an individual is able to find a graceful dance with the environment, that person is able to solve problems and develop successful cognitive abilities. If the adaptive process does not work, the person experiences a great deal of stress; he makes up answers, avoids and absents himself, says, "I'm not here," distracts himself, and is in a state of denial and rationalization. If, on the contrary, individuals function in concert, in cooperation, as a team, they face the future together, and develop a sense of "Self" in the environment. When not functioning, they become depressed and feel, "I can't solve this; I'm overwhelmed and paralyzed; I can't cope; I am out of it." The pathologies then become antisocial, schizoid, schizotypical, paranoid, eccentric, and suicidal (Ichazo, 1991).

The Father Wound

Kaplan (1978) noted that it was the mother, and she alone, with whom the infant child works through the initial separation drama. Ichazo's (1991) "conservation" phase (year one) emphasized the nurturing, feeding, gastro-intestinal aspect of the infant's first year of life. The child begins the first differentiation/integration developmental phase with the mother. The father plays a minimal role in this developmental stage. However, with Ichazo's "Relations — the paternal field," the father begins to play a more important role. In Ichazo's concept of "relations" (year one and two), the father more significantly enters the parenting role as the son begins taking his first tentative, independent steps out into the world. Now a boy becomes his father's son. The dad enters the picture and may take the child out of the unitary matrix, away from the mother temporarily, "determined to rescue him from the feminizing influence of the females of the household and teach him how to be a man" (Levant, 1995, p. 35). The periods when the small boy is taken to be with the father are also times of great potential benefit or loss. The benefit, when the father is safe, guiding, and patient, is that the child's affections open to another being outside the matrix. The experience is one of loss when the opposite is true, and the child is yelled at, physically oppressed, or demeaned. Such traumas result in the child's affect becoming imploded, contracted, fearful and vigilant; as the separation from mother it had become a fearful, contracted-closing experience. Therefore, once again, "when we started walking our dads made sure we started walking like a man" (Levant, p. 34).

The so-called golden age of fathering was in the nineteenth century, when families lived on farms. Sons were economic assets. Sons spent time in the fields with their fathers. Walking along beside dad was grounding, concretizing experience for the son. However, the father was gone from sunup to sundown, and the mother still primarily parented children until a son could go to the fields. The fathering of small children was still left to the mother. The greater number of men seeking custody of small children now evidences change. Dads are taking a more active role in the child-parent relationship, and in the training process, too (Gurian, 1999; Hanson & Bozett, 1985; Kindlon & Thompson, 1999; Kort & Friedland, 1986; Lamb, 1986; Lewis, 1986; Pleck, 1987).

Fathers often have more precise ideas than mothers about how children should behave. They exhort the son to be a man and not a sissy. They seem to be intolerant of a son's deviations from gender-appropriate behaviors (Palkovitz, 1985). Fathers are usually stricter than mothers in their definitions of appropriate gender-typed expectations and behaviors. Fathers, it appears, are especially intolerant of any hint of their son's deviations from gender-appropriate behaviors. More often than not, it is the father and not the mother who encourages the son to stand up against the neighborhood bully. A common complaint made to this writer by men in family counseling is that the mother is making a sissy of the male child; she's too soft on him. Men are intent on making sure their sons are taught to be men. They work at directing the child's temperament toward a masculine identity. And they tend to work a lot harder than mothers do to force-fit their children into stereotypically masculine and feminine molds. Levant (1997) noted this force-fit, as shown earlier in the literature review:

As for men of earlier generations, for male children of the post-war era, "being a man," meant conforming to seven basic tenets:

1) strict avoidance of anything feminine,
2) restricted emotions,
3) strength and aggression,
4) self-reliance,
5) pursuit of achievement and status,
6) disconnection of sex from intimacy, and
7) homophobia. (p. 6)

Going off with a father, then, who has been programmed to display the same constricted emotions, can deepen the internal wounding of the child. Such a father may be also emotionally constricted, and, with his high value on work and production, may be unavailable psychologically as well as physically. Men in counseling sometimes express grief, anger, regret, and hatred for their fathers for past hurts; for example, a 60-year-old client of this writer was still afraid of his 90-year-old father. This man, a client, was still waiting for some expression of love and acceptance. Some men in counseling have taken the initiative and have told their fathers that they loved them. An uncomfortable silence was the first response, and then after several attempts their fathers slowly began to return a forced and uncomfortable "I love you too."

In general, fathers treat their sons much differently than their daughters. Boys are handled less, punished more, and given greater freedom earlier by their parents than girls are. In our culture, boys are socialized earlier in their gender-appropriate behaviors and pushed away from parental dependencies earlier than girls (Doyle, 1983, pp. 106-110). Fathers teach boys to stifle their expression of emotions. Expressions of fear and pain, such as crying, are high on the prohibited list (Levant, 1995). The avoidance of fear is ingrained in the male psyche from centuries of antipathy toward it. Some 600 years ago male fear was associated with not deserving love from a woman. Chaucer (1952), in one of his *Canterbury Tales*, "The Nun's Priest's Tale," puts the following words into the mouths (beaks) of two chickens, a cock named Chanticleer and a hen named Lady Pertelote. Chanticleer dreamed a beast, a fox, came and carried him away, and he made the mistake of sharing his feelings of fear with the hen Lady Pertelote. Lady Pertelote's response to Chanticleer's fear was as follows:

"For shame," she said, "you timorous poltroon!
Alas, what cowardice! By God above,
You've forfeited my heart and lost my love.
I cannot love a coward, come what may.
All women long — and O that it might be!
For husbands tough, dependable and free,
Secret, discreet, no niggard, not a fool
That boast and then will find his courage cool
At every trifling thing. By God above
How dare you say for shame, and to your love,
That anything at all was at all to be feared?
Have you no manly heart to match your beard?
And can a dream reduce you to such terror?
Dreams are a vanity, God knows, pure error.
Dreams are engendered in the too replete
From vapors in the belly, which compete
With other, too abundant, swollen tight." (pp. 232-233)

Developing males, a thousand years later, are taught by their fathers to suppress the caring emotions, the ones that get expressed through gentle, nurturing, and affectionate behaviors (Levant & Pollack, 1995). Fathers were found to communicate their biases both through positive reinforcement and through punishment: by signaling disapproval to, or withholding affection from, their children, especially from older boys, when they witnessed gender-inappropriate play. Indeed, withholding physical affection from sons is one of the primary modes through which fathers teach sons to inhibit affectionate behaviors (Langlois & Downs, 1980). Some men have so internalized this prohibition against expressing caring feelings that they cannot acknowledge, to themselves or to anyone else, how much they hungered for their father's affection and how much the denial of that affection hurt. Sadder still, some men are so imprisoned by this conditioning that they cannot help repeating the pattern with their own sons — withholding affection just as their fathers withheld it from them.

According to Fagot (1985), Felson and Russo (1988), and Herzberger and Tennen (1985), male children receive much more punishment than female children. The punishment takes the form of the parents' withholding touching and emotional comfort, and sending the child off to play unattended in order to encourage greater independence. Independence is also furthered by the difference in degrees of punishment males receive as compared to girls. A female client of mine in her written social history related that when her mother became angry with her brothers she threatened to cut off their penises.

One can punish a child in a variety of ways. Here, again, parents use different types of punishment for each gender. Weitzman, Eifler, and Ross (1984) noted:

> Boys are subjected to more physical punishment, whereas psychological punishments, such as the threat of withdrawal of love, are more frequently used for girls. Children trained with physical punishment have been shown typically to be more self-reliant and independent. The other method of child training — the love-oriented or psychological method — usually produces children who are more obedient and dependent. As girls are most often trained with psychological methods they are exposed to more affection and less punishment than boys. (p. 173)

That added punishment brings about some negative consequences. Hartley (1974) noted:

> More stringent demands are made on boys than on girls and at an early age, when they are least able to understand either the reasons for or the nature of the demands. Moreover, these demands are frequently enforced harshly, impressing the small boy with the danger of deviation from them, while he does not quite understand what they are. To make matters more difficult, the desired behavior is rarely defined positively as something the child should do, but rather, undesirable behavior is indicated negatively as something he should nor do or be — anything, that is, that the parent or other people regard as "sissy." Thus, very early in life the boy must either stumble on the right path or bear repeated punishment without warning when he accidentally enters into the wrong ones. This situation gives us practically a perfect combination for inducing anxiety — the demand that the child do something which is not clearly defined to him, based on reasons he cannot possibly appreciate, enforced with threats, punishments, and anger by those who are close to him. (pp. 7-8)

What would a man who, as a boy, sustained such "gender-bifurcated socialization and early psychological hurt" (Levant & Pollack, 1995, p.

47) look like? It is likely that high on his agenda would be the elevated sustaining of a sense of independence referred to earlier in Pollack's (1995) work:

> He would have a panoply of intrapsychic defenses, such as unconscious anger or rage toward women, condescension toward anyone in a care-taking role, overvaluation of independence, devaluation of the need for connectedness, stoic denial of sadness or pain, with an inability to mourn or grieve loss and a walling-off of the core vulnerable self. (p. 47)

The Crossover

Haviland and Malatesta (1981), as noted earlier, contended that male children start out in life with a more sensitive affective experience, while girl infants are calmer. Then later in childhood boys "cross over" (Levant, 1995) and lose the earlier labile affect. How does this "radical change" come about?

According to Levant (1995), powerful influences of the mother, the father, and the culture work together and block this emotionality. Once blocked, the powerful emotions flow into three separate streams. One expression of these early-suppressed emotions takes on the form of what Levant calls "action empathy," the instrumental inclination to do and fix things. Another aspect of unlived and disowned emotions is that they get forced down into subterranean depths, resulting in emotional numbness; or they become the third aspect, the universal masculine expression, "the catch-all of male emotion — that of anger" (Levant & Pollack, 1995). Consequently, the historically sustained parenting models of motherhood and fatherhood wherein children were unable to receive and experience adequate emotional affect from their parents is transmitted from one generation to the next. These developmentally gender-linked, normative, separation traumas and losses leave boys and men at risk for lifelong psychological consequences that emerge as deficits in emotional intimacy, empathy, and the ability to make commitments in relationships (Belcher & Pollock, 1993). Furthermore, Pollack (1995) noted,

> Gender-bifurcated patterns of role socialization often exacerbate these unconscious traumas, shaming boys and men into suppressing the expression of a whole range of deeply felt needs — warm or sad feelings, so as to eschew being called a "sissy" and being viewed as shamefully

81

unmanly. Yet there is every reason to believe that male qualities of succor, care, sacrifice, giving, and, indeed, empathy exist that could form the terms of a positive, substantial, and proactive sense of masculinity (Levant & Pollack, 1995).

Similarly, in the forward to Robert Johnson's 1974) book, *He: Understanding Masculine Psychology*, Barnhouse stated:

Women often labor under the delusion that life is really pretty easy for men, at least when compared to their own lot, and have no idea what a complicated struggle is really involved in the transition from male childhood to real manhood. They have no idea of the long and arduous road that must traveled by the male child who must separate himself from the original indispensable, nurturing mother and venture forth into a way of experiencing himself that is not her way and that he cannot learn from her either by example or by instruction. Considered in these terms, it is easy to see that a girl just learns to be like her mother, while a boy must learn to be different from her without his difference deteriorating into either antagonism or fear. Unfortunately, the current conditions of Western culture all too often favor this deplorable outcome, with unfortunate social results. (Barnhouse, 1974)

Male Development and Violence Against Women
The previous explorations lead to the focal point of this discussion. O'Neil (1995), noted earlier, raised the question, "Why do men harass, rape, and batter women?" (p. 164). Of all the issues noted by O'Neil, it is upon the issue of male violence toward women that this research is focused. Why are men violent? Why are they violent toward women? These questions will be addressed by examining the work of Karr-Morse and Wiley (1997) and then exploring its link to the work of Pollack (1998). The previous discussion examined the record of male development through the approximate age of two or three years. Human development surely did not conclude at that point. Wilber et al. 1986) and many others, for example Gould (1978), Levinson (1978), and Sheehy (1976), set forth the multiple stages of adult human psychological developmental and growth. According to Karr-Morse and Wiley, by the time the child is two years old the predisposition for violence is already set. They explained:

In order to understand the tide of violent behavior in which America is now submerged, we must look before preadolescence, before grade school, before preschool to the cradle of human formation in the first thirty-three months of life. Those months, including nine months of prenatal development and the first two years after birth (33 months), harbor the seeds of violence for a growing percentage of American children. . . . Rage-filled adolescents only seem to come out of nowhere. They come, too often, from the nursery. (p. 8)

Karr-Morse and Wiley (1997) further delineated the factors they believe foment the roots and causes of violence:

1. Maltreatment during the nine months of the fetal growth and the first twenty-four months after birth.
2. Alcohol, drugs, and tobacco.
3. Chronic stress or neglect, which affects development of the fetal or early infant brain.
4. Early child abuse and neglect, which undermine focused learning.
5. Chronic parental depression.
6. Neglect or lack of stimulation necessary for normal brain development.
7. Early loss of primary relationships or breaks in care giving.

These are the beginnings of the growing epidemic of violence now coming to light in childhood and adolescence. (p. 15)

Karr-Morse and Wiley continued: "Through the interplay of the developing brain with the environment during the nine months of gestation and the first two years after birth, the core of an individual's ability to think, feel, and relate to others is formed" (p. 15). Significant in this regard are items three through seven above. Specifically, they note that the infant's brain develops in proportion to the kinds of stimulation it receives. Critical periods (windows of opportunity) exist for expansive brain development. An infant deprived during one of the windows of opportunity is deprived throughout life. They noted, for example, that "babies born with cataracts . . . who did not receive surgery in the earliest months grew up blind because the brain cells that would normally process vision died or were called to work elsewhere. By four months of age, babies totally deprived of vision from birth are blind" (p. 22). It is clear that the experiences of the developing infant shape it for life.

Pursuant to the study of male development, as has been noted by Rubin (1974), Verny (1981), and Doyle (1983), males begin life with a projected parental mindset that has already made decisions about how they should be treated and how they should act. Karr-Morse and Wiley (1997) stated,

> All of our senses are fully installed and are being test driven pre-natally . . . all sensorial capabilities will be employed before birth, which is why, to anyone paying attention, the infant is capable of his or her incredible menu of skills and emotions upon arrival. Long before we are born we are experiencing. Our early brain is hard at work recording sensual input. (p. 51)

Prior to a male child's birth, parental beliefs are already programming male infant behavior.

Male infants are talked to differently than female infants. They receive less emotionally laden communication than their sisters. Karr-Morse and Wiley (1997) pointed out that the way a mother talks to a small child determines its prognosis for brain development: More talk equals more brain development. Mothers touched, talked to, and handled their daughters significantly more than they did their sons (Doyle, 1985; Katz, 1986). The male infant's brain development suffers and male infants often come up short in this regard. The experience was one of abandonment.

This traumatic experience of abandonment occurs so early in the life course that the shameful memory of the loss is likely to be deeply repressed. The male loses touch with his emotional self as if it never existed (Pollack, 1995; 1998). These infant male traumas point to the fact that violence becomes more probable. Karr-Morse and Wiley (1997) noted that

> Through the interplay of the developing brain with the environment during the nine months of gestation and the first two years after birth, the core of an individual's ability to think, feel, and relate to others is formed. . . . When we seek to understand violent behavior from the perspective of brain anatomy, we find some surprising realities. First of all, violent impulses are generated in the lower parts of the brain, particularly the limbic system. Under conditions of extreme threat or rage, when the

brain is flooded with stress hormones, the "fight or flight' human is not under the governance of the analytical cortex, the seat of rationality and wisdom. Under those extreme conditions, it is the limbic brain and midbrain, which are quickest to respond to mobilize the individual. (pp. 15, 33)

Perry (1997) pointed out that this dominance of the fight-or-flight tendency preempts the rationality, the desire to think before we act, of the neo-cortex.

Any factors which increase the activity or reactivity of the brainstem (e.g. chronic stress) or decrease the moderating capacity of the limbic or cortical areas (e.g. neglect) will increase an individual's aggressivity, impulsivity, and capacity to display violence. (pp. 124-129)

Consequently, a young child's lack of adequate stimulation of the neo-cortex, which provides a modulating and tempering of the lower brain's fight-or-flight reaction to the overstimulation of the alarm reaction stress experiences, may result in the acting out of violence (Karr-Morse & Wiley, 1997). The discomfort and reaction to the emotionally charged stress experiences in the infant, in lieu of adequate infant bonding, attachment, and emotional regulation, results in the life-long influence of that trauma as ongoing impulsive violence. They continued,

It is the belief that fetuses and babies are not sentient that is a fundamental reason that we have not been successful in stemming the roots of violence. Tomorrow's violent criminals still lie in their cribs today. To prevent one in twenty of today's babies from exchanging the slats of their cribs for prison bars in their adult lives, babies must be in the forefront of our concern. (p. 294)

The current developmental process of many, if not most, males raises concern in many quarters. That concern is revealed in summations of this problem. Pollack (1999) indicated that America is facing a gender Armageddon, and in *Real Boys* (1998), Pollack listed the following:

1. From elementary grades through high school, boys receive lower grades than girls.
2. Eighth-grade boys are held back 50 percent more often than girls.

3. By high school, boys account for two thirds of students in special education classes.
4. Fewer boys than girls now attend and graduate from college.
5. Fifty-nine percent of all master's degree candidates are now women.
6. The percentage of men in graduate-level professional education is shrinking each year.
7. Boys experience more difficulty adjusting to school, are up to ten times more likely to suffer from "hyperactivity" than girls, and account for 71% of all school suspensions.
8. Boys are lagging behind in reading and writing.
9. Boys' self-esteem as learners is far more fragile than that of most girls. (pp. 15-16)

Additionally, Gurian (1999a) considered the male developmental journey as a moral emergency in America. He noted:

1. We have the most violent non-war population of children in the world. More people in the U.S. per capita commit violent acts every day than any other country, and 90 percent of them are male.
2. More of our children per capita get arrested for crime than in any other country. Ninety percent of arrestees are boys.
3. After Russia, more of our citizens are in prison than any other country in the world. Ninety percent of these incarcerated individuals are male.
4. Our young males make up 80 percent of drug-addicted and alcoholic youth.
5. Our boys constitute the majority of children who are homeless, murdered, in foster care, neglected, and institutionalized.
6. Our rate of mental disorders in the male population per capita is one of the highest in the world. For instance, 90 percent of the Ritalin used on children in the world is used on ours. Approximately 3,000,000 kids are on Ritalin in the U.S. — 90 percent of them boys.

7. The child suicide rate has gone up over the last decade with increasing acceleration, mainly among adolescent boys; by nineteen, males commit suicide at a rate of 6 times greater than girls (video, The National Desk: *The War on Boys*).

8. Our teen pregnancy rates are among the highest in the industrial world, and we provide the least extended family support to teens that have babies. Ninety percent of males who impregnate a teen girl abandon her and her family.

9. Our schoolchildren are arguably the most undisciplined in the world. Ninety percent of the children who require discipline in schools are boys. As one educator recently stated, "After teaching in Hong Kong, Japan, and Australia, then returning to the United States, I felt something like despair when I saw what had happened to the American middle school classroom."

10. Our boys and young men also comprise the majority of child-abuse victims and are the less likely victim to talk about and get help for their suffering. In a 1998 study of 7,000 children, 48 percent of boys, compared to 29 percent of girls, said they would never tell anyone about the abuse they had experienced. As psychologist Aaron Kipnis explains: "it is egodystonic — not in accord with their self-image and traditional gender identity — for boys to complain about pain." Thus our boys are becoming more and more at risk for abuse, neglect, violence, addiction, psychiatric illness, and all the pains of childhood lived in broken homes and confusing worlds, pains that never appear in statistics. (pp. 4-5)

Intimate Partner Violence and Its Treatment

Simple awareness attests to the universality of humans' inhumanity to each other. Explorations into intimate partner violence here involve a brief overview of violence history under matriarchal and patriarchal systems, and some historical examples of violence toward women. The revolt against the abuse of and violence toward women will be examined, with an overview of the dynamics of intimate partner violence and implications for treatment.

Intimate partner violence is a shocking event for the whole community. Information about its severity and extensiveness comes from the National Family Violence Survey and the National Crime Victimization Survey. At least two million women are beaten by their partners each year (Bachman & Saltzman, 1995; Berry, 2001; Flowers, 2000; Groetsch, 1997; Stets & Straus, 1990), and evidence from the National Crime Victimization Survey indicates that one-fifth of the time a weapon is involved. Intimate partner violence resulted in twice the injuries of stranger violence (Berry; Flowers). As many as half of all female homicide victims are killed by their husbands or boyfriends (Groetsch; Kellerman & Mercy, 1992).

Violence surveys indicate that women assault their partners at least as often as men do (Cook, 1997; Stets & Straus, 1990; Straus et al., 1980). Parity between intimate partners seems to end, however, with the severity and results of aggressive acts. Studies found that assaulted women were several times more likely than men to require medical care after severe assaults and were significantly more likely than assaulted husbands to experience psychological injuries related to their abuse (Groetsch, 1997; Hammer & Itzin, 2001; Herman, 2001; O'Leary & Maiuro, 2001; Weiss, 2000).

Violence in History

It seems impossible to conceive of a time when violence and murder did not exist. McNeill (1963) noted that up until 12,000 B.C., hunting, killing for survival, dominated human life-styles. After 12,000 B.C., sophisticated ideas of planting, growing, and harvesting developed in early membership societies. Around 9500 B.C., towns of about 200 people emerged; and from 4500 B.C. to 1500 B.C., towns of 10,000 to 50,000 people developed, producing the great city-states and civilizations. Farming provided the surpluses that allowed segments of the population leisure and time for reflection. The issues of death and survival still dominated thinking, however (Eisler & Skidmore; 1987; McNeill; 1963; Mickunas; 1973; Neumann, 1973).

Early farming membership societies employed ritualistic magic in the form of cultural activities, monuments, and rites to facilitate survival and avoid death (Boss, 1963). It was not such a leap from killing animals for human survival to the bloodletting of human sacrifice (Becker, 1975). Human sacrifice was a ritualistic practice also designed to offer the other's body to stave off one's own death (Becker, 1975). If the blood of a human was spilled, it was believed it would take powerful magic not to be the victim of blood revenge (Fried, 1967). The magic of rituals served to "defend against it [death] and deliver it to others" (Campbell, 1949, p. 126). The shocking and horrendous rites of human sacrifice were universal. The following is an example:

> The particular moment of importance to our story occurs at the conclusion of one of the boys' puberty rites, which terminates in a sexual orgy of several days and nights, during which every one in the village makes free with everybody else, amid the tumult of the mythological chants, drums, and the bull-roars, until the final night, when a fine young girl, painted, oiled, and ceremonially costumed, is led into the dancing ground and made to lie beneath a platform of heavy logs. With her, in open view of the festival, the initiates cohabit, one after another; and while the youth chosen to be last is embracing her the supports of the logs above are jerked away and the platform drops, to a prodigious boom of drums. A hideous howl goes up and the dead girl and boy are dragged from the logs, cut up, roasted, and eaten. (Wirz, 1925, Vol. II, p. 40)

Matriarchy

The question arises as to the origin of such sacrifices, to whom were they made, and why. Enter the Great Mother/ Great Goddess myth. According to Campbell (1959), dominant in the consciousness of the early cultural mythology were the composite naturalistic/biological, the Great Mother, and the metaphysical/mystical, the Great Goddess. It was to appease her that the human sacrifices were made. The Great Mother and the Great Goddess seem to be a fitting consciousness awakening point in historical culture similar to conscious awakening in human development (Campbell).

Kaplan (1978) noted a common belief in contemporary psychology: The infant at birth does not have a personal identity. For the first four to six months, the baby is enmeshed with the mother and its physical surroundings — Klein's (1975) concept of projective identification. The individuation process continues as various stages (1) physical, 1-12 months; 2) emotional, 12-36 months; and 3) cognitive, 36-60 months of the separation process) are negotiated (Mahler, 1975). The development of the sense of self is worked out with the mother, now loving, now terrifying (Campbell, 1959). The mother as the biological basis of the family becomes the whole world to the child (Brown, 1959). Thus, the mother, if she is appropriate to the stage-specific needs of the child, can be thought of as the Great Mother, the Great Environment, or the Great Surround (Neumann, 1973); or if her approach is inappropriate, she is the vengeful Destroyer (Fenichel, 1945). She is the Good Mother and the Bad Mother (Sullivan, 1953). Human cultural history, like human developmental psychology, worked out its separation drama with the mother.

Two basic principles played significant roles in the cultural separation drama acted out with the Great Mother. Science being absent, myth and metaphor ruled the day (Campbell, 1959). The first principle was the association between the moon and the womb, for both lunar and menstrual cycles run a 28-day course:

> At the end of the monthly lunar cycle, the moon "disappears" or "dies" — it goes dark; it goes into the underworld or netherworld. But within three days, behold: the moon is reborn and resurrected! In fact, the moon must die if a new cycle is to begin. The moon is also a consort with the earth. Hence, the first symbolic equation that emerges is: *the consort of the Great Mother is the three-day-dead-and resurrected god.* (Wilber, 1981, p. 123)

The second basic principle is more gruesome. Early history was void of scientific knowledge regarding human reproduction. People did not associate sexual intercourse with pregnancy, as they experienced ubiquitous intercourse and few pregnancies. It was not male semen that caused pregnancy, birth, and new life. In fact, males were and are insignificant in the human separation drama and in the human historical cultural mythological drama. Males selected by the Mother/Goddess were merely phallic consorts (Neumann, 1973). They held no significance (Campbell, 1959). New life was perceived as being the result not of male semen, but of the cessation of the menstrual flow. It was the cessation of menstrual blood flow that was being converted into the life form of a new baby (Neumann). The Great Mother needed blood in order to bring forth new life.

> When we put these two symbolic equations (of the dead and resurrected lunar-god consort and the blood sacrifice for life) together, we straightforwardly arrive at the perfect

logic of the early rites of human sacrifice: the symbolic consort (human or animal) is sacrificed in blood to the Great Mother, dies, and is resurrected (after three days, according to many myths) . . . . To put it all in a nutshell: what was the way to appease the Great Mother, to keep her as Protectress and prevent her wrathful indulgence? Give her what she demands — blood! And likewise, invent a precise way to do it — ritual! So goes paleologic: like magic, it works with partial truths; and, like magic, since it is unable to grasp higher perspectives or wider contexts, it arrives at barbaric conclusions — [human sacrifice]. (Wilber, 1981, p. 126)

The sacrificial ritual of early membership societies served to appease and expiate death guilt and ensure the fertile future of a separate self. The embodiment of the mythological Mother/goddess, "the queen of heaven, the daughter of God, goddess of the morning and evening star, the hierodule or slave-girl dancer of the gods — who, as the morning star, is ever-virgin, but, as evening star, is 'the divine harlot,' and whose names in a later age were to be Ishtar, Aphrodite, and Venus" (Campbell, 1959, p. 412) — was worshiped. The male consorts of the Great Mother/goddess were incidental and expendable via self-mutilation and suicide as part of an elaborate sacrificial ritual. "The ritual served as a magical substitute for transcendence and immortality, a magical rite to ensure fertility, ensure the future, ensure in fact that death will not grin in at the harvest, while simultaneously presenting the self as central to the cosmos and all-favored among the otherwise vengeful elements of Mother Nature" (Wilber, 1983, p. 128).

The sacrificial ritual — the moon-womb, need-for-blood, three-day-dead-and-resurrected god, appeasing the Great devouring mother to preserve life — becomes extroverted and logically leads to murder. Extending the sacrificial death ritual outward toward the other completes the transition of sacrifice to homicide (Brown, 1959). Some consider that murderous hostility is pre-eminently the substitute sacrifice, a killing of others to magically buy off the death of the self. The original death-terror becomes the death-dealing; "One arranges the substitute sacrifice of actually killing somebody else, thus acting on, and appeasing, the terrifying confrontation with [one's own] death" (Wilber, 1981, p. 154). Wilber continued:

But let us note the logical priorities herein involved: under the desire to kill lies the extroverted death impact, and under death impact lays the pull of transcendence. Murder, that is, is a form of substitute sacrifice or substitute transcendence. . . . The deepest wish of all is to sacrifice one's self — "kill" it — so as to find true transcendence. . . . The logic of killing others in order to affirm our own life unlocks much that puzzles us in history . . . from scapegoating to mass war to Roman arena games to Nazi blood sacrifices. . . . And the simple fact is that, around the third millennium B.C., especially in Sumer, those early city-states of Ur, Uruk, Kish, Lagash, and all — modern, massive warfare of one state against another was born. (pp. 154, 157, 159)

Patriarchy

Violence and bloodletting accompany human history. For early hunters, they meant survival. In the transition from the Mother/Goddess to patriarchy violence was there. With the familialization of the male as evolution moved beyond the hoe, violence was a consort of patriarchy. Patriarchy is viewed as male domination based upon the familialization of the male via the role of the father that has been present with humans from the beginning (Jaggar, 1988). Patriarchy is also viewed as that shift from the ideal matrifocal (or equalfocal) horticultural societies dominated by the Great Mother ideal to a patrifocal mode existent for five thousand years (Chavetz, 1984; Eisler & Skidmore, 1987; Gimbutas, 1991; Neilson, 1990). "The Great Mother represented the totality of nature: matter, instincts, body, crops, earth, fertility, sexuality, emotions, desire, magic, and the beginning of myth" (Wilber, 1981, p. 122). History progressed from the perception of Mother Nature to that of human nature, "and this marked the beginning of patriarchy" (p. 122). Patriarchy has dominated history and culture since the Mother/Goddess ideal. It has also furthered the phenomenon of violence among humans. This is especially true regarding women. Since its evolutionary emergence, patriarchy and the males who have governed it have — sometimes with female compliance — dominated, hurt, and killed women. A few notable examples stand out.

Chinese Foot Binding

Russell (1983) noted that for over a thousand years footbinding in China crippled women. Chinese footbinding originated as a practice among the Imperial harem dancers between the 9th and 11th centuries in China (Dworkin, 1974). The practice was universalized to most Chinese women. Footbinding extended by emulation from the Imperial Palace to millions of Chinese women over ten centuries (Dworkin). The toes of the feet were curled under and bound into the soles of the feet. The feet, in addition to suffering excruciating pain, were crippled. Women had to walk on the outside of their toes. Toenails grew into the skin, calluses formed, circulation stopped and the feet became infected. Women hobbled along, taking small steps, actually falling as they went, with the need of external support to "walk." A distortion of the female body resulted, with the thighs and buttocks becoming swollen, which men called voluptuousness. Men also assumed a sexual outcome of footbinding: "The smaller the feet, the more intense the sex urge" (Levy, 1966, p. 141).

Footbinding limited the mobility and ensured the chastity of women. Faithfulness to the husband and the legitimacy of children was guaranteed. Being born a woman was payment for sins of a past life and footbinding might spare such a further incarnation. For males, the bound foot resulted in the total dependence of the woman upon the male: "To her I am the world, I am life itself" (Levy, 1966, p. 89). Consequently, for 1,000 years the patriarchy of one sex mutilated and enslaved millions of "the other sex in the name of the art of sex, male-female harmony, role-definition, and beauty. . . . Brutality, sadism, and oppression emerge as the substantive core of the romantic ethos" (Dworkin, 1974, pp.111-112).

The Burning of Witches

Throughout the middle Ages, when Platonism was expressed as Christianity, multiple shades of religious "truth" hammered out their meanings (Thilly & Wood, 1957). This was especially true of the notion of the Devil or Satan (Dworkin). In that process, until the 10th century Devil worship was anathema to the church, which, however, did little to contest it other than issue some proclamations (Dworkin, 1974). Women were mostly charged with the practice of Devil worship, and they were designated as Witches.

The pursuit of witches was relentless. On December 9, 1484, in the Bull of Innocent VIII, a prescriptive decree, the Pope assigned "Heinrich Kramer and James Sprenger as Inquisitors to define witchcraft, describe the *modus operandi* of witches, and standardize trial procedures and sentencing" (Dworkin, p. 125). The witch-hunt began. Because women were viewed as the entrée of sin into humanity, they were tried and burned as witches (Dworkin).

Estimates differ as to the number of women witches that existed. In the 13th century it was estimated that some 1,758,064,176 were devil-driven. A more conservative estimate put forth by "Jean Weir, Physician to the Duke of Cleves, estimated the number to be only 7,409,127 . . .[and] the ratio of women to men executed has been variously estimated at 20 to 1 and 100 to 1. Witchcraft was a women's crime" (Dworkin, p. 130). It is estimated that some nine million women were executed, often by being burned alive. One sex, whatever the theoretical justification, murdered the other sex.

Purdah

Purdah is a widespread practice today throughout the Muslim populations of Middle East, North Africa, and Asia. Purdah is the practice of isolating women from contact with men outside of the immediate family. Frequently women become prisoners in their own homes (Russell, 1983). Until recently, in the capital of Afghanistan, women were still kept in medieval lifestyles. When the Taliban, in 1996, began to reinforce a version of Koranic law, women were returned to a form of imprisonment. Women couldn't work outside the home, girls couldn't go to school outside the home, and women could leave the home only when accompanied by a man; in effect, women were barred from public life. In such restrictive societies suicide levels go up, along with despair and depression (Amanpour, 1997).

Clitoridectomy

Clitoridectomy (excision of the clitoris) is still practiced on millions of pre-pubescent girls in Egypt, Sudan, Somalia, Kenya, Yemen, Saudi Arabia, Iraq, Guinea, and Ethiopia (Eisler, 1987). Female circumcision, the practice of cutting away all or part of a girl's external genitalia, usually without the use of anesthesia (Brownlee & Seter, 1994), prevails even where modern African governments endeavor to restrict or prohibit it. The practice is believed to diminish a woman's sexual appetite in order to maintain her virginity and make her more marriageable (Brownlee & Seter). Circumcision of both males and females is considered crucial to children's socialization. It is seen as a symbol of a group's stability and as a means of reinforcing respect and authority (Samad, 1996). According to Maina and Oyaro (2000), girls in Kenya's Masailand embrace female circumcision because of fears that they will be isolated and that no one will marry them. In 1998, some 89% of Masai women between the ages of 15 and 49 were circumcised. Every year, an estimated two million girls undergo circumcision (Cheakalos, 1998). Maina and Oyaro (2000) noted that circumcised women are twice as likely to die in childbirth and are more likely to have stillbirths than other mothers.

The results in some cultures reveal that circumcised women had lower childlessness, lower infertility by age, and higher total fertility than women who were not circumcised; although in some cultures, the opposite was true (Larsen & Yan, 2000). Although 15 of the 28 nations that practice ritual female genital circumcision, plus some six European nations, have banned the practice, it is a persistent tradition that will not be readily eradicated (Anonymous, 1999).

Rape

A significant expression of the exercise of male power and control over women is the phenomenon of rape, which is as old as history. When Israel invaded Canaan, virgin women were taken as the spoils (Numbers 31: 32-35). Rape has been the norm for invading armies. Rape, within and outside the family, is one of the crudest and most brutal ways in which Western patriarchal societies seek to maintain the sexual status quo. The National Crime Victimization Survey of the Bureau of Justice Statistics expressed the belief that women experience twice as much sexual violence in their lives as had been reported. The Rape in America study, conducted by Crime Victim Research and Treatment Center of the Medical University of South Carolina, reported that some 12 million adult women have been victims of at least one forcible rape during their lifetimes, that approximately 6,000,000 women are raped annually in America, and that many women have suffered from rape-related Post Traumatic Stress Disorder and other psychological disorders (Martin, 1976).

Suttee

"Suttee" (a term borrowed from the Indian name for the immolation of widows) or "sati" (Banerjee, 1999) is the practice of placing alive the widow and children of a dead chieftain in his grave to be buried with him. According to Eisler (1987), the Kurgan invasions into Old European cultures changed the pastoral horticultural open-towns into a Kurgan culture of war. The Kurgan invasions from the northern European steppes around 2500 B.C. brought "bronze weapons, daggers and halberds, together with thin and sharp axes of bronze and mace heads and battle-axes of semiprecious stone and flint arrowheads, coinciding with the routs of dispersal of Kurgan people" (Gimbutas, 1973, p. 166).

With the cultural "Kurganization" came the practice of suttee. Many graves dating from the fourth millennium B.C. reveal the status of males and their possessions placed in their graves, documented in Kurgan burial practices. The strongly male-dominated culture that followed involved a marked change in burial rites and practices of the Old Europeans. These "chieftain graves" indicated a radical shift in social organization, with a strongman elite at the top. Old European burials showed little indication of social inequality, but with the Kurgan influence marked differences occurred in the sizes of the graves as well as in what archaeologists call "funerary gifts": the contents of the tomb were other than the deceased. "Among these contents, for the first time in European graves, we find along with an exceptionally tall or large-boned male skeleton the skeletons of sacrificed women — the wives, concubines, or slaves of the men who died" (Eisler, p. 50). Women, as wives, concubines, and slaves, were buried and burned alive with their deceased husbands.

Banerjee (1999) linked what he calls the heathen practices of widowburning with the punishment by witchburning of Christian societies. Widowburning in some communities, as amongst the Calcutta Marwaris, takes on a life of its own and has become the focal point of worship, which shapes certain traditions, associated with the ideals of female domesticity (Hardgrove, 1999). This practice in some cultures has continued (Gimbutas, 1973). Suttee has political and economic ramifications and Western scholars are strongly recommending reform (Ansari, 1997).

The Objectification of Women

A strong male dictum is to avoid anything feminine (Levant, 1997). The statements "No sissy stuff in this house," "If you are going to cry I'll give you something to cry about," and "Quit acting like a girl" often strike familiar chords in a male's memory. Men, due to developmental experiences, often carry two internal ego states regarding women. From the practicing phase (12 – 24 months) men carry the ideal of the goddess expressed as euphoria and self-giving love, and from the wounds of the rapprochement phase (24 – 36 months) men may carry revolting trivializing contempt for the "bitch" and the "whore" (Goldberg, 1976; Levant, 1997; Pollack, 1998). When the woman transfigures from the goddess, by virtue of disagreement and disapproval, to the bitch, the man can depersonalize her into an object, and objects can be beaten (Pence, 1985). "In interviews with 22 victims of battering in Duluth, the women listed the most frequently used verbal insults they experienced; leading the list were slang words referring to female genitals, followed by slut, whore, dumb bitch, ugly bitch, fat bitch, and lazy bitch. All of these insults increased in use prior to an assault" (Pence, 1985, p. 3).

It takes significant ongoing effort for men to personalize the women in their lives in treatment groups. Objective references to the female partner as the "old lady," "the little woman," and "the wife," are ingrained concepts difficult to transmute into "Jane," "Mary," or "Sue." Moreover, the Madison Avenue employment of women and women's bodies to sell products further objectifies women. Pornography is a multimillion-dollar business (Pence, 1985). Women as objects sell, they are beaten, and they become victims.

The Revolt Against Violence Toward Women

Subtle changes began to shift the cultural consciousness regarding intimate partner violence as the twentieth century approached (Pence, 1996). According to Pence, the notorious examples of woman abuse previously mentioned were consonant with the pervading underlying social presuppositions of male ascendancy supported by the dicta of religious institutions, educational institutions, and government. The profound negative impact upon women continued. Many women were illiterate, nurturing children and fulfilling the mother role was a never-ending task that limited their roles in the public social structure, and they mostly accepted their assigned role in the family division of labor (Chodorow, 1974). The natural order or natural law belief systems, which positioned the man over his partner with entitled rights of obedience and service, still prevailed. This notion was heavily reinforced abroad in American life, and by existent hierarchical structures (Pence).

For hundreds of years, concomitant with patriarchy in West, it was man's responsibility and duty to control his wife with beatings as necessary (Dobash & Dobash, 1979). Male privilege was recognized by the courts as a legal right perpetuated by the male judicial system. Wife battering was an accepted practice (Pence, 1996). Under English Common Law husbands could physically discipline their wives (Jones, 1981). A good husband was one that "ruleth well his own house" (I Timothy 3:4).

However, during early colonial history in the 1600s and 1700s, the husband's right to discipline a wife was taken away and given to the civil authorities (Jones, 1981). The civil authority took over the obligation of judging a women's behavior regarding her husband and arbitrating family disputes. After the American Revolution, the husband reasserted his right to discipline his wife. In 1824 the Mississippi Supreme Court ruled that a man had the right to chastise his wife moderately if it was done discreetly, not to bring shame to either party. The North Carolina court ruled that a husband had a right to discipline his wife, and that it was no matter for the state. The law was not to enter into the privacy of the man/wife relationship (Jones, 1981; Pence, 1996).

Toward the end of the century, however, states began to overturn the practice. In 1872 Massachusetts and Alabama led the nation in passing legislation criminalizing wife abuse. By the beginning of the twentieth century, the legal and public approval of wife beating had declined to the extent that most Western countries and all 48 American states had outlawed the practice (Pence, 1996).

Battering continued, according to Pence (1996), but was hidden from the public eye. By the second decade of the twentieth century, society had progressed far enough that a husband was no longer permitted to beat his wife. Men's assumption and expectation of the women's subordination was so strong that changing the law did not result in its being enforced. Despite laws on the books specifically designating wife beating as an assault like any other assault, the state continued its policy of non-interference simply by looking the other way, unofficially sanctioning the subordination of women. Wife beating, in some quarters, has been against the law, but the police, the courts, and public officials have winked at it (Pence). The issue of wife-beating finally gained international media attention and the extent and severity of the problem began to be recognized in 1972, with the opening of the first shelter for abused women in Chiswick, England (Jones, 1981; Pence).

Beginning in the 1960s in the United States, battered women's programs were organized to provide safety for women who had been assaulted, and to confront police, the courts, and institutions that took a light view of woman abuse (Pence, 1996). In the 1970s people involved in these programs began to take action in defense of women. They set up rape crisis centers. They exposed incest and sexual harassment. They started the shelter movement, creating places where abused women could go for support in helping to heal their physical and psychological wounds (Pence; Walker, 2000a). Battered women's shelters and programs organized throughout the 1970s greatly impacted the judicial systems and community awareness and focused intense attention on the intimate partner violence problem (Pence, 1983). The growth of interest in the problem has been in response to the "social construction" (i.e., public recognition) of intimate partner violence as a major problem. This recognition occurred as a result of major changes in society and in the social sciences (Finkelhorr, 1984; Straus, 1992).

According to Dobash, Dobash, Wilson, and Daly (1992), Straus (1973), Yllo and Bofrad (1988), and Yllo and Straus (1990), the pathway to these changes may be noted in approximate chronological order. Beginning in the 1960s, growing social activism extended to the causes of women and children. The rising incidents of homicide, rape, assault, political assassination, and terrorist activity, along with the Vietnam War, sensitized people to the issue of violence. The burgeoning divorce rate and growing number of single parent homes in the 1980s and 1990s increased the negative aspects of family, including violence. The growth in the financial viability of married women lessened their need to tolerate abuse for financial reasons. Violence was a factor in 40% of divorces (Berry, 2001; Flowers, 2000; Lovinger, 1966; O'Brien, 1971). Social service professionals grew rapidly in number. "Social activist baby-boomers were entering graduate school and they wre interested in using social science as a means of social activism" (Jasinski & Williams, 1998). According to Finkelhor (1982), the American Association of Marriage and Family Therapists went from having 3,375 members in 1975 to having 25,000 in 1995. Straus (1975) noted that the women's movement, beyond its establishment of rape crisis centers and women's shelters, was ideologically important because feminists crystallized and publicized phenomena that had previously been ignored. The conservative political agenda for "law and order" in the 1980s converged with the sociologists' and the women's movement's demand to end the immunity of wife-beaters. Violence came to be recognized as a conflict tactic. Sociology and its debunking tradition (Berger, 1973) contended with the concept that marriages were made in heaven and families were a haven when oppressed women resided therein. Women have been outstripping men in academia (Pollack, 1998, 1999), bringing research prowess to the topics of gender roles, male oppression, and the male dominator role.

The Expanding Field of Intimate Partner Violence Research

Consequently, the interest in intimate partner violence, though recent, has resulted in an explosion of research articles and resultant knowledge that may be unprecedented (Straus, 1998). The 25-year history of research on violence in the family has contributed to an increasing awareness of the scope and significance of this problem (Jacobson & Gottman, 1998). In 1975, the first National Family Violence Survey was conducted to measure the extent of violence in the family, in an attempt to understand what the violence meant to the participants and to determine what caused the violence to take place (Straus, Gelles, & Steinmetz, 1980). This was the first attempt by researchers to measure intra-family violence in a large, nationally representative sample. This survey found that individuals faced the greatest risk of assault and physical injury in their own homes, perpetrated by members of their own families. The Family Research Laboratory at the University of New Hampshire, a research group, published some 35 books and 300 articles on domestic violence from 1974 to 1996.

Articles on domestic violence number in the hundreds. The fact that ten new journals on this topic began publication since 1985 (Jasinski & Williams, 1998) provided an insight into the interest in domestic violence research. Although each new insight into intimate partner violence raises new questions and controversies, all the attention and political effort seem to have been fruitful, for the available evidence suggests that intimate partner violence has been decreasing (Straus, 1986, 1994).

The Root Causes of Intimate Partner Violence

The nomenclature for male/female violence progressed through a developmental process (Sonkin, personal communication, July 17, 1998). It has been called family violence, domestic violence, and spousal abuse. Intimate partner violence was chosen as the most appropriate term for this study. In its limited expression, it refers to partner violence between two married or cohabiting adults. Intimate partner violence may generally refer to other types of violence in the family, including child abuse. A review of the literature explores violence in the context of the entire family and expects that the term "intimate partner violence" is related to, and must be viewed from, the perspective of intimate partner violence, child abuse, and sibling violence (Jasinski & Williams, 1998).

Intimate partner violence etiologies abound. A cursory examination of the literature notes the following lenses through which it has been viewed: historical, biological, psychological, sociological, and feminist. Conventional wisdom in the treatment community reaffirms some popularized views. Intimate partner violence has been attributed to sexism (Worley, 2000), a belief in male superiority over women (Ramirez, 1994), the male desire for power and control over family members (Pence, 1986), and the belief that intimate partner violence is a learned behavior imitated by males who watched their fathers do it to their mothers (Cousin, 1997) — all of which, to varying degrees, ring true and find some substantiation in the research.

The Historical Etiology. A review of the historical developments of the male/female roles leads to the historical etiology for intimate partner violence. Doyle (1983) noted the historical development of the masculinity stereotype. Out of the survival instincts sustained by male physical strength, patriarchy unavoidably emerged (Wilber, 1996). Male and female diverse characteristics yielded a pattern of division of labor, hunting and mothering respectively, that sustained the tribe. Historical survival practices set a precedent. That precedent led to a pattern, and the pattern led to the prescription of how things ought to be done, as in Kant's categorical imperative or deontological ethic, from "is" to "ought" (Kant, 1962). The male dominator role, sustained by practice and perpetuated as patriarchy, is considered a convention destined to perpetuate intimate partner violence (Walker, 2000b).

Centuries of human and societal survival became ingrained belief systems and patterns of behavior. A man, due to his sexual/gender qualities, a natural order, according to Pence (1989), sustains the societal and family order and internalizes his position and universalizes it to include not just the role of sustainer, but that of progenitor, director, guardian, protector, leader, teacher, disciplinarian, and controller with entitlements. According to Doyle (1983), the woman was the nurturer of the children who became dependent, supportive, a "helpmeet" (fitting help) (Genesis 2:20), and subservient to the head of the household. Most institutions in American life sustain this concept in a natural and hierarchical order: religious institutions, educational institutions, government, and organized sports all contribute to the system. A man's sense that he must be a man, and do what a man is supposed to do, has led to the use of force, abuse, and violence to maintain this perceived natural order (Pence). A video presentation of a participant in a perpetrator treatment program voiced this belief as follows:

> I have been taught all my life that in my family I am in charge. If I am in charge and I tell you to do something — you do something. But when my partner says "no," which is the standard response that causes the signs of "fatal peril," then I feel worthless. I've never been told in my whole life I'm supposed to feel worthless. I've been told I'm supposed to be in charge — I'm supposed to figure crap out. When she says "no — forget it — I ain't doing it" — I'm worthless as shit — I might as well be dead — wouldn't be anything lost if I were dead, then I'm not worth anything. (Ramirez, 1994, video)

Feminist intimate partner violence theory attributes much of the problem to the societal construction of patriarchy (Donavan, 1985).

However, many researchers affirm that patriarchy was not some conspiracy hatched by men against women, but a logical outflow of behaviors that perpetuated the survival of the village and became an ingrained pattern of belief and behavior (Goldberg, 1973; Wilber, 1996). The historical etiology of intimate partner violence served as a matrix for other views.

The Bio-chemical Etiology. The most important element of male behavior throughout history, according to Doyle (1983), was the factor of aggression in the survival of the social group. A kind of bio-chemical phenomenon (testosterone) was at work from the beginning in male aggressive behavior that was different from the one at work (oxytocin) in the female nurturing role (Gray, 1996; Wilber, 1996). Observers note that, when considering the human species, violence and males are given mutual definitions. To explain violence is to explain maleness and vice versa (Miles, 1992). "Most violence, most crime . . . is not committed by human beings in general. It is committed by men" (Archer & Lloyd, 1985, p. 124). Testosterone is seen as a key factor that endows men with a biological propensity for higher levels of aggression than women (Goldberg, 1973; Kipnis, 1994). A summary of several sex studies notes that males are biologically predisposed toward greater aggressiveness (Maccoby & Jacklin, 1974).

Men and aggression may be understood from the biochemical process of male development, i.e. hormonal factors predispose males to violence (George, 1997). Male hormonal development, a key distinguishing factor between males and females, explains patriarchy, male dominance, and male attainment of higher-status roles (Goldberg, 1973). The testosterone hypothesis was pursued from three perspectives: the role of the chemical in male neonatal life, its effect at puberty, and its impact on adult males (George; Hines, 1982). Studies found that multiple factors are involved in testosterone levels: time of day, environment, positive circumstances, and stress, and that no simple link could be assumed between testosterone and violent behavior (Albert, Walsh, & Jonick, 1993; Archer, 1991; Rabinow & Schmidt, 1996).

However, despite the fact that no simple link between testosterone and male violence and dominance may be certain, the hormonal differences between males and females over centuries do play a role in intimate conflict (Goldberg, 1973). First came the familialization of the male (Habermas, 1976); then began "the one, single, enduring, and nightmarish task of all subsequent civilization: the taming of testosterone" (Wilber, 1995, p. 156).

The Psychological Etiology. The scientific search into the nature of human behavior provided the psychological etiology of intimate partner violence. The study of human behavior, according to Goble (1970), was basically the purview of theologians and philosophers. Wundt (1832-1920), however, is credited with the first scientific study of human nature in founding the first formal laboratory of psychology in 1879 and the first psychological journal in 1881. Other schools followed: Functionalism (William James); Gestalt (Wertheimer & Kohler); Psychoanalysis (Freud); Behaviorism (Watson); and Human Potential (Maslow et al.). The psychological perspective has an extensive history. The view of individual responsibility and the lack thereof led to the cataloguing of human characteristics and individual psychopathologies (Loseke, 1993). Gender roles and gender differences accumulated a growing theory base of differences.

The psychological etiology for intimate partner violence has received a reasonable amount of empirical documentation in different laboratories (O'Leary, Malone, & Tyree, 1992). These studies document personality traits such as poor impulse control, poor anger control, conditioned emotional arousal, weak personality development, or emotion-focused coping (O'Leary, 1993). Early inquiries into causes led to the examination of the misnavigation of the rapprochement phase of human development — the psychological birth of the human infant (Mahler, 1975) — that resulted in significant personality disorders directly affecting intimate interpersonal relations (Masterson, 1988; Wilber et al., 1986).

Men charged with intimate partner violence, when evaluated with the Millon Clinical Multiaxial Inventory, were found to have the following personality profiles: schizoid/borderline, narcissistic/antisocial and possessive/dependent/compulsive disorders (Hamberger & Hastings, 1986). Great numbers of such men show evidence of personality disorders (Hamberger & Hastings, 1988). Seventy-five percent of documented abusive men had significantly elevated scores on aggressive/sadistic personality disorders tests, and 62% had elevated scores on the antisocial personality disorders tests (Murphy, Meyer, & O'Leary, 1992). Abusive men are aggressive, dependent, defensive, and easily offended by their intimate partners, as assessed on the Jackson Personality Inventory (O'Leary et al., 1992). As the physical abuse increases, a correlation exists to the degree of personality dysfunction (O'Leary, 1993). According to O'Leary et al. (1992), empirical evidence does support the psychologically dysfunctional nature of human males as a contributor to intimate partner violence (Gottman, 1994). Intimate partner violence is the result of "Early Experiences" (Starr, 1983, p. 20) or the abuser's psychological history. Numerous theoreticians subscribe to this position (Groetsch, 1997; O'Leary, 1993; Karr-Morse & Wiley, 1997).

The Sociological Etiology.   The context of an individual's life, according to Gelles (1993), becomes the raw materials employed to construct an individual's consciousness. The major societal structures exert significant influences upon a society's members. A key element in the social structure is the family, its givens, and the givens of each member's age, birth order, sex, socioeconomic level, race or ethnicity. Society's institutions shape the behaviors of members of society. This is especially true regarding the nature of the family structure and intimate partner violence (Gelles).

Starr (1983) provided an overview of some of the most basic views as to the causes of domestic violence. She noted that one of the perceived root causes of intimate partner violence is what she called the "societal" viewpoint (p. 9). The societal view posits that individuals in a society absorb the cultural milieu. In this case, violence is a part of the American way of life — a socially condoned method that allows some persons in power to maintain their privileged positions. Abusers are not emotionally ill; they are functioning in accordance with societal norms and standards. Star also concurred with the belief that "family systems" (p. 9) contribute to spousal abuse. According to Gelles (1993), a conflicted member of a family, sometimes the female parent, transmits that violent trait, as she is "more likely to maltreat the children" (p. 32). Moreover, abusive traits, wherever they originate, are passed to other members of the family (Burgdorf, 1980; Gelles; Straus, 1980; Wolfner & Gelles, 1993). Intimate partner violence is a learned response to managing conflict. Star noted that the "socialization" (p. 9) process, once learned, can be modified and tempered with psycho-education and relationship skill building.

Gelles (1993) noted that the psychological perspective "ignores the special, and unique structure of the family as a social institution" (p. 34). The risk of stranger violence is minimal in comparison to the threat of family violence. The family is society's most violent social institution (Straus et al. 1980). The sociological perspective offers a broad context and an inclusive perspective that neither excludes nor diminishes other areas of focus. The sociological perspective provides a place for other perspectives in a broad framework, allowing for the examination of the impact of social institutions and social structure upon the social phenomenon of intimate partner violence.

A Feminist Perspective. Feminism is a perspective for viewing reality. This viewing point looks at the problem through many lenses. Donavan (1985) provided a history of the movement. Muraskin and Alleman (1993) explored four major perspectives on feminism: liberal feminism, Marxist feminism, socialist feminism, and radical feminism. Cahoone (1996) observed that feminism fit into the post-modernity movement along with multiculturalism and eco-feminism as a rejection of the "ideology of a privileged sexual, ethnic and economic group with the aim to undermine established educational and political authorities and transfer their powers to the previously disenfranchised" (p. 2) and led "eventually to the feminist critique of male power" (p. 6).

The key expression of male power is patriarchy or male domination. Patriarchy has been viewed from different perspectives. According to Wilber (1996), Patriarchy 1 position asserts that male dominance has been a part of history from the beginning (p. 570), from the earliest familialization of the male (Jaggar, 1988). Patriarchy 2 position affirms that patriarchy was a shift from the matrifocal or equifocal realities of the horticultural societies as they gave way to the plow and horse societies. This view of patriarchy has existed for 5,000 years (Eisler, 1987; Gimbutus, 1991). According to Wilber (1996) there is a developing body of research he called "a third wave of feminism" (p. 270) that has "relocated and rediscovered female power in the patriarchy, research that demonstrates that female power was indeed a strong, conscious, intelligent co-creator of the patriarchy, a co-creator of that (and in every) stage of human development" (p. 570). Furthermore, with the androgyny influence of Pleck (1995) and his male role strain paradigm, the polarity between males and females may be lessening. Both genders may wrench their identities out of the ante-postmodern (modernity) certitudes (Kristeva, 1981) and argue for the emancipation of all marginalized and compartmentalized members of society (Nochlin, 1988; Rabinow, 1984).

Nevertheless, as in human development, an experience of trauma or fear may elicit compensating behaviors that persist far beyond their usefulness. Far beyond the differentiation, inclusion, and expulsion of phenomenon in Western history there is a lingering dominator consciousness among many men that feminist researchers are attempting to address.

Intimate partner violence is related to many males' desire for this dominance and control. Gender studies reveal that males who experience a greater need for intra-personal safety and predictability seek to manage and control unpredictable external events and the result is that intimate partner violence is more common (Coleman & Straus, 1990; Levinson, 1989; Straus, 1980; Yllo & Straus, 1990). Threats and violence are used to maintain males' dominant position (Babcock, Waltz, Jacobson, & Gottman, 1993; Fagan & Browne, 1994). Just the male attitude of consent to use violence correlates highly with the use of violence (Jasinski & Williams, 1998; Kaufman, Jasinski, & Aldarondo, 1994; Straus & Gelles,

1990). Furthermore, higher levels of power and control are positively correlated with the use of violence (DePuy, 1995; Hamby, 1998).

From the feminist perspective, therefore, intimate partner violence cannot be understood unless male gender and male power are confronted (Yllo, 1993). As a growing field of study to provide a lens through which to view intimate partner violence, though it may not be a sufficient theory to explain the totality of intimate partner violence, the feminist viewpoint is a necessary perspective. Patriarchy is a system of male power and male control over women in society, and feminist researchers often view the patriarchal system as having laid the roots for perpetuating the expectations of masculinity vs. femininity that get expressed in a violent society (Yllo).

Feminism has developed a broad, inclusive perspective regarding violence. According to Dobash et al. (1992) and Hammer and Maynard (1987), domestic violence is not just a historical phenomenon, a bio-chemical difference, an individual problem, or a social dilemma; it is a political issue and must be addressed politically. Violence is a means of social control over women that is at once personal, institutional, symbolic, and material (Yllo, 1993). Often, feminist researchers are not content to see violence as psychological and sociological. It is a political issue that demands political action.

In sum, according to O'Leary (1993), with regard to the etiologies of intimate partner violence, "the most well-developed sociological, feminist, historical, and biological theories do not by themselves provide adequate basis for an understanding of family violence" (p. 7). The field of intimate partner violence is new and developing. Many camera angles provide for a broad conceptual differentiation and synchronization. Yllo (1993) recommended caution about the potential development of chasms and counterattacks among the theorists. She holds out hope that a welcoming stance may exist toward challenges to and development of many viewpoints

Typologies of Intimate Partner Violence

Studies have explored the style, severity, and pervasiveness of intimate partner violence with varying outcomes, depending on the populations and study methodologies (Jasinski, 1998). Many distinctions have been made regarding the nature of perpetrators and the abuse. One key concept that pervades the conventional wisdom in the domestic violence field is the cycle of violence.

Walker (2000a) looked at batterers from a psychosocial point of view. She affirmed the dominance of the "power and control" concept (p. 6). It is the learning in early life that shapes the batterer. She pointed to the social learning theory origins of battering, among many other insights. She affirmed the common reality expressed by many a batterer who says that he came from a home with a "strict," wife abusing "father" (p. 12).

Also according to Walker, intimate partner violence is viewed as a recurring cycle involving stress buildup, explosion, and the honeymoon phase. The cycle may explain some aspects of events that happen more than once; it may not explain change and learning between events. Other views of recurring events may be more helpful. The cycle may be expressed as a biorhythm of psychological expansiveness and implosion. Relationships breathe with alternating states of tension and resolution of tension, from polarity to intimacy (Ellis, 1990; Goldberg, 1976). With imperfect listening and communication skills, the unresolved problems become more loaded over time and uncontrollable frustration explodes in the relationship in increasing degrees of severity and ultimately becomes a terroristic form of abuse (Johnson, 1995). Personality disorders that prevent satisfactory resolution of problems contribute to intermittent abusive rage (Dutton & Starzomski, 1993). As problems remain unresolved, violence becomes more deliberate, dangerous, lethal, and premeditated. Partners attack each other "in ways that diminish self-esteem, create feelings of vulnerability, and activate fears of rejection and abandonment" (Douglas, 1991, p. 528). Stress over unresolved problems precipitate conflicts in intervals; hence the concept of the cycle.

Gottman (1999) conducted extensive research on couples and their relationships. He established a "bed and breakfast" where couples go for a day or so. All of their activities are monitored: three video cameras record their every activity, urinanalysis and blood tests are taken frequently, and polygraph and other "psychophysiological recording devices" (Jacobson & Gottman, 1998, p. 20) are used to monitor the emotional levels of batterers in states of marital conflict.

The findings of these scientific physiological studies placed male batterers in two categories. Category-one perpetrators includes men who are psychopathic, have severe antisocial behavior, demonstrate criminal-like traits, are highly sadistic in their aggression, are less dependent, use violence as a punitive measure, and usually stay in the relationship over a longer period of time. The researchers called this category of batterers "cobras" (p. 28).

Some of these men in the midst of marital conflict had heart rates that lessened. They were violent not out of emotional arousal but out of calculated vengeance. They also found some men who became physically activated, high tension, heart racing, and so forth, when in marital conflict, and they observed that these men were more emotionally dependent upon their partners. These men demonstrated a slow burn, and they were very insecure. Their level of terror and jealousy usually led to the dissolution of their marriages within a couple of years (Jacobson & Gottman). The researchers used the concept of "pit bulls" (p. 28) to designate these men. The ability of researchers to measure the physiological arousal of a person in an intimate conflict goes a long way in providing clues to understanding the adverse physical affects of marital conflict (Jacobson & Gottman).

Intimate partner violence is also viewed as being on a continuum, from the least abusive "remorseful batterer" on the one hand, to the most abusive, the "terroristic violent offender–the serial batterer" on the other (Groetsch, 1997; Jacobson & Gottman, 1998; Johnson, 1995; Saunders, 1992; Straus, 1990). The ability to distinguish the difference is key to appropriate treatment (Straus, 1993). Sonkin (personal communication, July 17, 1998) views these categories as follows: 1) one-third of the perpetrators are high functioning non-pathological, with the ability to change; 2) one-third of the perpetrators are borderline individuals with multiple diagnoses who may be able to benefit from treatment (Dutton & Starzomski, 1993); and 3) one-third are psychopathic, and treatment does not work.

Groetsch (1997) viewed battering as falling on a continuum of three increasingly lethal categories: Category One as the least dangerous; Category Two as moderately dangerous; and Category Three as most dangerous. According to Groetsch, the Category-one batterer is least dangerous and is represented by eight factors:

> 1) a normal man in abnormal circumstances; 2) abuse is
> situational, isolated; 3) cause of aggression: 90% external
> 10% internal; 4) previous relationships with women were
> not violent; 5) no premarital abuse; 6) no use of weapons;
> 7) feels genuine remorse; 9) very treatable (p. 9).

The Category-two batterer is more dangerous. Designators for Category-two are:

> 1) a male with several character defects; 2) abuse is
> neither isolated nor ongoing; it's sporadic; 3) cause
> of aggressions: 50% external 50% internal; 4) some
> previous relationships with women were violent; 5) some

premarital abuse; 6) some use of weapons; 7) feel limited remorse; 8) might be treatable (p. 9).

Category-three batterers are very dangerous. This category is represented by the following factors:

> 1) a male with a personality disorder; 2) abuse is ongoing, systematic; shows a chronic pattern; 3) cause of aggressions: 10% external 90% internal; 4) all previous relationship with women were violent; 5) frequent premarital abuse; 6) frequent use of weapons; 7) feels no remorse; has no conscience; 8) not treatable. (p. 9)

It is not possible to look at intimate partner abusers through a single lens. Human uniqueness defies that stance. Flannery and Huff (1998) discuss four types of violence: 1) situational (contextual factors such as alcohol, poverty, or stress play a role); 2) relationship (family patterns); 3) predatory (muggings, robbery, or gang assaults); and 4) pathological (mental illness-caused violence). Nothing less than a national cultural change in every phase of human life, according to Flannery and Huff, will re-educate a culture to prevent violence.

The developmental history of individuals, viewed as the causes of interpersonal violence, has received much attention. The violent potential begins as early as babyhood. If a child is raised in a stress-ridden home, that stress impacts the child in its brain development and may become a predictor of an adversarial stance toward others. This phenomenon is based upon the quality of the home environment and is fairly fixed by the time the child is two years old, according to Karr-Morse and Wiley (1997). Those early experiences of fear, guardedness, and vigilance become ingrained personality traits that live on beyond the childhood years. According to Perry (1997), they contribute to an individual's inability to manage stress, conflict, and tension throughout his or her life. Those early stressors show up as aggressiveness, impulsivity, and the possibility of violence.

Consequently, violent behavior must be viewed from the broadest of perspectives. It must be understood from the perspective of internal moods, compulsions, and urges that have a long history. This history can surface as anger and rage in a crisis, and these crisis episodes can be universalized to men in general (Levant, 1992). The work with violent men requires an in-depth understanding of many of these factors, and therapy work needs to be accompanied by an in-depth empathy for men (Levant & Pollack, 1995).

These leading theorists outlined the territory of perpetrator characteristics. Other theorists focused upon treatment and prevention of domestic violence. Hammer and Itzin (2000) focused on confronting the abuser and the process for dealing with repeat offenders. Several studies focused on the nature, effectiveness, and evaluation of intervention treatment programs (Decker, 1999; Fall, Howard, & Ford, 1999; Feder, 1999; Roberts, 2002; Roleff, 2000; Said, 2001; Vincent & Jouriles, 2000; Wexler, 2000).

The male batterer, therefore, has been examined from many viewpoints. This research examines and categorizes batterers. Much of the research involves observing, categorizing, and attempting to employ extrinsic measures to stop the violence. The extrinsic nature of violence control is demonstrated by seeking methods to find, arrest, fine, imprison, punish, educate, and train men out of their violent behavior. The Washington State Governor's Intimate Partner Violence Action Group (Halpert, 1999) reveals this approach. The upsurge of treatment programs and the numerous treatment manuals (Sonkin et al., 1985; Paymar, 1993; Pence & Paymar, 1993) all seek a solution. It is sometimes supposed that all batterers fit into a crisp clear category — that a batterer is a batterer is a batterer. On the contrary, each person in a relationship is unique, and his or her relating style is unique. Consequently, intervention must be multi-dimensional. The question then becomes, do other approaches exist for dealing with male violence? For example, is there an intrinsic approach?

Implications for Treatment

The cultural awakenings in the 1970s and efforts of the feminist movement focused upon the need to move beyond the goal to provide shelters for abused women. People sought to do something about the abuser (Pizzey, 1974). Programs for treatment of batterers have grown rapidly in twenty-five years. The first program designed specifically to treat batterers opened in 1977 (Adams, 1994) and then became prevalent in most major metropolitan areas (Edleson and Tolman,1992). Mandatory arrest laws advanced the proliferation of treatment programs in many states (Adams, 1994). According to Sonkin (personal communication, July 17, 1998), in 1976 the issue was what to call these programs.

Then throughout the 1970s, questions arose about who should offer these programs. In 1979, the first jail diversion programs, consisting of 52-week programs, began in California. Ultimately the question of who would control these programs and what philosophical or psychological theory would be used in the treatment programs arose. For example, is domestic violence a sociological problem or a psychological problem? Sonkin et al. (1998) noted that many favored the Duluth Model, a sociological approach, although others held that domestic violence is a psychological problem, i.e. attributable to Post Traumatic Stress Syndrome, as is the Battered Women's Syndrome (Walker, 2000).

Prompted by the need to insure the safety of the victims by controlling violent men, community-based programs grew. Mandatory arrest laws increased, resulting in most batterers' being court-ordered to attend gender-specific treatment programs. Men often don't self-refer to such programs, and nearly 100% attend because of judicial order (Finn, 1987). Men attending such programs, according to Bodnarchuk, Kropp, Ogloff, Hart, and Dutton (1995), are considered the most violent 1% of the U.S. population.

Even though a wide range of behaviors of violent offenders, few treatment centers adjust their programs to address individuals along a continuum (Hamby, 1998). The primary goals of almost all batterers' programs are as follows: 1) ensuring the female partner's safety; 2) altering attitudes toward violence; 3) increasing the perpetrator's sense of personal responsibility; and 4) learning non-violent alternatives to past behaviors (Edleson & Tolman, 1992). Treatment theories impact the programs by virtue of the beliefs, temperaments, and life experience of the presenters.

Program treatment theories come on the scene, gain attention, and fade away. Program presenters bring to their programs their underlying theoretical psychological presumptions, their therapy theories, their philosophies of man, their philosophies of education, and their beliefs about intimate partner violence.

Early on, behavioral modification programs in the form of anger management provided many valuable conceptual approaches combined with skill building components involving assertiveness training, systematic desensitization, and cognitive restructuring (Saunders, 1984; Sonkin et al., 1985). In the 1990s, explorations into better treatment approaches were conducted. Most early treatment programs fell under the broad term "anger management." Grassroots self-help groups with an anti-sexist, philosophical resocialization method and a group facilitation process existed. Some programs followed a highly controlled didactic psycho-educational modality, and others a loosely controlled discussion group aimed at a more therapeutic approach (Gondolf, 1987).

The Emerge program and the Duluth Model were developed. The Intervention Project in Duluth, Minnesota, in 1984, relied heavily on the anger management approach and traditional counseling to control intimate partner violence. The Duluth facilitators conducted interviews with Ann

Ganley and revised their curriculum to its "Power & Control: Tactics of Men Who Batter" model (Pence & Paymar, 1986). Their model is based upon the underlying belief held by large numbers of those working in treatment programs — that physical violence is an intentional method men use for maintaining control in relationships (Adams, Bancroft, German, & Sousa, 1992; Common Purpose, 1996; Pence, 1993). About one-fifth of treatment programs focus primarily on power and control issues (Tift, 1993).

Violence is also seen as a criminal issue, and Criminal Justice System-Based Reform Projects in Massachusetts and San Francisco have employed judiciary-based case management approaches to deal with perpetrators. Arrest is the first intervention; protection orders, regular reporting, and program attendance further confront intentional male behavior (Buzawa & Buzawa, 1996; Clark, Burt, Schulte, & Maguire, 1996; Soler, 1987).

Do batterers' programs work? Some believe that whether an abuser attends a treatment program or not makes little difference (Rosenfeld, 1992; Tolman & Bennett, 1990). No single type of treatment has been found to be better than any other (Tolman & Bennett, 1990). Others have found a high cessation rate of violence among less severely violent men even when no programs were attended (Aldarondo & Sugarman, 1996; Field & Straus, 1990). This also has been the case with more severely violent men (Toleman & Edleson, 1995). When several studies were analyzed, it was found that the recidivism rates across the board were in the 27% to 36% range (Rosenfeld, 1992). However, it is generally thought that men benefit from treatment programs (Davis & Taylor, 1999). Consequently, treatment programs are widely used.

With regard to curbing the domestic violence problem in society, the main question is whether the current intervention system is effective. This is an extremely difficult question to answer because the variables for making such a determination are so extensive that it is difficult (if not impossible) to block out a control group. The many variables include: 1) the training, philosophy, and commitment of the law enforcement officers who must make an instant diagnosis, based on limited information, about who is at fault in order to make an arrest; 2) the training, philosophy, and commitment of the judicial system; 3) the training, philosophy, case load, and commitment of the Correction/Probation officers; 4) the fact that only a small percentage of batterers in many locations are required to attend a treatment program; 5) the typologies of batterers on a batterers' lethality continuum who become the mean in any treatment group; 6) the ethnic, cultural, and education level of participants; 7) the training, philosophy (e.g. social, therapeutic, behavioral intervention), experience, and commitment of the treatment providers; and 8) the setting, group size, training materials, fear/trust levels of groups, dropout-rates, and program length. All of these factors work against precise program evaluations and precise measurement of batterer intervention (Clark et al., 1996; Edleson & Tolman, 1992; Gondolf, 1990; Shephard, 1992). The success rate of treatment programs is often in the eye of the treatment provider.

Implications for the Future

Research into intimate partner violence has been going on for 25 or more years. The implications of this research are still very vague (Jasinski & Williams, 1998). Nevertheless, researchers and providers press forward. The social variables of this population being what they are, the effectiveness of intervention activities remains unknown. For example, work is being done to begin much earlier to identify and provide treatment with interpersonal conflict resolution skills for school children who give evidence of violent tendencies (Johnson, 2000).

With regard to future treatment for violent offenders, several suggestions have been made: 1) Intervention upon arrest needs to be immediate and follow some basic guidelines: early evaluation to determine the range of violence by trained professionals, close contact with the offender, and close monitoring of the defendant through the judicial and treatment system; 2) Treatment should take into consideration and be appropriate to the degrees of lethality; 3) Stages in the life cycle and risks of re-offence should be considered; 4) Provisions should be made for young witnesses of the violence as well as for the victims of the violence; 5) Finally, general interpersonal and conflict resolution skills training should be made available to broad community populations (Jasinski & Williams, 1998).

Specific needs for future research involve longitudinal studies to attempt to discover patterns for the escalation and cessation of recidivism. Additional research is needed with regard to ethnic minority communities and alternative life-style communities. Research is needed to discover community resource systems and to formulate protocols that may be applied among other communities. Finally, further research is needed, from a qualitative perspective, to explore the internal psychological world of males who are violent toward intimate female partners.

Herb Robinson, Ph. D.

Summary

This discussion of the literature began with the origins of the idea of the human male in contrast to pre-humans. His emergence as a human from pre-human hominids was the result of his identity, according to Habermas, as a father. Throughout history males have carried with them certain basic ideals as multiple nuances of male identities have appeared, merged, been modified, and perpetuated the male ideal. The concept of the epic, heroic, or warrior male as the embodiment of physical strength and action emerged in the classical Greek and Roman era. The Christianizing of Plato's ideal became a "divine" blueprint of all particular entities and brought man to a special relationship with, and representation of, God. Man became the priestly arbiter of otherworldly realities to the real world.

With the demise of the Roman Empire and the emergence of feudalism, the chivalric ideal of man became the protector of woman and the weak. When the culture reaffirmed the ideals of ancient Greece and Rome, the lofty ideals of intellectual reason, order and balance found expression in the idea of manliness. The focus upon the physical world and the burgeoning discovery of the intricacies and predictability of scientific discovery enabled man to multiply himself beyond the production of his mere brawn. With the division of labor and production, man became truly manly as he succeeded in the realms of business, property, and money.

The Industrial Revolution and the use of machines multiplied man's power and control over nature immensely. The masculinity ideal in the United States somewhat mirrored the development of masculinity ideals in Europe. Early in the 1700s the early colonial landowner, via the advancement of patriarchy, became the image by which men measured masculinity. Then, with the expansion of the factory, the male prototype become earthier, with the ideal being a hard worker with common sense who had an eye for advancement in practical matters, the common man.

The opening of the Western United States provided the potential for the development of the adventurous man, the He-man. Throughout the twentieth century men have had to deal with having their role encroached upon and, to some extent, usurped by women. This led to the blurring of traditional gender roles and has resulted in Pleck's (1995) androgyny. No longer does the physical strength differential between men and women economically provide an advantage to men. With the birth of the information age, both genders discovered an equal footing for any accomplishment sought.

Contemporary culture in the United States is a composite of most of the ideals accumulated throughout history. Not all males have adapted to the androgynous idea. One ideal that is still present, having persisted throughout history, is that of patriarchy.

The masculinity stereotype is an accumulation of the views of all the ages past. The manly ideals of bravery, fearlessness, daring, being cool "Never let them see you sweat", physical strength, toughness, skillfulness, and dexterity still remain. Furthermore, a real man is honorable, honest, and courteous, and he must not complain. He must be in control of his emotions — he must not cry. With the blurring and melding of gender roles, many of the above dictates persist; yet the long-standing idea of middle-class respectability, one of the foundations of the masculine norm, has been cracked and battered, and males are not dealing well with the blurring of the masculinity ideal (Mosse, 1996).

Strangely, although men have been looking in the mirror for centuries, it was the result of the feminist research regarding women that in the later half of the twentieth century evoked philosophical questions about the nature of the male gender. Throughout the centuries, the necessity for survival conferred assumptions about who a man was. The male identity emerged from the early research regarding the psychological understanding of persons.

Pleck (1981) noted that the research into the nature of males took the form of what he called the Male Sex Role Identity Paradigm. Pleck stated that the basic template for identifying the Male Sex Role Identity Paradigm involved using terms such as "insecure" or "inadequate"; gauging psychologically harmful consequences of a man's relationship with his mother; and viewing homosexuality as the worst misfortune that can befall a man. He proposed instead the Sex Role Strain Paradigm. The Sex Role Strain Paradigm held that the Male Sex Role Identity Paradigm adversely affected men as they tried to fit themselves into a ready-made definition.

The Sex Role Strain Paradigm suggests that a prescribed role identity should include an opening of role identity to include all positive qualities attributable to humans. As such, androgyny seems to open the possibilities and has proved to be an important transitional concept in moving to a whole new way of viewing sex roles that has emerged both in the social sciences and in society. Nevertheless, a great deal of research is still documenting factors that continue to support the Sex Role Identity Paradigm. Ongoing study into the male gender role socialization process documents the male journey to manhood that results in what Levant (1997) calls the Normative Male Alexithymia, an inability in men to express feelings.

The difference between the developmental experiences of males compared to females was explored. Male children have experienced a traumatic separation drama during the rapprochement phase of their development. Consequently, that trauma has squelched their emotional capabilities and has caused difficulties in adult male/female relationships.

Specifically, Chapter I began by stating that attempts to address the problem of domestic violence began with a focus on safety for women victims. The focus soon shifted attention to the perpetrators of the domestic violence, usually the male member of the relationship. Consequently, the attempt to better understand men has become an imperative. That quest drove this inquiry. The examination of the masculinity stereotype throughout the sweep of western history revealed an accumulation of ideals, beliefs, and behaviors that have been internalized by many men in contemporary society. It was surmised that men are more external than internal psychologically; that they are more independent than they are intimate emotionally and socially; and that they are more action-oriented than present-centered behaviorally. This ingrained behavior stereotype has been perpetuated in the socializing of male children. It is also belived to hold a clue to the underlying historical phenomenon of the abuse and murder of women by men. As such, these factors prompted the inquiry into the internal landscape of men to explore further these assumptions.

CHAPTER III
DESIGN OF THE STUDY

The purpose of this study was to examine the stories and experiences of six men who abused women. The nature of those behaviors, similarities of the thematic patterns, socialization processes, ramifications of the behaviors, and possibilities for prevention were explored. This chapter describes the general principles of qualitative research, followed by a development of phenomenological and heuristic methods used for this study. Also presented in this chapter is a description of the research participants, data gathering and analysis. It also provides the limitations and ethical implications of the study.

Qualitative Research

From the 1930s through the 1960s, many Americans learned to read from the *Dick and Jane* series (Gray & Arbuthnot, 1940). Fulghum (1989) noted a key concept from the Dick and Jane books. He said, "Remember the Dick and Jane books and the first word you learned — the biggest word of all — 'look'." Looking is a part of a cluster of human information-gathering procedures, the five senses, called empiricism (Thilly & Wood, 1957). The phenomenon of wonderment and the process of figuring out how to satisfy that urge became a branch of philosophy called epistemology (Katsoff, 1953). Epistemology investigates the origin, structure, methods of acquisition, and validity of knowledge (Stroll, 1971). A brief examination of the history of "looking" follows.

Plato's ideas inspired the development of Western Civilization. "The themes, the questions, and even to a great extent the terms of all subsequent Western philosophy lie in germ in the writings of Plato" (Barrett, 1962, p. 79). Plato affirmed that all physical things are temporary; they come into existence and go out of existence (Thilly & Wood, 1957). The real world exists in a hierarchy of blueprints, of which things in the physical world are representations. These blueprint archives could not be perceived by "looking" in a physical sense, only by thoughts in the mind (Thilly & Wood, 1957). Augustine later applied a similar view to Christianity, similar to that of the Bible in Hebrews 9:23, that the things of the physical earth conformed to "the patterns of things in the heavens." Consequently, for nearly 2,000 years (300 B.C. to 1500 A.D.) the prevailing focus of human thought and attention was upon the mind; this was called idealism. Attention was focused heavenward, on the spiritual, on God, an examination with the mind or heart; and physical realities were not as important (Thilly & Wood, 1957). The debates of the day were focused on which was real, the spiritual or the physical (Stroll, 1971).

However, that began to change. St. Thomas Aquinas incorporated Aristotle's concepts of entelechy into his beliefs, which meant that the essence of the thing is not in some lofty blueprint but in the physical object itself (Thilly & Wood, 1957). Thus the mental focus shifted from the lofty heavenly blueprints to the physical realities themselves (Sprague, 1961). The beginnings of the actual physical sense of "looking" emerged. When the focus was on the physical world, profound discoveries resulted. The how and what of looking ensued. Several British thinkers, Locke, Berkeley, and Hume, developed a branch of philosophy affirming that knowledge was gained through the senses: sight, smell, taste, touch, and hearing (Thilly, & Wood, 1957). Once the focus shifted from the ideal to the real and from the spiritual to the physical, significant advances were made in understanding all aspects of the planet (Jones, 1961).

Other thinkers in Europe began to overlay knowledge through the senses with a mental process of verifying raw data by way of reason. That, according to Searles (1968), resulted in another branch of epistemology: rationalism. The quest for accurate information expanded epistemology to include not only empiricism and rationalism but also, to a lesser degree, intuition, mysticism (non-mediated knowledge), and kinesthetic knowledge (Gardner, 1993; Thilly & Wood, 1957). With the development of science, great strides were made in knowledge in all fields. This scientific approach to understanding reality stated that valid knowledge consisted of accurately representing or "mapping" the world of reality (Wilber, 1995), which resulted in "Truth." Great optimism regarding the potential for solving problems by way of science resulted. By "looking at" the real world through the process of weighing, measuring, comparing, and testing, answers to problems could be found (Cahoone, 1996; D'Andrea, 2000; Wilber).

Gradually, however, the map-making paradigm was brought into question (Wilber, 1995). Post-modernity resulted from thinkers who believed the mapping representation paradigm was very naïve (Cahoon, 1996). A shift took place as people moved from credentialing the map-making process of the real world to exploring the developing interiority, viewing points, and shifting perspectives of the map maker (D'Andrea, 2000).

The map-making paradigm implied an external viewing point from which reality could be observed, identified, described, investigated, weighed, measured, compared, and explained. Moreover, another perspective on "looking" exists, especially when it comes to humans. This perspective is what might be called "looking with" a person, through his or her eyes. For example, to clarify this distinction, note the difference between the brain and the mind. A great deal might be discovered from looking at the human brain (Wilber, 1995). The brain can be examined in numerous scientific ways, through EEGs, PET scans, MRIs, and so forth, until an extensive amount of information is gathered. However, no amount of observation of the brain can determine what is in the mind. To determine what is in the mind of another, one must "look with" that individual. That involves talking to the person, dialoging, communicating, interviewing, interpreting, and sharing interior worlds from the person's knowing (Stets & Straus, 1990). To look with a person one must talk and share and interpret in order to understand them.

Several factors are involved when it comes to the attempt to understand the world of another person. The listener must be able to: 1) trust what is being said (does the person tell the truth?); 2) obtain accurate information (how well does the person being interviewed know his or her mind?); 3) understand the person based on the person's ability to communicate inner aspects of consciousness (does a vocabulary exist capable of communicating inner realities?); 4) grasp the degree of congruence (do the communications really reflect the inner world?); and 5) obtain a view of the person's multi-levels of inner consciousness (Wilber, 1996). When interviewing and attempting to understand the experiences of perpetrators, these several factors come into play.

A qualitative approach was chosen for this study. Straus (1990) noted that qualitative research is important for many reasons. Unlike quantitative research methods that sample large populations in order to gather information through "statistical procedures" (p. 17) so that the information can be generalized to broader populations, qualitative research methods seek to understand the inner reality of a select, often small, group of people. A qualitative research method is open-ended, unbounded by precise categories. It gathers information about "people's lives, stories, behavior" (Straus, 1990, p. 17). It is useful for exploring subtle inner realities and details of inner experience unavailable to quantitative research. Its focus is to obtain insight into deeper levels of intra-psychic experience. Qualitative research "attempts to uncover the nature of a person's experiences . . . understand what lies behind [their behaviors], gain novel and fresh slants . . . and intricate details" (Straus, 1990, p.

19) of inner consciousness that are difficult to convey with quantitative methods.

Similarly, Patton (1990) explained that the qualitative approach offers more "depth, detail, and meaning at a very personal level of experience" (p. 18) than does a quantitative approach. Qualitative research focuses on discovery, description, depths of meaning, openness; and is unconstrained by prescripted categories of analyses. Quantitative categories, measuring, controlling, and predicting do not prescribe it. Qualitative researchers tend to work with smaller samples and try to understand the meanings and inner life-world of the participants.

For these reasons, a qualitative methodology was chosen for this study. Qualitative research also encompasses a broad variety of methods such as ethnomethodology, ethnography, symbolic interactionsim, ecological psychology, naturalistic and field research, heuristic inquiry, hermeneutic methods, phenomenology, and research based on systems and chaos theories (Patton, 1990). This study will employ the phenomenological aspect of qualitative research.

Phenomenology

The concept of phenomenology had its origins in the 1700s and the writings of Johann Heinrich Lambert (1728-1777). Lambert was a mathematician, physicist, astronomer, and philosopher. In 1764, he spoke of a discipline called phenomenology; he called it the "Theory of illusions" (Schmidt, 1967, p. 135). Lambert believed the word "phenomenon" referred to the illusory features of human experience. Kant was a contemporary of Lambert's, corresponded with Lambert, and was impressed with Lambert's work. Kant used the term "phenomenology" two times. His use of "phenomenology" presented the term in a new light, expanded its meaning, and promoted a redefinition of the term (Schmidt, 1967). Kant used the term "phenomena" to distinguish objects and events, as they appear screened through one's experience of them. He used the term "noumena," or "things-in-themselves" to refer to the way objects and events appear, as they are in themselves, separate from any external cognitive overlays (Schmidt). Kant subscribed to the concept of "phenomena" because we can't know things-in-themselves, only our experience of them.

Hegel modified and expanded further the concept of phenomenology. Hegel's focus was upon the nature of the mind. The mind develops in successive refining stages until it becomes aware of itself as it is in itself. For Hegel it is the mind that relates to objects in reality by an illumination of living in those objects spiritually (Thilly & Wood, 1957). Phenomenology, for Hegel, is the study of the mind in which we come to know the mind as it is by observing the ways it appears to us (Schmidt). Consequently, for Hegel, phenomenology was a science designed to understand the human mind.

The term "phenomena" then came to represent the early stages of mind development and "noumena" came to represent an advanced stage of mind that knows itself. By the 1850s "phenomena" came to be known as whatever is observed to be. Sir Willam Hamilton in *Lectures on Metaphysics* (1858) and Edward Von Hartmann in *Phenomenology of Moral Consciousness* (1878) noted that phenomenology was a descriptive study of the mind and a complete description of moral consciousness. Hartman's major work dealt with the human unconscious, out of which came self-consciousness, consciousness of the transcendent, and ultimately led to identifying with the cosmic drama of redemption (Schmidt).

Since Edmund Husserl, the term "phenomenology" has referred to a way or school of doing philosophy. Thus phenomenology became a method. Members of the phenomenological school were philosophers in German universities before WWI, and between 1913 and 1930 several volumes of phenomenological studies were published. The editor in chief was Edmund Husserl.

Husserl was a significant philosophical mind of the last century. He is known as the forerunner of Gestalt psychology and existentialism, a thinker in the field of logical theory, an investigator of the structures of experience and its objects, a promoter of the rigorous science of philosophy, a leader in the idealistic tradition of philosophy, an effective teacher, and a philosopher who influenced scholars in the fields of law, psychiatry, mathematics, religion, sociology, psychology, and philosophy (Farber, 1966). As a phenomenologist he was interested in the descriptive science of essential structures and objects of human experience. His focus was upon the "pure experience" and "not on the particular facts or events or in the factual accounts of origins." The phenomenological method "begins with the individual and his stream of experiences" (p. 13).

Phenomenological inquiry seeks to know human experience by attending to inner consciousness, experiences, feelings, and emotionality. Farber noted that phenomenology was concerned with "all things being viewed from the point of view of one's own experiencing of them, and only in so far as they have meaning in and by one's experiences" (p. 14).

Polkinghorne (1989) also noted Husserl's view that "knowledge of the structures of consciousness was not a matter of induction or generalization from a sample but was the result of a 'direct grasp' of 'eidetic seeing' [meaning that images are extremely detailed and vivid]," and "descriptions

121

of those essential structures that are inherent in consciousness" (p. 42). Similarly, Patton (1990) related that Husserl's assumption was "that we can only know what we experience by attending to perceptions and meanings that awaken our conscious awareness" (p. 69). Phenomenology, then, attempts to understand the flow of the participant's stream of consciousness captured in time as the participant experiences and interprets his or her world.

Heuristic Phenomenology

Etymologically, "heuristic" is derived from the Greek *heuriskein,* "to discover" or "I have found it" (Vine, p. 100). It involves the process of internal exploration and discovery. The discoveries form the building blocks for additional explorations and refinement of methods for additional investigation and analysis. Heuristic research involves the researcher throughout the research process in an ongoing involvement with the subjects, which contributes to greater understanding of the self. The discovery process is twofold: It increases the researcher's understanding of the topic of study, and it also expands the internal realities of the researcher. The researcher monitors his or her growing awarenesses, knowledge base, biases, and attunement with the subjects (Moustakas, 1990).

Heuristic inquiry was popularized by the publication of *Loneliness* (Moustakas, 1990). Moustakas expressed his indebtedness to authors that preceded him: Jourard's (1971) inquiry into self-disclosure; Maslow's (1971) study of self-actualization; Polanyi's (1958) tacit dimension of epistemology, indwelling, and personal knowledge; Buber's (1958) investigation of mutuality, the "I-Thou", and dialogue; Gendlin's (1978) concept of focusing, and the felt sense; and Rogers'(1961) humanistic psychology.

The strengths of heuristic inquiry lie in "its potential for disclosing truth. Through exhaustive self-research, dialogues with others, and creative depictions of experience, a comprehensive knowledge is generated . . . [that can lead to] a systematic and definitive exposition" (Moustakas, 1990, p. 40). Heuristic research and data analysis, to be discussed later, involves a process for finding truth: "engagement, immersion . . . incubation, illumination, explication, and culmination . . . (into) a creative synthesis" (p.18). The internal activity of the researcher in the heuristic process involves identification with the research population, subliminal vocalization (self-dialogue), intuition, indwelling, focusing, and the tacit dimension of epistemology (Hawka, 1985; Moustakas, 1990; Patton, 1990).

Phenomenology and heuristic research, however, involve some major differences. Heuristic research emphasizes connection and immersion of the researcher in the experience, unlike the detachment of the phenomenological researcher. Heuristic research attends to the subtle realities of the interview subject while the phenomenological researcher seeks structured, clear, descriptive categories. Heuristic research employs the researcher's intuition, and tacit knowing of the experience, and the phenomenological researcher seeks more precise experiences. Heuristic research tends to focus on the person as a whole, and phenomenological research tends to focus on the outcomes. Heuristic research posits the researcher as his or her instrument in the inquiry process and is less oriented toward pure scientific objectivity than phenomenological research.

> Personal discovery, so central to the heuristic researcher, covers a wide range of subjective perceptions, ideas, feelings, sensations, desires, and actions. As a result of exploring widely and deeply in the internal sense, discovery becomes possible. The subjective experience is further expanded through involving other participants. Others will shed light on the researcher's self-experience and also stimulate flashes of knowledge with him or her. (Hawka, 1985, p. 10)

This study, then, will employ a qualitative, phenomenological method with a heuristic orientation for the research design.

Participants

In the city of Spokane, Washington, from available statistics, in 1998, 17,000 911 domestic violence calls came to the police; in 1999 there were 14,000; and in 2000 there were 13,000 (Blocker, 2001). Of these numbers, about 4,000 cases per year are adjudicated, and of those 4,000 cases a very small percentage of the perpetrators are court-ordered to attend a Washington Administrative Code 388.60 prescribed treatment program. Normally, the defendant receives a one-year jail sentence, which is suspended; receives a $5,000 dollar fine, which is also suspended; and is court mandated to attend a Washington State Certified Perpetrator Treatment Program. The Washington Administrative Code 388.60 stipulates that the treatment program may not define satisfactory treatment solely as a period of time or number of sessions, and then notes that treatment involves a minimum of 26 weekly groups plus weekly sessions for the remainder of a one-year minimum. All of the participants in a perpetrator counseling program attend weekly group sessions for more than nine months throughout the one-year program. The counseling sessions involve individual and group sessions that provide psycho-educational material, conflict skill-building and communication abilities, and training in the ability to differentiate feelings in order to respond rather than react to conflict situations.

The participants in this study were selected from men who presented themselves via a court order to attend such a treatment program. Even though many participants share experiences of deep personal grief in their relationship conflicts, some exhibit the ability to describe those experiences with greater clarity. Many of those with greater ability to explicate the inner realities were purposefully chosen by "intensity sampling" because this method provided greater information-rich cases for the study (Patton, 1990). Due to the fact that there are no rules for a sample size in qualitative research (Patton, 1990, p. 184), an arbitrary sample size of six men was chosen. Six men were chosen because it seemed that the resultant data would be manageable.

Each participant signed a release of information and granted permission for the researcher to include information about his case in a research study (See Appendix A). Furthermore, each participant attended and graduated from the program as prescribed by the Washington Administrative Code: 388. The program involved self-awareness and a behavioral modification model.

Data Gathering

Data were gathered in many ways. The data gathering process began with the initial interview. The initial interview began the induction processes into the program. This interview is important in that it initiates the therapeutic process. The goal is reassure the client, alleviate whatever fears may exist, attend to their presenting narrative of what happened to them to initiate the referral to counseling, and provide them with information about some of the initial steps of the intake and evaluation process.

The notation of the person's story began with the first interview. The person's story, information about his social/psychological history, was gathered throughout the program. A significant amount of information about the person's social history was also gathered during the intake/evaluation process. The intake/evaluation process involved the accumulation of the following information: the precipitating episode that caused the arrest, the nature of the violence, the name of the current partner and the name of the victim, early family life (places, parents, siblings, education, physical abuse history, and sexual abuse history), employment history, military history, relationship history and children/spousal abuse history, substance abuse history, legal history, counseling history, and the kind of relationship the person hoped to create through the help of the program. This information was collected in the form of hard-copy notes.

After the evaluation, the person began to attend the weekly therapy groups. The weekly groups and the experiential training exercises provided ongoing information to the clients and the therapist regarding the client's ability to appropriate the new skills. Throughout the training program each member of the program prepared and read aloud in the group a series of self-report documents. Each member responded to every other member's reports and practiced a formula for providing feedback. The self-report documents were written throughout the time of treatment as follows: 1) a statement of the episode that resulted in their arrest and their culpability in that incident, 2) a statement of their life history emphasizing their lifelong hurts and beliefs acquired in childhood and persisting into adulthood regarding women, 3) a simulated statement as from their partner to them describing the partner's experience of the abuse incident (this was called an empathy letter), 4) a statement of their internal physiological experiences preceding, during, and after the abuse incident (this was called a quotient of pain letter), and 5) a statement of the new skills they would be employing in their relationships, noting several goals and two or three activities to accomplish those goals (this was called an action plan for healing).

The self-report documents averaged from one to five pages, and each man read his documents aloud before the group. The letters provided a significant opportunity for processing the information and developing a relationship-building theory base. The sequence of the letters each man read was very close to the order presented above. Upon completing the program each person gave a graduation presentation summarizing his experience in a format similar to the above five categories. Additional individual sessions, taped interviews of their life stories, completed the data gathering process. The data were stored in the individual files of the participants in a secure, separate file-room in the office complex.

Data Analysis

The analysis of the data involved a multi-phased process. The steps in that process are as follows. The first step in the data analysis process involved gathering together all the pieces of information regarding each participant. This gathering process included documents and notes regarding the participant from the first initial engagement, the intake/evaluation, the weekly impressions, the self-generated documents presented by each participant, internalized impressions of the participant by the researcher based upon interactions in the group setting, and the participants' graduation presentations. This began the process of leading the researcher into the inquiry on human interiorities, where one "encounters the self, one's autobiography, and significant relationship within the social context" (Moustakas, 1990, p. 27). Every bit of data regarding each participant was gathered, compiled, organized, and studied.

The second step in the data analysis process then began. This step involved the immersion of the researcher in the accumulated information about the participant. This was a lengthy process; it was a personal process on the part of the researcher to indwell, experience, and absorb the nuances of the participant. This indwelling process went on throughout the time the participant was in treatment. The goal in this second step was to allow all the data to filter through me until I began to experience, as much as possible, a profile of the participant.

The third step involved a stepping away from the material for brief periods of time. I slept on it. In my times away from the data I designed ongoing formulations of the personality profile of each participant. When I returned again with fresh perspectives to the accumulated data I not only reviewed the data, but also began to clarify the profile of my experience with the participant. I kept checking to see whether my profile was justified by the data. Hunches got explicated. In heuristic inquiry background, vague and fuzzy moods become well-formed, crisp, and clear figures of meaning (Moustakas, 1990). In tacit epistemology (Polanyi, 1966), answers to questions emerge as non-mediated "knowing." The incubation process is continuous.

The fourth step involved a return to and review of the data. This time, from a new viewing point, significant themes and sub-themes began to emerge for review and clarification. The goal was to refine the major themes and modify or omit factors that were not essential to the experience.

Once the researcher has conducted the interviews, taken the notes, and explicated the question, the heuristic researcher must allow time for internal germination. It is a time for the cognitive data "out there" in the notebooks to be taken in and filtered through the multi-levels of the researcher's interiority. The researcher cannot repeat the case notes. The researcher must indwell, absorb emotionally, be melded with, breathe, and exhale the data. They become the researcher and the researcher becomes the data. In this study I was the facilitator of the treatment program and met with the participants on a weekly basis. My goal was to "meet" the participants with as much of my personal authenticity as was appropriate. All of this changed the researcher, and new connections emerged between the "self, other, and world" (Moustakas, 1990, p. 32).

The fifth step was to initiate the same process with each of the other participants. The goal at this level was to explore and develop common qualities and themes among the participants.

The sixth step was to further elucidate the profile of each of the individual participants, and explore how the expanding experience captured the moods, imprints, spirit, and quality of life that emerged from the experience. The seventh step involved the summarization of the above processes to formulate a composite portrait of each participant.

The eighth and final step involved an effort to compile a "creative synthesis of the experience . . . . It invites a recognition of tacit-intuitive awarenesses of the researcher, knowledge that has been incubating over months through process of immersion, illumination, explication of the phenomenon investigated" (Moustakas, 1990, p. 52).

Explication involves the merging of thoughts, ideas, themes, night hunches, and numerous attempts to "say" what one believes about the experience. The writing and re-writing yielded new and emerging themes. The process was continuous. It involved Gendlin's (1978) "focusing," Polanyi's (1966) "indwelling," Grof's (1990), "self-searching," and Powel's (1969) "self-disclosure." It was a going within to listen, trust, attend, and attune to those inner realities.

As the writing process continued, various themes began to emerge. These themes seemed to point to underlying realities that were revealed by the themes but also disguised by the themes. These underlying realities were undifferentiated, fuzzy, and unclear. They were analyzed according to Polanyi's (1966) principles for addressing the tacit through illustration, paradigm, metaphor, example, and the mirroring effect in the explicit. Some vague images of constructs began to form. "The entire process of explication requires that researchers attend to their own awarenesses, feelings, thoughts, beliefs, and judgments as a prelude to the understanding that is derived from conversations and dialogues with others" (Moustakas, 1990, p. 31). The growing inter-relevancy of the parts yielded an insight into the whole and new insights emerged and became a part of the outcome.

Limitations of the Study

One of the limitations of the phenomenological study involves the sampling of the experiences of the research population. Sometimes the ability of a participant to provide information is limited for the following reasons: 1) the authenticity of the participant: For example, does the person tell the truth? 2) the degree of accessibility of the participant to the interior information: Can the person access his interior reality? 3) linguistic limitations: Does the participate have an adequate vocabulary to articulate aspects of interior consciousness? 4) congruence of statements: Is there an accurate representation of the participant's inner world? and 5) since the interiority is so complex and multidimensional, can the participant verbally represent such complexity (Wilber, 1996)?

Another limitation has to do with the blind spots or selectivity of the participant's disclosure. Earliest memories, often traumatic memories, set the tone or become a template from which a person views many other events in life; consequently, personal vision is selective. "This 'subjective reality' includes the individual's beliefs, views, perceptions, and conclusions. Behavior is understood from the vantage point of people's cognitive perspective" (Corey, 1986, p. 47).

The limitation of the population from which the sample was selected is noted as the fact that the research participants were adjudicated, court-mandated perpetrators. Therefore, a significant limitation of the study involves the very nature of a qualitative study. Unlike a quantitative study, no inferences may be drawn regarding the population in general. The conclusions may not be representative of other men in general. The design of the study does not permit application to the general population. The goal is to obtain a deep insight into the realities of several men. These insights may or may not have universal applications.

Finally, as a heuristic study, the presuppositions of the researcher have an impact upon the study. My own history working with this population, research regarding the masculinity stereotype, and viewpoints based upon my experiences shaped the view-lens for this study, to note some of the limitations.

Ethical Considerations

The fact that the participants in the Certified Perpetrator Treatment Program are court mandated to attend did not automatically include them in the research project. Participation was an individual choice. Each individual signed a separate release to participate in the research project.

The participants were briefed on the nature of the study, the breadth of the study, and implications of the study. They gave their informed consent to participate.

Another consideration of prime importance was insuring that no aspect of the research project would embarrass participants or "endanger their home life, friendships, or jobs" (Babbie, 1995, p. 449). Maintenance of the anonymity and confidentiality of the participants was practiced. Anonymity, in the most refined definition of the term, does not yield itself to this phenomenological research project. A broad application of anonymity was applied. The participant's names were not used. Identifying delimiters and other demographic information that might identify the participants were carefully considered. This also is commensurate with the general confidentiality requirements of the treatment program. Specifically, the Washington Administrative Code 399.60.140 and the Revised Code of Washington 70.02.030 and RCW 70.02.050 set general standards for confidentiality. It was the underlying intent of this inquiry that no one participating should experience any resultant harm.

CHAPTER IV
RESULTS OF THE STUDY

The purpose of this study was to examine the stories and experiences of six men who abused women. The descriptors of those behaviors, how those behaviors expressed similarities of the thematic patterns across the research population, the socialization processes, the ramifications of the behaviors, and possibilities for prevention and treatment were explored. Each person participated in an extensive initial evaluation and several self-disclosure interviews, as noted earlier.

Each participant had been arrested for domestic violence. Each was sentenced to a year in jail and a five thousand-dollar fine, both of which were suspended. Each was court ordered to attend a certified perpetrator treatment program, and each signed a release to participate in this study.

The program they were assigned to complete involved a weekly session for some thirty-six months and contact with the program for a period of one year. Each person successfully progressed through the treatment program. The goal of the program was to insure victim safety. The participants confronted their abusive behaviors and their belief patterns that led to their abusive behaviors, and formulated a responsibility plan for improving future behaviors. The program focused on skill development that would facilitate each person's ability to absorb and buffer anger and dissaproval projected upon him, skills to manage conflict, and communication skills to further ongoing win-win decision-making.

Each person shared significant aspects of his life. Each story was mainly a description of historical events. The profile of each person will be presented, followed by information provided regarding specific life events. Shared similarities of events across the six participants' lives were evident. These similarities involved outcomes of their behavior, emotional experiences for each person, and options for growth and change. Several themes evident in their stories serve as insights to the interior world underlying the surface events.

Arvil Stimpson

Mr. Arvil Stimpson was court ordered to treatment due to a domestic dispute with his wife of less than one year (Initial Interview). Mr. Stimpson is a 70-year-old white male. He was born and raised in the Midwest, the eldest of four children. He has a brother aged 61, a sister aged 59, and a brother deceased at 50. His father passed away at 57 and his mother passed away at 75 years of age. Mr. Stimpson shared the story of his early family life (Intake/evaluation).

His father was ten years older than his mother when they married. His mother was 18 years old and his father had high expectations for his mother. His father seemed always to be upset about something. His rage and filthy language at times of stress were unbearable for his mother and as a child he was also a recipient of this madness. The father once threw a radio down the basement stairs because Arvil had cut his head falling into it as a toddler. He would come home from his work and when dinner wasn't ready and on the table when he thought it should be, he slapped the mother around, throwing dishes and food all over the kitchen. As time went by and WWII arrived, the mother took a job in a local defense plant. The father was jealous of her as she was quite attractive at age 32, and she was making more money than he. He used her working as another excuse to hurt her with more verbal and physical abuse.

While working at the defense plant the mother met a married man at the plant and started seeing him on a regular basis. One night she came home while the father was working a second job in the war effort. Arvil watched her get out of a car with this other man. They stood kissing each other. Arvil stated, "I had my first taste of jealousy and anger" (History of Hurts and Beliefs Letter). He informed his father the next day. A very short time later the parents divorced.

After finishing high school Mr. Stimpson joined the military. He retired after 22 years, having spent three years of that time in Korea and three years in Vietnam. He retired with a physical disability, a hearing loss due to working around the loud noise of motors. Mr. Stimpson married in the late 1950s. His wife was mostly compatible with Mr. Stimpson and he expressed little difficulty with the marriage. He seemed to be able to have a lot of liberty and his wife was seemingly okay with that. They had three children. After 41 years of marriage his wife died of cancer.

About two years after his wife died, Mr. Stimpson married a woman in her early sixties. Three months into the marriage Mr. Stimpson was abusive to his wife; she was afraid and called 911. Mr. Stimpson was arrested and put in jail. He was then court ordered to attend a perpetrator treatment program.

The domestic violence incident happened shortly into the marriage. Mr. Stimpson, being a military man, used some salty language. He described the pervading temperament carried with him into his new marriage:

131

I never realized until recently why this "Generation Curse" has followed me all of my adult life. It has caused me trouble and grief with the women I tried to become serious with. Jealousy, anger, suspicion, doubt have been as much a part of my life as it was my father's. I would meet an attractive lady and everything would be going along just fine until some small offense, imagined or real, would cause me to react towards her in much the same way my father acted toward my mother.

I use to believe that the problems I was experiencing with the women in my life was always their fault, but very seldom did I take responsibility unless it was after the fact; then I was sorry. This mind set has now followed me into my present marriage. (Responsibility Letter)

The description of the incident is as follows:

I believe all of us, from the time we are at puberty, have a mental acceptance or belief about the one person we would consider spending the rest of our lives with. When you [re: his new wife] and I met, I was walking around looking at you through my expectations. I actually expected you to act and behave in a certain way, but it didn't take long for me to decide that you were not meeting my expectations.

I became very jealous, suspicious, and angry, doubting almost everything you told me. I attempted to control your every move, stalking and accusing you of being with other men. We fought and my language and accusations became unscrupulous, unreasonable, and excessive. We had no peace or joy. Strife from anger and rage became the order of the day.

Then we planned that trip to Seattle. We were going to take care of the grandchild while your daughter and son-in-law was out of town on business. I remember all too well the day we were to leave. A great deal of tension and fear was building in you at the time. I did not realize how much until I walked into the kitchen and you unceremoniously told me that I was not going with you on the trip that you had decided to go alone.

At this point I flew into a rage. I kicked things, threw things, slammed doors, cussed, and pushed you around. I remember your fear of me when you ran into the bedroom to call 911. I was so enraged that you would want me in jail that I started pulling telephone leads out of the wall. The next thing I remember I was being cuffed, put into a patrol car, and carted off to jail.

In retrospect I'm glad no children were involved. I did notice when we were leaving that your daughter had arrived and was entering the house. It pained me to realize that now she would get all of the sordid details. I just knew my marriage was now over.

I blamed you for deciding that I wasn't to make the trip. I felt you had made an arbitrary decision to get me out of the way and with the 911 call I was definitely out of the way. I believed at the time you were the one responsible for the entire incident. I was jealous and angry so I flew into a rage to let you see my displeasure with your decision. I was released from jail and had my court date. (Responsibility Letter)

Mr. Stimpson spent two and a half days in jail and was ordered to attend a Certified Perpetrator Treatment Program. That was when he came to my office to keep his required appointment.

Mr. Stimpson described his physiological experience when his new wife told him he could not go to Seattle with her, including his trauma following the arrest.

A year after my first wife died of cancer I received the manifestation of one of my prayers. I had prayed for a Christian woman to come into my life. About mid-March of 1999 we met at the church for the first time. I realize now that when I prayed for a Christian woman I didn't have a clue. I remember you were wearing a woman's Navy blue dress jacket with lieutenant bars. Since I more or less grew up in the military, my approach and the ensuing conversation with you came rather easy. I was immediately attracted to you. Your smile and laughter was fascinating. I was captivated by your beauty, exuberance, and charm. I could hardly take my eyes off of you.

Our first meeting eventually led to our first date. I was happily surprised when you agreed to go with me after church for a sandwich and coffee before you went home. This was a scary time for me. I was clumsy and embarrassed and I felt guilty since you were the first woman I had been out with in 42 years except my wife. Your lovely smile and the easy conversation did finally bring us together on future dates. In July you accepted my engagement ring and in October we were married in our church.

Our marriage has been anything but bliss. We seemed to fight all the time. Our pushing and shoving with my abusive, vile language was the essence of our quarrels. I brought a lot of old baggage into our marriage from my past. Jealousy, suspicion, doubt, control and anger. After a few months of marriage we had our most serious quarrel. I can remember your fear of me that day. I also remember spending three days in jail. Jail, for me, a successful member of society, was the most degrading, terrifying experience of my life. After I got out of jail we continued to disagree over everything. In June you left me to go stay with your daughter.

It was a frightening time. The stress was almost unbearable. I had no appetite and I took nighttime sleep aids like they were candy. There was a lot of confusion and my thought process was a mess. I would call you but you either weren't there or didn't wish to speak with me. T.V. was out the question; so was reading. I just couldn't stay focused. It surprises me now that since I've already experienced three heart attacks in my lifetime that I didn't have another. I don't now (*sic*) how I could have been so foolish. (Quotient of Pain Letter)

When Mr. Stimpson came to my office for the first time I observed him to be about five foot ten and 160 pounds. His hair had been blondish but now it was mostly gray. He had it combed in a large wave on top. His body structure was symmetrical; there were no somatic breaks, i.e. bulges, disproportionately large or small parts of torso, arms or legs. There was no evidence of any deficiencies or handicaps. His body structure was straight and mildly vigilant. He eyes were appropriately contracted, not protruding or squinting. His eye contact was direct; he was observant. His chin and jaw were fixed, not tight or fluidly mobile. His diaphragm and pelvic area were fixed, closed, conjoined (not flat, sucked in, jerky or too immobile). There was a steady rate of breathing. Mr. Stimpson's clothes were casual. His general grooming was neat and in good taste; sometimes he wore a tie and blazer.

His speech and vocabulary were fluid and smooth. His vocabulary was moderately well developed, and he sometimes made oblique references to his old military language without actually using the words. His speech was couched in a remorseful tone, with an expression of disgust with himself, even apologetic, for having to be arrested and be in this program. The pitch of his voice was low, direct, moderately paced, and assertive. His response was one of alertness, and his face was not overly expressive, but he would laugh uproariously from time to time. His presenting style was warm, accepting, optimistic, relaxed and casual, sensitive, available, responsive, businesslike, and down-to-earth. He responded positively when he caught a new idea that impressed him and would share those openly with the other men in the group. He shared his own story openly and unashamedly.

In the group setting he would often lean forward and cup his hand over his ear in an attempt to hear more accurately. He would jump into the group conversations with "Oh boy, I'll tell you what I have come to learn." His new wife was, in his words, a "seven days a week, 24 hour a day Christian." He always idealized her. Sometimes in the group, in order to affirm him, I would ask how many days a week and how many hours a day Christian was he? Sometimes in the group he would share his Christian beliefs. It was a self-disclosure and no one took umbrage at it. He would affirm that his new wife could get to him in ways he could not understand.

Mr. Stimpson was successful in the program. He was eager to learn and to participate. He returned to court to notify the judge of his completion and returned to our office the same day to express his gratitude for the help he received. He expressed sincere gratitude for all he had learned and the fact that his marriage had turned a corner and was much improved.

Art Yount

Mr. Art Yount was arrested for a domestic violence episode and court ordered to attend a certified treatment program. Mr. Yount was a 24-year-old white male (Initial Interview). He was born in a moderately sized city in central Washington State and later moved and was raised on the west side of the state (Intake/evaluation). Regarding Mr. Yount's early years, he stated,

> That was where I really remember some of my first experiences with women. I know very little about my grandfather (on my father's side) because my dad told me it was better we forget about his parents and most of his past. What he has told me is that his father was physically abusive and died at a fairly young age from cancer. My grandmother and stepfather took up where his father left off and both sexually and physically abused him and five brothers and sisters until he left home at fifteen years of age. My dad and his siblings were all physically abused and lived in a very poor part of town where they literally fought constantly to stay alive.
>
> My mother tells me stories of growing up with an alcoholic father who used to whip them on a daily basis, which might explain why my mother always expected me to do better than everyone else. She was always pushing me to get better grades, and screaming at me if I struck out or had an error during a baseball game. Nothing was ever good enough.
>
> My dad and mom rarely spoke civilly after we moved to Seattle and for three years were constantly at each other's throats. They argued mostly about money and about my sister and me. My mother was a workaholic and my father didn't work at all. Very rarely did we do anything as a family that didn't end up in an argument. I felt like I was the mediator, and at the same time, had to take care of my sister.
>
> I played baseball and had a 3.8 grade point average, and I did everything I could to please them. No matter how hard I tried, with my mom nothing was ever good enough. Her expectations continued to worsen until it got to the point where she would embarrass me in front of my family and friends if I committed an error, struck out at the plate, or brought home anything less than a "A" from school. Probably because I related so well to my father; I could almost feel his pain. I would hear her call him

names. Call him a loser, a bad father, and a worthless piece of shit. I saw women as vicious, self absorbed, and cruel. It felt that no matter what my father did or said he was worthless, and thus I would be too. I was just like him. (History of Hurts and Beliefs Letter)

Those experiences served as a backdrop for Mr. Yount as he began to look for a partner to begin his own family. He stated that his early childhood experiences impacted his expectations about what kind of woman would come into his life. In spite of what he had seen and heard, Mr. Yount held out a belief that "this woman would love me unconditionally and see me as a god in a sense. I thought she would do anything for me." Mr. Yount illustrated both of these internal states. He related his early experiences with women:

I dated quite a few women in high school and found myself doing everything I could to please them. I was always watching what I said when my girlfriend was around. If there was an argument, that was the end of the relationship. Just out of high school I started to think that lashing out would better suit the situation, so I started yelling and threatening my girlfriend; I ended up losing her too.

As I grew older I began to think that all women were the same. I believed that they only wanted to mold men into their ways and that what they wanted was all that was important. Women had to be watched constantly because you never knew what they might do. At the same time, I longed to find someone who would love me. I dated a few women that were great for a few months, but eventually would start trying to control me. They would get upset and yell, telling me how worthless I had become. The more I got to know a woman, the more I was reminded of my mom, the more I was reminded of the days when my mom would scream at my father for no apparent reason.

Many outside influences affected my beliefs about women; watching my mother and father, hanging out with friends in high school that treated women like crap and knowing many people who had been through a divorce. As much as I wanted to believe that there might be someone out there for me, I never thought I would find her. When I found my wife and married I considered her one of the problems.

It wasn't long ago that I remember feeling as though the world owed me something. I had a chip on my shoulder a mile high and I felt as if I had been through things in my life that nobody could possibly imagine, especially a woman. Women never had to deal with pain; they didn't know what it was like to grow up looking over their shoulders. I mean hell; one even tormented my dad for sixteen years. Every time a girlfriend would so much as raise her voice at me, the hair on the back of my neck would stand up and I would immediately lash out. In short, I had a "screw them" type attitude and felt that women needed to be "put in their place." (History of Hurts and Beliefs Letter)

Mr. Yount then describes the series of events that led to his domestic violence episode and subsequent arrest. Mr. Yount shared the following when he wrote (as if to his intimate partner) in a therapy exercise.

The events that led up to my arrest and the court order to attend classes here, is something that I will never forget.

For the last month or so everything I asked of you seemed to be too much to ask. Things just weren't getting done around the house. It was nearing the weekend and I thought I would offer to buy you a beer so we could sit down and talk. You showed up there with my sister after you'd been shopping all day and proceeded to tell me every last detail. Needless to say we didn't get to talk much. We ended up at another bar where we argued because a man made an obscene gesture at you and my sister. You said I was stupid and a jerk because they were just playing around.

I pushed you and grabbed you by the hair. I told you to take your stupid ass home; you called something and said you were going home. I stayed about 45 minutes longer, had a few more beers, and left with my sister.

Once home I asked you what your problem was and why you were such a fucking mental all of the time. We couldn't ever just go out and have a good time, and proceeded to let her [he shifts from first to third person] know that it was no way to treat a man who was paying her rent, and buying her groceries. I then told her that if she didn't like it I was going to take our son and move the hell out. At that point that the statement had been made I couldn't see you standing there anymore. She hit me a couple of times in the face and before she had a chance to blink I hit her back, knocking her back a couple of feet. I was so engulfed with rage you were no longer my wife, much less a human being. I hit you twice in the face, picked you up, ran you down the hall and put you through the wall in the entryway. As she lay there crying I remember being numb, angry, and feeling detached from her as a person. I kicked her in the head and walked outside. The police showed up just a few minutes later. (Responsibility Letter)

Mr. Yount reflected on his behavior and explored every detail in front of many other men in the therapy group setting. He presented it as if he were talking to his intimate partner and concluded with the following statements.

After I calmed down enough I started to become overwhelmed with feelings of guilt.

I know that I must have hurt you, that what I've done is wrong, and I can never go back and change what has happened. I hope that by paying attention to your needs and wants, goals, and ambitions I can somehow gain back some of your trust. I enjoy my life with you and our son and will never jeopardize that safety net you said I had once created. I love you.

Looking back at the beliefs I had as a young man, having a few enlightening experiences and this class as reference, I can see now that I had been misled. My parents are not to be blamed directly, but indirectly were responsible for their actions, which I believed, was the way things were meant to be. Women bitched, and men either went out to the garage or told her flat out to shut the hell up. I know now that there are many more choices than these and that our "letting go of the rope" statements are a guide, not necessarily commandments. Women need us to listen to them, to show compassion, and to feel empathy as they might for us, in their time of need.

My action plan will include some changes I feel I must make to ensure that my family feels safe when I'm around. For the last few years, looking back, it's obvious now that by intimidating my wife I never got the chance to know who she really was. I spent all my time controlling her and convincing her that her lazy ass needed to stay home and take care of our son. I will stop trying to control her by telling her to have a great time if she goes out with her friends, and possibly hand her some money to show her that I'm okay with it.

I will no longer spend every waking hour wondering where she's at and to make this easier I can occupy my time by doing something with my son. I've wasted a lot of valuable time, time that I could have used to focus on the relationship with my son so that he can grow to be a strong, understanding man one day. I'm determined to change to better my family, but most of all, for the chance to see my son break the abusive cycle and have a family of his own.

I'm starting to see now just by listening to her and handling problems calmly and rationally that there is hope. (Responsibility Letter)

When I first saw Mr. Yount, even though he was 24 years of age, he looked much older. He was about five foot eleven with a slender build. His hair was brown and a little rough-cut, not smoothed down. His body was slender; it seemed tightly bound, stringy muscular and tense. He always seemed to sit leaning forward. His face was narrow, somewhat drawn tight. His eyes were inset, observing. His diaphragm and pelvic area were fixed and rigid. His clothes were casual, jeans and blue-collar worker shirts. His demeanor was concrete, complemented by a concrete, matter-of-fact communication style.

His vocabulary was adequate in describing his life experiences. The pitch of his voice was low, a little halting, cautious, and searching for the right words, sometimes restating things for additional accuracy. In the group setting Mr. Yount was quiet and sometimes when he would read his responsibility or empathy letters he would lean forward with his face in his letter and he would cry while he read about his violent behaviors toward his partner.

Sid Belini

Mr. Sid Belini was arrested for domestic violence and was on probation with a Community Corrections Officer. Mr. Belini recounted the record of his childhood years.

> I was born in California, where I lived for about three years, on March 20, first day of spring, 1973. My dad, Alfred James Sampson, was a biker, and my mom, Lidia Louann Clemmons, was a hippie chick out of the 60s, and they were back together through an arranged marriage that was arranged over in Ireland before they probably were even born, through both of their parents.
>
> My mother left when, actually my mom and dad split up when I was about two and a half. At the age of three, my father married my babysitter, and mom was pushed totally out of the picture. And my father died on his motorcycle on their honeymoon night. He was in a coma for about two weeks, and you know, that was that. She [my babysitter now stepmom] found out she was pregnant after my dad was killed. When I was three she had my stepbrother, Walter Belini.
>
> Well, my babysitter really wanted custody of me, so, in the State of California, her and my biological mother had a battle in court and California State Supreme Court Justice and everything else got involved, and it was a big newspaper event and all that stuff. My babysitter, stepmom, eventually won custody of me.
>
> We then moved to central California, and she met another biker, Mr. Mac Belini, that lived in southern California. He used to ride his Harley up every weekend to come and see her. She was working at this hotel there in town, and he did that for a year or so before he finally said, "To hell with it. I want to marry you." So that was kind of neat. I

141

> was four years old when they got married, and he adopted
> me and I took his name — Belini. I basically just took his
> name and started writing his last name, and it's been that
> way ever since. (History of Hurts and Beliefs Letter)

Mr. Belini stated that he didn't remember too much of his childhood. It was confusing. He stated, "I never knew exactly who I was or where I belonged, you know. I was always around bikers and stuff, which was pretty cool, 'cause that's what I knew, you know, familiar faces and machines and everything, and that was all right. But it's, I don't know, as far as family life, though, it was always kinda weird" (Session Notes). He continued and talked about his dad.

> My dad? I still call him my dad; he's the only guy I've
> really known. He was always a, a pretty neat guy, you
> know, I'd watch out for him 'cause he's, he's a good-sized
> guy and had a pretty, pretty bad temper, but he was always
> real nice to us kids, you know. He could talk to somebody
> in a suit and tie, or wearing a full set of leathers, and it was
> no big deal 'cause he'd carry on a normal conversation.
> (Taped Interview)

Mr. Belini related that he was physically abused. His dad whipped him with a belt. He got whipped for teasing his little brother and teasing animals. His father was the disciplinarian. He was close to his mother. He lived for a while in a bad neighborhood, about which he said, "If you're a small, white kid, basically you don't belong there. It's the type of neighborhood, you know, gunshots every night, sirens. It was pretty scary, but I was a pretty fearless kid, really" (taped interview).

He related that he had a lot of freedom and could come and go as he pleased.

> At about five I had a little, used a little scooter some of the
> bikers had built out of spare parts, lawn mower engine,
> and stuff and put a little set of ape hanger handlebars. It
> just had two basically like smaller wheelbarrow wheels
> on it. I used to fill it up with gas at the corner gas station
> for about 50 cents. I'd ride all the way out to the beach,
> which was probably; I don't know, 15, 20-minute drive in
> a car. Took a lot longer on a little scooter.

I used to have people at the local machine shops, they'd call up my mom or my dad and say, "Hey, I just saw your kid cruising down the main street here, you know, just wanted to let you know."

With regard to my younger brother, Walter, it just seemed like as a kid that my mom and dad always paid more attention to him, you know, was always concerned what he was doing and stuff. You know, I was just kind off back here in the background somewhere. Oh, yeah, yeah, it was one of those gut-wrenching deals, you know, it was kind of painful. I'd cry sometimes. I've always, I've always been pretty emotional in some ways, on the edge of my seat, trying to hold everything back. Don't let too many people in that door. I'd, oh, you know, I'd be a wreck, you know. Let me watch Charlie Brown or whatever. If it's a sad deal, you know, I mean, it rattles me, and I'd have tears on my face.

I was, just, just lonely. There was a gal I went to school with, all the way from, it's kind of funny, she bounced around to all the same schools I did throughout my entire life with the exception of my final two years in high school. Glenda Eades was little, blond hair, blue-eyed thing, you know, I always kinda had a crush on her. After second grade, I went to a Catholic/Christian school over, just in the next town, because it was, it was a little bit nicer, and you didn't have to worry about your kid getting shot with a stray bullet or something in a bad neighborhood.

My mom [stepmon] was basically like my own personal protector. She had been there from day one when my mom and dad first needed a babysitter. She just hated to see this cute, little kid basically and, you know, get a raw deal. She was great, great.

Oh, it's, my mom still, to this day, I lovingly call her the biker bitch from hell, you know. Nicest woman you'll ever meet, I love her to death, but if you ever get on her bad side, that's a whole different ball game.

Glenda Eades and I were best of friends here and there, but she pretty much bounced around at the same schools that I did all the time. Seventh grade, she was a hot little ticket, you know. Every guy in the school was after her. She, it was basically you have the upper social level, and you had a head cheerleader and the cheerleading squad, and that was her. I didn't fit into her social class. Pretty much I didn't really want to deal with anyone. I just hung out with the misfits — you know, kids with long hair. Felt accepted there.

She was always a good friend of mine, and during seventh, eighth and ninth grades, she was pretty much larger than life for even herself. She didn't really take notice of anyone else that had been there with her growing up. It was all about bigger and better things, but later on in high school, she kind of mellowed out and came back down to earth and started talking with everyone she grew up with.

I kept in touch with Glenda Eades. Our last year of high school, she got mixed up with a drug dealer who had graduated two or three years prior. Got pregnant, had a kid. She just, you know, was always just bright and shiny and glowing, you know, just a real beautiful girl. And just something happened to her, you know, and when she kind of dulled a little bit, things started going downhill for her. She started looking like hell, you know. Basically one of those deals I was trying to get away from. That's why I left California.

I did something I never thought I'd do. I got married to a woman. I was, basically what I saw was, I saw blonde hair, blue eyes, two-piece, and G-string bikini walking up the dock. There was probably, I don't know, 100 yards of dock going out to the marina where I had a crew, three or four guys under me, trying to, you know, kept them "get busy" and everything, rent out the rental boats, ran the gas dock. I'm looking around, you know, where in the hell's all my guys. I'm just swamped. I popped around the corner, and they're all standing there on this pontoon boat, looking at what's coming up the main walkway. So,

I take a look, and it's this gal in a little, two-piece, G-string bikini, and I said, "You guys might as well go back to work 'cause I'm gonna marry that woman someday," and sure as shit, Herb, I did. And I was just, holy smokes, Constance Baker. Or Connie for short. I married her, shortly after moved to up north, that's where her family originated. And after probably eight or ten months, and we split up.

I had quite a few fights in school. I remember one kid, Don Avis in grade school. He was messing with that Glenda Eades, and I roughed him up a little actually.

My dad is still alive. He's considerably toned down. He was major, both my parents were major drug users growing up, and just big time partygoers. They'd be Harleys all over the front yard, and they've both toned that down. Probably when I was in about junior high, I guess, the last time I remember any big parties or anything like that.

When I look back over my whole childhood my greatest experience was getting my first motorcycle. That was great.

My worst experience was the day I turned 16. With regard to my natural mother and father, and everything else, you know, that was, I was kind of always looking for the missing pieces, because I didn't have anything figured out really. Everything happened pretty early in my life. When I turned 16, I went to do a job at a local community college. They needed someone to do their flyers, their advertising. It was a regular, legal job, you know. I had to go and get my birth certificate. So, I called my step mom and told her I needed my birth certificate. I need some proof of who I am basically. So, she gave it to me, and I was pretty excited about the job and everything, but I just wanted to check, as I went out the door that everything was in order. And I pulled out this birth certificate, and I'm looking at it. I remember falling down on the steps. I was reading as far as my mother's maiden name, Lidia Louann Clemmons, and the woman I'd always known as my mother was Teresa Lou Belini. I looked down to where it said father. It said Alfred James Sampson, and my dad that I've always known was Mac Belini, Jr., you know. I was pretty much devastated.

You know, I, you know, they'd probably tried to explain things to me earlier in life, but as a small child, you just don't fathom a whole lot, you know. It was pretty emotionally draining. It probably, I think I was in shock for probably about a week. You know, it's just like if you walked up to a socket and stuck, jammed a safety pin in there. It's pretty much that shocking.

I don't know where my natural mother is. I've tried to track her down. The last thing I ever got from her, see I was always told that she was my best friend; she used to send letters and little packages and stuff. Last time I ever heard from her was sixth grade or seventh grade, summer. She'd sent a letter saying she was moving to New York with a new boyfriend of hers. I tried to track her down since, you know, with no luck, and hell, that was quite a few years ago.

Now, I'll tell you the truth. I'm still kind of confused about the whole deal. You know, it just gets kind of difficult when nobody's got any answers. When I look at my birth certificate or Social Security number. I actually have two names and two different Social Security numbers.

My birth name was Sid Allen Sampson, and I didn't know I had the middle name Allen until I was 16, and then just recently, in the last probably three years, started using my whole name.

Prior to that I was just Sid Belini. My natural mother and father named me Sid. My adopted father was Belini. (Taped Interview)

When Mr. Belini first came to my office I observed a man in his late twenties about five feet ten inches tall and about 180 pounds in weight. My initial experience of him was that he was closed, constricted, and tight. He was very unexpressive. He talked in a monotone with minimal eye movement. He was very concrete and matter of fact. The most significant bodily feature was his pectoral muscles. They were well defined and seemed to stand out high on his chest. It seemed as if he were holding his breath, or as if he were blowing up and ready to explode. He was dressed casually in laborer's attire, jeans, blue-collar shirt, and heavy work boots. He often wore a visored baseball cap with the visor pulled down close over his eyes from which he peered out at you. He would sit in the group quiet and observant and as time progressed he would talk, and when he talked what came out was a caring, sensitive, interested, discovery-oriented person. He became very good at demonstrating many of the skills presented in the group.

Mr. Belini recounted the events that got him arrested and sent to a treatment center. He recorded the events as a letter to the victim.

Dear Winnie:

When we first met, I thought you were everything I wanted in a woman. These ideas were formed at a very early age. I expected you to act and behave in this manner.

For two years, we had a lot of good times, and with my new job, I looked forward to the future with high expectations.

I thought that my expectations would become your own. When they did not, I became resentful. I thought you were spending too much time with friends partying and not enough time with me.

I started drinking excessively and degrading you whenever possible to make myself feel better.

One day I came home early and started drinking. We decided to go to the bar to see friends. On the way, you started talking about our finances, and this upset me. I called you a stupid bitch and told you to shut the fuck up. When we reached the bar, you said that we should break up. This enraged me.

I asked for the car keys, and you said no. So I walked outside, got into the car and pulled the fuse box. I was so angry I punched the rearview mirror and broke the windshield. Some people said they were calling the police, so I started walking home. When I arrived, I started drinking heavily, hoping to feel better about the situation. I then started destroying the house to get back at you. The next day, I woke up to two police officers standing above me. They got me on my feet and took me to jail. I could only image the disappointment of my friends and family.

As I sat in jail, I felt ashamed and abandoned. No one came to visit or help.

I wanted you to understand my frustration, but you didn't, so I took it out on you.I blamed everything that had gone wrong on you, when in reality, it was me that was out of control.

I can only imagine your terror when I destroyed our car and home and how hurt you must have felt. I just wanted my pain to stop.

I know what I did was wrong and I have taken certain steps to prevent this behavior in the future. Since then I have stopped drinking and doing drugs. I also attend a DV Perpetrator program. These things are to better get to know myself and to understand my destructive behavior. I want you to know that I am responsible for my own actions and that none of this was ever your fault.

Sid

Rondel De Marco

Mr. De Marco is a 27-year-old Hispanic male. Mr. De Marco was arrested for a domestic violence episode, went to jail, and was sentenced to a year in jail, suspended, and a $5,000 fine, suspended (Initial Interview) if he attended the Certified Perpetrator Treatment Program.

Mr. De Marco was born in central Washington. His father was from Texas and his mother was from central Washington. His mother was Irish and his father was Hispanic (Intake/evaluation). Of his father Mr. De Marco related:

My dad fills my memory base with being a real hardass. Since I was two years old, my dad expected too much out of me. He used me to get himself out of the military, by having custody of me while he was still enlisted. He was released from the military on a hardship, because he had to take care of me. From that point on, it was hell living with him. He somewhat neglected me, because he was still young and into marijuana-hippy stage, etc. It seemed like all he did was smoke it and sell it, and I'd just be there to fetch things.

We moved back to Washington State with nothing and arrived from California to Washington on a small, Honda 250 motorcycle. He pinched me and hit me all the way to Washington, just to keep me from falling asleep at times. My whole life he made me feel scared to talk to him, be around him, etc. I hated him because he was always so mean and irritated. I had to listen to how he was beaten by his dad, and I don't have any idea how easy I had it. He kicked my ass all the time. When I was in kindergarten, I still remember him bashing me into the wall, and he broke the sheetrock with my head. He was never like this towards my stepmom, but only me. I hated him, and I usually avoided him by staying away from home or in my room, pretty much hiding. I walked on eggshells when he was around. (History of Hurts and Beliefs Letter)

Somewhere along the way Mr. De Marco' parents separated and both remarried.

Both my moms were not even as extreme, but still whipped me when I needed it. My dad always stressed the point that you never raise your hand to a woman, and I believed it totally. My stepdad beat me worse than my real dad and also beat my real Mom extremely. I hated him with all my heart. I grew up believing I would someday do something back to him, something he would not like or perhaps even remember due to being a vegetable or worse. (History of Hurts and Beliefs Letter)

Mr. De Marco described the nature of his intimate partner relationships.

I had several girlfriends in my life, and all were very good relationships. They would end due to my needing or wanting another, but always ended on good terms. I

soon got older and fell deeper for my high school fling. I
went to the Marine Corps, and she tried to wait for me.
She did cheat, and I never was the same towards a woman
again. Trust has always been out the door when it came to
women after that. I become more suspicious, possessive,
and I would let them go easily. Yet, I would go back to
them even after the fact. I always had to bring up the
incident, which caused a fight. This is still my biggest
flaw. I don't yet have the ability to not bring up the past,
let it go or forgive. The thought stays in my mind, and I
start to get myself worked up.

I just wish the girls knew how much it hurts me or that I
have a jealousy problem. I feel someday I will find one
that will not ever make me feel like that again, one that
will be with me from the moment I date only her and her
me. I sometimes feel that all women are lying, cheating
hookers, but deep down I hope there is one out there that
is an exception to this. I don't want to be alone anymore; I
want a family. I still have hope that I can change to make
a better partner for that special person, whoever it may
be, if anyone at all. (History of Hurts and Beliefs Letter)

After high school Mr. De Marco went into the military. After he
was discharged at age 22 he met a woman who was 19. He began an
important relationship with her. He talked about this relationship in his
Responsibility Letter to her.

Dear Sonta:

I was brought up with the conception that an intimate
relationship could only be carried out with honesty and
respect for your partner. In all my past relationships, I
carried high expectations of my partners to not disrespect
me around other men and to not lie to me. If a girlfriend of
mine in the past did this to me, I automatically distanced
myself and the relationship would eventually end, as I
would find another companion.

When I met you, I fell in love instantly and wanted to
give you my best, my honest and my full commitment. I
expected you to be my only love, and for me to never have

to lie to you or you lie to me. I wanted you to put me in the place as your man and your one and only. I usually expected that past partners came and went, but once they went, they stayed gone. However, in our relationship, I soon found out that this wasn't always the case.

Our relationship started out just about as wonderful as one can hope to wish for. I loved you more than I had loved any other human being before. I would tell you this, and I also stated that I believe you were my soul mate. You were very young at the time, and I was fresh out of the military, age 22; you were 19. I had an edge that either worked for me or against me, due to my having a lot of experience, experience of relationships that worked and did not, experience of how I acted when I was your age and very naive and inexperienced, been around the world, etc., discipline, etc.

When I met you, I was ready for you to give me your best. We were going to make this work, and perhaps marry each other. I never once took into consideration your age, past experience or anything of the liking in that matter up to this point. To me, it didn't matter as long as you were with me now. We both had daughters of the same age, only one month apart. We soon found out that dealing with the children's other parent became an issue. We both became possessive and limited our relationships with our children's parents.

I never felt like I couldn't trust you, until you confronted me about my relation with my child's mother. I fed into your request, but I could never seem to do anything right in your eyes when it came time to deal with my baby's mom, Rachel. I, in turn, did the same and expected the same of you or demanded it, rather. One of the biggest problems that started chopping at our beautiful tree of love was other people's influence. I started hearing about how big of a liar your personality was. I was hearing rumors that I did not like. No matter how much I tried not to hear the talk, I still would dig for more information about you. I soon became involved in hearing about the way you treated past people and how you still were in contact with all of the most recent men. When I confronted you about the rumors, you lied about it all.

We lived together right away, and I had never lived with a girlfriend. I saw this as a pretty big step in letting you know, as well as myself, that I was in love. You would still get phone calls from several ex-partners. At the time, you lied and said they were just friends. I trusted you and had no problem with guys as friends. It became a problem when they were still calling and sometimes your visiting them when I was at work, etc. for six months and then some.

I started getting uncomfortable about this situation and could see through your lies. Small lies led to my getting upset. This led up to our first physical confrontation, and I remember it like it was this afternoon. The incident started by my asking you some questions about your afternoon after I left home for lunch. When I got home from work at 5:15 p.m., I wanted to talk about how I was feeling. I wanted you to know I didn't approve of your hanging out with my guy friends when I'm not there.

Without even knowing your ex-boyfriend Jim was there after I went to lunch, I asked for an example of what happened this afternoon. I think you thought I knew he went there and felt you had better 'fess up. You told me, "Oh, yeah, he came by to pick up some of this things that I still had of his." This wasn't even the last boyfriend or your baby's dad. I was having to deal with him on different matters you were keeping as secrets also.

You were starting to do things without telling me. I felt like you were not being true or were afraid to tell me even the smallest things, afraid I would get upset. You chose to lie and chose to keep things from me. After we argued about this matter and you accused me of all kinds of lies and rumors, I thought you thought the rumors up yourself in order to justify your actions lately. I got so angry and hurt that you were lying to me that I threw the cold water that I was drinking in your face. You just sat there in awe and then smiled with disbelief. I remember I felt like an out-of-control freak.

You left the house, and I eventually looked for you around town. Lo and behold, you were parked at Jim's house. When I knocked, a girl told me you weren't there. It appeared she had been crying, too. I left and went back to your house. I started packing my belongings and was moving out ASAP. When you showed up, you must have been shocked that I was leaving, because the look on your face showed it. You asked what I was doing, and I told you. You started being mean and calling me names. You bumped me in the hall, and I called you a lying, cheating bitch and some other bad names.

You started to help me out with my stuff, but in the process, you broke some of my valuable possessions. When you would grab something of mine from that point on, I would grab it from you, until it became a struggle over it. You slapped my chin and tried to kick me anywhere you could. I squeezed your arms and lifted you and threw you on your couch. After you came at me again, I grabbed your wrists, also squeezing them hard, to try and hurt you until you calmed down. You started tearing my clothes, and I pushed you on the bed really hard, then grabbed your legs and pulled you to the ground, and you hit your head on the floor. I said I was sorry, but you were very upset and hurt.

I stated I am calling your mom; this is way out of hand. You took your phone from me and unplugged it from the wall. I used my cell phone, but she was not home. I called my ex-girlfriend, Rachel, and asked her to call an officer immediately to mediate this situation, so I could get my belongings in a peaceful manner. I made myself leave to avoid any more physical contact, so I drove to my dad's.

On my way there, my dad called and told me the police were there at his house already. When I arrived, they asked what happened, and they stuffed and cuffed me in front of my family. Your child heard us cuss and yell, and she saw us shove each other around. This has probably affected the way she sees me in her eyes now, due to my making her mommy cry. Since then, we have argued and called each other names without any regards for her feelings and emotions, as if it were fine. Our daughters miss playing with each other.

I wanted so much for this not to happen this way. I felt so cheated, disrespected and disgusted that my lover would lie or cheat, if you had, on me. My whole world went down the tubes, and I felt like getting so far away from you. After time went on, you called me, and we talked about how much we were sorry. I made it known that you hurt me and how. I let you know how sorry I was to see you get hysterical, and sad that our relationship went to a physical conflict. I stated I was not a very good person to try and talk when it came to girls, and that I usually flee if they made me look stupid or feel betrayed.

I went to jail and got very embarrassed when my name hit the paper. We lost a special bond from that point on. I never have been able to fulfill the trust in my heart. I feel all the court costs, days missed from work, counseling and emotional problems were not worth it. I could guess how you must still feel when you think back on it. I believe you feel we lost a special something, due to us showing hate towards each other. I feel we both hated each other at the moment, and it took away from our love from that point on. Because I still feel pain and humiliation, I felt like I could never refill that space.

What I have to offer you from this point on is my sincere apology for losing control. You may never see me in your eyes as you did when we first connected, but I will dedicate my life to trying. I want to be the spark in your eyes forever, and I don't want anything like this to hinder that possibility. If I can't ever refill that space of trust in your heart, then I have failed yet another relationship. I promise to seek treatment for my own self-assurance. I need to be able to know I will never lose control, and I need to change my ways of thinking you are my property or that it needs to be perfect or nothing.

I promise to give you space and benefit of the doubt. It was not your fault totally that the argument took place. I should have approached it in a different manner. You don't deserve to have water in your face, shoved, squeezed, thrown or to be called names that are vulgar. You are very special to me, your daughter, and to our new boy. I want you to see that we can get through this evil and disgusting chapter of our lives. It will just take my full dedication and realization that relationships need to be worked on every day. I promise to try and be the person you fell for from day one. I promise to be there for you until you say you don't need me anymore. God forbid that ever happens. I *will* work on this, day by day.

Love, Rondel

Mr. De Marco also wrote a letter to himself as if from his partner. It is called an Empathy Letter. This letter is a means by which men are able to begin to stand in their partner's experience and understand what the abuse was like for them.

Dear Ron:

In 1998 we had our first fight. You began to be a very suspicious and controlling person. You blamed me, accused me and intimidated me. Your actions and words hurt me emotionally, and you also hurt me physically. My wrists were squeezed; you threw me around like some worthless piece of meat. I felt like a person to whom you've grown to hate as your worst enemy.

You used to be so special and such a prize for me to be with. I treated you very good and tried to be the person you wanted to be with. I wanted to be loved, hugged and be your everything. I feel I forfeited a lot of bad habits, as well as actions that I knew you wouldn't like about me. Even though I tried my best, it wasn't enough for you.

I lost a big amount of love, trust and intimacy towards you. My self-respect was even in question, just because of your words and the way you looked at me from that point on. I turned very cold towards you, and I don't know if I can ever let it go. We both blame each other,

155

but I wish you would just let your pride go and try and let the past go.

I want you to know I still hurt from those words. I want you to know I feel like you look down upon me, and I hate it. I want you to leave your past behind and listen to me for who I am, here and now.

Sonya

Shane Sagen

Mr. Shane Sagen presented himself for treatment due to a domestic violence episode. Mr. Sagen is a 25-year-old white male, the only child of a 32-year-old father and a 30-year-old mother. He was born in California. After a couple of years in California, Mr. Sagen's parents move up the coast to Washington State and eventually to eastern Washington. When Mr. Sagen was about five years old his parents divorced and Shane stayed with his mother. He was close to his mother. He related,

> Well, when we came here, my dad started drinking a lot, according to mom. And I got both sides of the story so they did for a little bit. Anyway things weren't going too well. They hadn't been for a while. Dad was drinking a lot and, you know, bringing strange people to the house, doing weird stuff like that and so they got a divorce. She told him that she wanted a divorce. I don't remember much about it. I saw my dad every weekend for a while, then it got real sporadically and briefly over the years, nothing substantial. My mother and I moved back to California and I didn't see him for over a year.

> Then when I was about six my mom and dad got back together, I don't know, a year, something like that. Then that went sour, and then it got real sporadic. I didn't see him much anymore. When I was with him it was a good experience. He was a good, what I remember of him, I don't remember much. When he was angry it was pretty scary. Uh, he'd get right up an inch in your face, and scream in your face, tell you what you're doing wrong, and he's got those eyes that look right through ya. Scares the shit out of ya. (History of Hurts and Beliefs Letter)

Mr. Sagen remembered that there were about 30 kids in the first grade and he remembers his first grade teacher. In the fourth grade, when he was about nine years old, they moved back east, and he went to school there. His parents split up again. His mother died in 1998. He still wanted to see his father. He noted,

> He lives over in Renton. I went to go see him, what was it, last summer, because I just wanted to get some questions answered. Eh, it was weird. Lookin' at this guy sitting across from me realizing, you know, that he could be either levitating or he could die right there in front of me and it wouldn't make a lick of difference . . . just some guy, you know. But it was weird because that was, that's my dad, but yet, there's absolutely no emotional pretense whatsoever. It's just like some dude, you know, well, so. . . . (History of Hurts and Beliefs Letter)

Mr. Sagen talked about his patterns of discipline:

> She [mother] couldn't really discipline me. Once I got to be about nine years old, there really wasn't nothing she could do. I mean I'd just do whatever I wanted. I did that until I was about 19. I just did whatever. (History of Hurts and Beliefs Letter)

Mr. Sagen went to junior high school and dropped out of high school in the ninth grade. He said he partied, drank, and smoked pot most of the time with his friends. He did go back and got a GED, and he attended some college. He had his first meaningful relationship at age 16; it lasted about eight months. He noted,

> Let's see, at 16, I drank, 17, I started doing meth real bad, you know...pretty sporadically at first and then pretty much constantly. Oh shit, I used to slam it, so I used to use needles. You know, it's like, a fuckin' orgasm multiplied by a thousand. That's why it's so addicting. Oh yeah. You don't think of nothing else. You're just that and it's like that for like a half an hour. You're just; you're just cooking, gone.
>
> When I was 16. That was the best. Well, I mean, it's bad, but it was good to me at the time. You know, Connie, the first girlfriend, I had wanted to go out with her since

157

like the fourth grade. I was like so in love with her. She was so cool. And that's when I first started smoking pot. And I really like smoking pot, but I didn't have no money. So I started growing pot in my mom's basement. So, I wanted two things: I wanted to be able to have pot and have 'em grow right and I wanted to have Connie. And I got it all that year! And it was so cool. That was the best time in my life. That was the best time in my life. I can remember I had no worries, no bills, 16, my mom was O.K.... My mom never did drugs, she didn't drink, nothing.

I would never really come down off of it. I always had enough to where I never really came down. I would just like power nod and eventually pass out wherever I was at. Eventually you just fall asleep. Yeah. I mean the shortest times I used to stay up was about five days. The last time I ever got high was before I went to jail, was for fifteen days.

Oh, fuck, when I quit I was like 104 pounds. I was tiny. I had fucking jaundice. I had a lump on this side the size of a golf ball just from missing so many times. All many friends were turning up dead and it was bad, bad, bad, bad. It was not good. Eventually, your body just shuts down. After ten-twelve hours, you'd be starving because you haven't eaten anything. Eat and go back to bed. I can't count how many glasses of milk I spilt on myself. I'd be sitting in the chair after I got up and you know eating cookies or something and all of the sudden, gone, wake up ten hours later again. Oh, this is nice. Then I always had some when I woke up. Always. I mean it was just there. It was always there. (Taped Interview)

Later he met another woman whom he married in 1998 when he was 19 and she was 18. Shane continued:

I didn't really fall in love with her. I mean we got together and two weeks later, she got pregnant. I mean we had both just got off drugs. She was doing the same thing. You know and since I quit and I heard she quit then it been like two or three weeks since she quit, and I figured well if you need anybody to talk to, she can always call me, because I was dead set on ever doing it again. So, I'd, well give me a call. Well, we…she ended up coming over and watching a movie with me, and that was it. Then two…three weeks after that, that's when she got pregnant. No, that's sick. We had to move into her dad's house. That really sucked. That was not fun at all.

We lived with her dad and her crazy step mom. Yeah, that was neat. Her mom, her stepmom suffered from like dementia, so they'd be constantly fighting, you know, and her drugs, and we'd be in the room with her, God, oh, it so sucked. And then she always had a pile of animals. I don't know why. I don't know what her deal was, but she would always have all these dogs and cats and it was just horrible. It was a nightmare. I loved her, don't get me wrong, but it was a nightmare. I grew to love her after time.

Her dad was German and an electrician so he ended up moving out, and we took over the place. We stayed there for about, I'd say, two, three years. Then we had a baby boy and then a baby girl. I worked for a tree service. I'd climb those big trees and cut them down. I also worked in a sawmill. (Taped Interview)

Mr. Sagen had two children. He went to engineering school and his wife was also attending college. He then got a supervisory job and has been there ever since. The relationship was very conflicted.

We'd fight constantly. Get along, fight, get along, and fight. It was almost as if there had to be like a…it was weird with her. We'd never like talk or go do anything, you know. If we fought, we'd be close. She was a lot like my mother. She and I would fight like I did with my mother. If we got in an argument, then she'd talk more. I don't know. The arguments took some of the charge off so then you could kind of connect. It was almost like there'd have to be an adrenaline dump, you know, for us actually to feel close to each other. It was weird. It was weird. I just got sick of it. Years and years of that just wore me down.

I told her that if we keep fighting, I'm going to leave. And I had been talking with this other girl at work at the same time and it was a lot more...you know I liked this girl at work. She was really nice. And it wasn't like that, but you know, it was to the point where I wanted to get to know her. You know, I didn't really give a shit. I was sick of fighting with Andrea. That's all it was. It was just stupid.

So we got into a fight and well, I'm leavin.' Packed my shit and left, which surprised her all to hell because we'd done this hundreds of times, you know, hundreds of times. So, I left, and then I started seeing Karen. Everything was fine until she found out about Karen. And then she wanted me back. Because she was all for the divorce before she found out about that. When she found out about that, she wanted to get back together. "You gotta give your family a chance." And, you know, I thought about it. Fine, I'll give them a chance. Then we were together for about six months, then in February of 2000, that's when a guy came home for dinner and she said, 'Well, I met somebody else and I'm leaving ya,' and that was it.

Well, actually, when she first told me about that, she actually laughed. I thought she was joking. You have got to be fucking kidding me. After all that fucking hassle last summer. You have fucking got to be kidding me. You're fucking psycho, whatever. So that's how it went. And it just progressively built and built. I stayed there day after day. I lived with this new information.

Unbelievable pain. Oh, just like somebody let off a nuclear weapon in my stomach. It was bad. I was always shaking, couldn't eat. I was just on edge. Oh I was freakin.' Yeah, it was bad, 'cause my mom and grandma were the ones that raised me, and they both had died the previous two years, so I had no family, none, except Andrea and the kids. So it was like losing them was like losing your arms and legs. I lived in that for about three months. It was nothing really, 'cause I had to stay over there all the time. Oh I was going crazy. There was no doubt about that. I was just jittering. Couldn't focus on nothing, nothing. I couldn't do shit. Work was just a joke. I couldn't even function there. That went on for seven or eight months.

We had gotten into a fight. Oh, God. It was on a Saturday. That's when I pushed her. We had gotten into a pretty heated argument. This was into a week after she was saying she was taking off. So I mean I'm just going nuts. I'm just goin' nuts you know thinkin' about this guy. Then I'm working nights on top of it. So it's even worse. All I want to do is find this dude and cave his face in. That's all I thought about. That was the only thing on my mind. I want to put this dude in the ditch. He's dead. I never did anything aggressive toward him. Andrea and me got in a fight one night. That's when I pushed her and she started hitting me and I ripped the phone out of the wall. Then I smashed the table in half. And, uh, then she called the cops and I left. I still lived in the house with her at that time. I began to feel rage and sadness. Oh, it was indescribable.

Yeah, it was bad. Well, 'cause Andrea, she would go back and forth. It would be like, when I finally moved out, it would be like, and maybe we need to talk. And then, jerkin' me around with the kids, you know, constantly. That's still not over. That's still goin' on. So I mean it was just constant. I wish I'd never met that woman. It's bad, that bad.

Yeah, yeah, when you thought of another guy holding your kids, you know, sleeping in your bed, and then Andrea peeled [sanded down] my mom's dressers. My mom had these antique nice dressers. I mean this is not cheap stuff. This is nice stuff. Well, she peeled 'em. She got 'em. She kept 'em; I didn't get to take them when I got all my stuff out of the house. She kept 'em. So and all their stuff's in there, and I mean it's a minute thing but it's just one more wound nagging thing. You know. It was bad. Then I came here.

There was no fear in her. She spit in my face, came right up to my face and told me, "I'm gonna have T.J. kick your ass." That's why I broke the table. It was either that or

161

her head. It was one or the other. I just had this image
of poppin' her on the head. And then, so the table's right
there, and I just destroyed it, just fuckin' destroyed it. It
was in about four or five pieces. I was just crazy. It was
insane. It was insane. The whole thing was psycho. It's
just nuts. (Taped Interview)

About a month after the physical incident Mr. Sagen got a letter from
the court telling him to come down there for a show cause hearing for
city-fourth degree assault for interfering with a 911 call and malicious
mischief. So Mr. Sagen went to court with a lawyer and he received a
stipulated order of continuance.

Oh yeah since then I was all over the place. I mean I can't
even remember last summer. I remember I was drinking
all the time, sleeping with anything that moved. I mean
it was just bad. And then I got the DUI last summer. It
was pretty bad.

And, I shit half pound of adrenaline. I hardly worked at
all. I mean I'd go for maybe one, two, three hours and
then I would leave. I did that for like a year. I mean I
got paid [he was supervisor of a crew—they carried on
for him]. I just was never there. This went on week after
week after week.

Yeah, which wasn't fair to them. I don't know, but I'm
kind of takin' care of that now, but have been for a while.
But they understood. Actually, I'm really close...see
the cool thing is one of the guys, I've known him for
thirteen years. We've actually been best friends since we
were little kids. So it's cool to work with him. And he
understood what I was goin' through. He picked up the
slack. He never bitched about it.

I can't remember half their names. They were nothing.
They were just pieces of meat to pass on, which isn't nice.
You know, that's wrong, but what I was going through, I
could care the fuck less about what they wanted. At that
time, all women were fuckin' whores and I didn't give a
fuck. They were the fuckin' Antichrist. That's the way
I looked at them. Okay fine, I can't beat ya. I'm grudge

fuckin' and see how you like that. And then leave 'em. So, it's more of an emotional battering is what I was doing then. I just didn't care. I was mean.

They never had a chance to call me. I wouldn't call them. I would give them fake numbers. One of them, I told her my name was John. I just didn't care. I could just care less. I would tell them everything they ever wanted to hear. Everything. I'd look into their eyes and I would lie – lie like a fuckin' carpet. I was horrible. Then they would just, "Oh, you are so sweet." And as soon as I got that act, I was gone. Fuck you. You're filtered out. It was bad. But then, then, then I don't know. I just got to the point where this ain't gonna fuckin' work, then I stopped doing that altogether. I haven't done that since last September.

Some things began to change. I don't know. Probably time. Coming to terms with everything. Realizing that I don't know, anyway Andrea had it set in her mind that I was the biggest piece of shit on her, that there was nothin' lower than me. I was never a good father. I was never this. I was never that. Once I came to terms with, you know, that's all bullshit. Then, things started getting better. That and I started getting' sick of the quality in my life. It was getting bad. It was stupid. So it's progressively gotten better. But it's still fucked up. I mean, now, I'm going through the contempt court thing with Andrea, file all that paperwork, the modification of the parenting plan, you know. And now, it's to the point where I don't even want to see her again, ever. I never want to speak to her again. I never want to have anything to do with her again. And that's one of my requests on the modifications of the parenting plan, that we drop 'em off but leave before the other one gets there or something like that. I don't even want to have any contact with her ever again. So, but it went from desperately wanting her to this. So, that's been a year and half's time. (Taped Interview)

When Mr. Sagen came to my office I observed a man about 25 years old. He was about 5 feet 10 inches tall and weighed about 165 pounds. His body structure was symmetrical, in that no part was out of proportion with the rest. He seemed tense, not from the meeting, but as if his tenseness was a life pattern. His eyes most often avoided contact. His communication style seemed to be concrete and somewhat distant. It seemed that behind his matter-of-fact communication was a withdrawn, even guarded disapproval of having to be there. That seemed to continue on into the weekly sessions. He seemed not to have too much confidence in his reading and writing skills. He would piggyback on another's statement with his own expressions of disgust with the whole process: courts, the program, divorce, all of it. Later on he seemed to push through his disgust and become more authentic in laying out his feelings of despair and conflict over not getting to see his kids.

Mr. Sagen wrote his Responsibility Letter as follows:

> Angee:
>
> We were together for years and I could not believe you would leave me for someone else. On Monday you told me you were leaving me for someone you had feelings for at your work. I was devastated. All the next week my frustration grew and the lack of communication you would give me. I should have given you more space.
>
> The boiling point for my anger grew all week to a climax on Friday and Saturday of that week. On Friday I thought you wanted to talk to me because you asked if I could stay home from work. You then asked if I could stay home so you could go out with this new guy no more than four days after you said you were leaving me. I was crushed.
>
> On Saturday I went out that night with some friends to have a couple of beers and blow off some steam which was probably not a smart thing to do. When I came home I wanted to talk, to my happiness, you seemed really responsive until the conversation started going downhill. You then said you could not do this to the other guy you were seeing which really hurt me after all the time we spent together.
>
> You went into the bathroom and I followed you in there and we had a fight, which escalated, and I pushed you into the bathtub. You ran out to call the police and I followed you and yanked the phone cord out of the wall, you said

then that if T.J. found out I pushed you he would come and kick my ass. I felt so much rage at this I told you I would kill him and smashed the kitchen table in half and left.

You then called police and filed a restraining order against me. I understand now that you needed your space and did not have to justify your leaving to me. You had every right to leave. What I did was wrong and not something I will never be able to make up to you. But I will try in the years to come when dealing with   our children

Love Shane.

Mr. Sagen also wrote an Empathy Letter, a letter as if from Angee to himself.

Dear Shane,

When I wanted to leave. All you wanted to do was talk your way of it. I just wanted to follow my heart and you suffocated me.

On Saturday night you scared and angered me by pushing, not letting me call the police, and breaking table. You have broke many things over the years including my heart.

I do not want to be with you anymore no matter what you say or do. Just try to be a good father to our kids.

Angee

Robin Stemmes

Mr. Robin Stemmes was arrested for slapping his girlfriend (Initial Interview). Mr. Stemmes is a 75-year-old white male. He was born in eastern Washington in June 1926. He was the eldest of seven children. His mother had five children before he was five years old.   "Needless to say, she had a very hard time both physically and mentally coping," he noted. He continued, "Being the oldest, I was forced to take more responsibility than I was ready for. It was Depression years and we had very little money and no money to waste on babysitters or help of any kind. I was babysitter and sometimes cook for my younger siblings. I feel that this was my foundation for being bossy and take-charge, and somewhat intolerant of others' shortcomings."

Mr. Stemmes' parents didn't get along. When they argued Mr. Stemmes' father would go away on long walks or to the basement where he would stay for hours.

> Sometimes he would not talk to mom or the kids for days. So I did not have a very good relationship with my father. There was no touching or show of affection from my father. I am sure that then made it very difficult for me to show affection in later years for my wife and kids. I have a very good relationship with my six kids now but I still have difficulty forming warm and meaningful relations with women. To overcome my difficulties with women and to overcome my natural shyness, I drink more than I should. (History of Hurts and Beliefs Letter)

Mr. Stemmes separated from his wife when he about 65 years old. They never divorced because of Ms. Stemmes' protestations of suicide or homicide. Mr. Stemmes dropped the idea of divorcing her. Eventually Ms. Stemmes developed Alzheimer's disease. He noted that after his six children were grown and had moved, little was left to hold the relationship together, and that he had developed a relationship with an old friend. Of his relationship with Madge, he related:

> The first time I saw you was over 20 years ago. You and your family moved to the golfing community, small golfing community in Idaho. I thought then that you were very attractive. Over the next 10 years we were together often in group situations and became good friends. About that time my wife and I were not getting along well — the last of the kids married and left home and we had little left to keep us together. About the same time you and your husband were having you own problems and eventually ended up in divorce. We came together naturally and eventually moved in together. I had filed for divorce but ran into trouble with my wife did not want a divorce and fought it bitterly — threatening suicide and murder. So I dropped the suit and agreed to pay her enough so that she could live apart comfortable. (Responsibility Letter)

However, the fact that Mr. Stemmes never consummated the divorce with his wife resulted in ongoing conflict with his girlfriend Madge. He talked about the impact of his lack of divorce on his new relationship.

> Our situation being unable to marry legally has been a strain on both of us. Any problem that I can't resolve frustrates me. Madge always resented the fact that I couldn't divorce. From that time on we had a very rocky relationship. We fought often and broke up several times, once for a year. When she yelled at me I became so terrified and so full of rage I couldn't speak, I just had to leave the house. I went back to my wife. We tried counseling and I agreed to go to an anger management course, but nothing seemed to work.

> I remember Madge and I purchased the home on the golf course in Eastern Washington. We thought this would be the glue to make it work. I deeded you ½ interest in the home, and we were happy for a while. But the old problem, no divorce, kept coming between us. We drank more than we should have. (Responsibility Letter)

Mr. Stemmes then related the incident that brought him to counseling for domestic violence. He talked often of how traumatized he would become at the inability to solve his and Madge's problem. The pain would be so great that he on many occasions he just had to walk out and leave. He noted:

> The night that I slapped you, we both had been drinking. We had a particularly bad argument and I slapped you. After many heated words I just lost it. When you called 911 I didn't try to stop you; I knew I was wrong and had it coming.

> I went to jail and our lives changed for the next year. Going to jail was the most humiliating experience of my life and I vowed to never go back again. (Responsibility Letter)

After the arrest and jail time and a restraining order Mr. Stemmes moved back with his wife, who had Alzheimer's. She had to be cared for at all times. He noted that sometimes he had to hide her shoes or she would just walk off down the street and get lost. One significant event stands out in my mind. In one of the group sessions I had some music playing when the men arrived. That served as a query to them about any emotions they got in touch with listening to the song — I think it was a Willie Nelson song. Some began to tell of "their song" with a significant other. When it came to Mr. Stemmes' turn he said the song between him and his wife was *The Gypsy.* The lyrics say that in a "quaint caravan there is a woman they call the Gypsy. She tells you all your heart's desire." I just happen to have the CD with that song on it and I played it for the group. As the song played, Mr. Stemmes began to experience deep emotions. He lower lip quivered and the sides of his cheeks puffed in and out as he tried to contain his sobs. I identified with him and almost cried too. I still feel deep pathos as I recall that event. After trying to divorce his wife, living with another woman, and eventually putting his wife in a nursing home, here he was crying about the love he felt for his wife some 50 years before. He continued:

> Madge and I still see each other. After one year we are trying again to make it work; after all the problems we have gone through, I still love her and I think she still loves me. (Responsibility Letter)

Mr. Stemmes related his remorse and empathy for the pain he caused Madge and his plan for future healing.

> I can only imagine how hurt you were to be slapped by me. I knew that I would be terribly angry if the situation were reversed. I want you to know that whether or not we get back together, I am deeply sorry for what I did and that it will never happen again. I will try to listen to you and understand how frustrated you must be with our situation. My goals for the future are to control my anger; when arguments start to escalate – walk away and cool off. I will try to listen better when you want to talk, be patient and not try to offer solutions, but just listen. I will be mindful of my drinking. I plan to do things together instead of drinking, for instance play golf or card games. I want to give you more space and your private time. I will try to take a walk each day; we both need the exercise and fresh air. (Empathy Letter)

In conclusion Mr. Stemmes noted the following:

> My wife is now in permanent nursing care for Alzheimer's disease and we cannot divorce. Madge has learned to accept this: however, it is a subject that is not discussed any more than absolutely necessary. I lived with my wife until she found permanent care. She has been placed in permanent care as I am finishing my classes here. I am moving back to the home I purchased with Madge. I am working to be more loving and understanding of Madge and her needs. (History of Hurts and Beliefs Letter)

From the information provided by these six participants, insights will be explored about the underlying constructs that have a powerful influence on their lives and violent behavior.

CHAPTER V
ANALYSIS OF INTERNAL
PSYCHOLOGICAL CONSTRUCTS

What are internal psychological constructs? This section will examine the following subjects. 1) An introduction to the concept of constructs. 2) An introduction to the concept of internal psychological constructs. 3) The eight themes as they emerged from the stories of the participants. Themes one and two develop the origin, nature, and outcomes of the psychological constructs. Themes three through eight explore aspects and manifestations of the two major constructs.

An examination into the concept of constructs will begin with exploration of the concept of constructs in general. Reality's building blocks, from atoms to molecules to physical objects to biological life, lead one to the apex of biological life, the self-awareness of humans (Wilber, 1996). Human mental capabilities developed via the transcendence of the bicameral mind (Jayne's, 1976; Wilber, 1981) and resulted in the ability of humans to have self-observational awareness. Consequently, beginning with nature and progressing through ascending degrees of complexity, one arrives at the human physical organism as the beginning place of discovery. All knowledge in the form of experience is rooted in the senses and grounded in the physical organism.

Specifically, then, epistemology, the study of the origins of the knowledge, progressed through the realm of empiricism, where Locke, Berkeley, and Hume came up with concepts about gaining knowledge through the senses — sight, sound, touch, smell, and taste. Epistemology "progressed through" so we could go beyond the radical empiricism of Bishop Berkeley's *esse percipi*, "to be — esse, is to be perceived — percipi" hence: no *percipi,* no *esse* – for example, if a person is not being perceived by an outside perceiver, that person doesn't exist (Thinly & Wood, 1957, p. 360). It was then a possibility to move beyond David Hume's radical empiricism that might be explained as follows: All one can say with regard to the game of pool is that the cue ball travels to the eight ball and stops, a sound is heard, and the eight ball moves away. Empiricism does not account for the transference of energy from the cue ball to the eight ball. The transference of energy cannot be observed empirically. Of Hume, Thinly and Wood (1957) noted, "We discover nothing in our experience that justifies our notion of necessary connection or causation: cause and effect can mean nothing more than a regular succession of ideas" (p. 368).

The rationalists and subsequent thinkers provided a way out of this dilemma by positing mental map overlays of reality to provide a means by which non-empirical gaps may be filled and subsequently be discussed. So when the scientist wishes to address perceived realities not afforded by scientific observation, he "constructs" terms for those perceived realities. These terms are called the "language of constructs" and the "language of intervening variables" (Stanford, 1965, p. 40). Drop an apple *a la* Newton, for example, and it "drops." The construct of "gravity" initially is invented to account for the non-observable causation of the "drop." The same is true with human physiological phenomena such as hunger, thirst, sex, and pain (Sanford, 1961, p. 217).

Specifically, however, for the purposes of this study, interest was in the internal psychological constructs. A clue is taken via a "posthole" approach across the span of history that provides an insight into psychological constructs. Plato's Meno describes Socrates' response to Meno's question as to whether "virtue is acquired by teaching or by practice" (Seasons & Fleming, 19655). After some preliminary discourse Socrates calls one of Meno's attendants (a slave boy), draws a geometric figure, a square, on the ground, and elicits from the boy complex geometrical information merely by asking the boy questions. Socrates concludes, "This spontaneous recovery of knowledge in him is recollection . . . his soul must have always possessed this knowledge" (Seasons & Fleming, 1965, pp. 22, 23). Here we see a concept in the philosophy of education *educere* "e-" out, plus *ducere* "to lead," to lead or draw out, an early hint at internal psychological constructs.

Moreover, several centuries later St. Theresa of Avila described her mystical experience of how an angel pierced her heart with a flaming golden arrow, which caused her to scream but was accompanied with such sweetness she wanted it to last forever and resulted in her *Interior Castles* (Peers, 1961). *Interior Castles* describes seven internal mansions or seven spiritual levels of internal awareness—internal psychological constructs.

Gibb (1978) described a ten-level hierarchy of what he called the "environmental quality" (p. 40) of a person or group designated as a template for human consciousness. His hierarchy described a continuum with internal psychological trust at one pole and fear at the other. His ten levels of interior consciousness were expressed in individuals and society with the following terms:

1) punitive, e.g. the prison system — "Punishment as a form of control and socialization";
2) autocratic, e.g. military systems — "Power and authority used to maintain control and order";
3) benevolent, e.g. some Japanese corporations — "Parental nurturing and caring as a primary theme";
4) advisory, e.g. modern business consultative systems — "Focus on consultative help and data collection";
5) participative, e.g. work groups (such as Saab auto manufacturing) — "Focus upon participation, consensual decision-making, and choice";
6) emergent, e.g. "Rise of group and community as new and leaderless level of reality and interaction";
7) organic, e.g. "Rise of major role of empathic and intuitive modes of being and communicating";
8) holistic, e.g. "Integration of unconscious, archetypal and latent processes into enriched living";
9) transcendental, e.g. "Integration of altered and extra-sensory states into being and consciousness";
10) cosmic, e.g. no sense of separation as of a person praying to God for love, joy, or peace. In the cosmic level the person is one with love, joy, and peace, and has a "Focus on cosmic, universal, and nirvana states of community and being" (p. 47).

The determining factors for Gibbs's hierarchy are modulated by a personalized fear/trust continuum from which realities are perceived and actions evolve. Each level marks an interior hierarchy of constructs.

Also important for this discussion are the insights of Carl Jung (Adler, Fordham, & Read, 1953-1971), as evidenced in his discussion of archetypes. His archetypes are consonant with the use of constructs.

> Everyman carries within him the eternal image of the woman, not the image of this or that particular woman, but a definite feminine image. This image is fundamentally unconscious, an hereditary factor of primordial origin imprinted and engraved in the living organic system of the man, an imprint or archetype of all the ancestral experiences of the female, a deposit, as it were, of all the impressions ever made by woman .... Since this image is unconscious, it is always unconsciously projected upon

the person of the beloved, and is one of the chief reasons
for passionate attraction or aversion. (Vol. 17, p. 198)

More could be said of Mallow's (1978) hierarchy of needs: Berne's
(1961) parent, adult, and child ego states; Tart's (1983) transpersonal
psychologies; Keyes' (1975) levels of consciousness; Johnson's (1991) 1)
two-dimensional man (Don Quixote), 2) three-dimensional man (Hamlet),
and 3) four dimensional man (Faust); Perls' (1969) psychic "holes" (p. 39),
disowned or unlived aspects of the personality; Glaser's (1970) "ego gaps"
(p. 60); and Kurgan's "construct of shame" (Levant & Pollack, 1995, p.
96).

Wilber (1995) is a key leading synthesizer of human interiority. Many
insights regarding internal psychological constructs may be gained from
Wilber's hierarchy. Wilber (1995) presents his unified epistemology as
a four-quadrant model. He begins with the notion of one who observes
phenomena — an external viewpoint. This means *looking at* phenomena,
whether individuals or social collectives, as an outside observer. It is a
quantitative scientific approach — weighing, measuring, comparing,
and naming. On the other hand Wilber also examines the interiority
of individuals and social collectives. He uses a qualitative, interior,
looking with a view from within outward. He develops a hierarchy of
the possible interior consciousnesses of individuals. His hierarchy of
internal consciousness, from the bottom up, goes as follows: "prehension,
irritability, rudimentary sensation, sensation, perception, perception/
impulse, impulse/emotion, emotion/image, symbols, concepts" (Wilber,
1996). Of his model he states,

> Emotions pertain to the interior experience of the limbic
> system. These emotions and the awareness that goes with
> them are . . . *experiences from within*, on the *inside*, in its
> *interior* . . . . You can only *feel* these feelings from within.
> When you experience a sort of primal joy, for example,
> even if you are a brain psychologist, you do not say to
> yourself, Wow, what a limbic day. Rather you describe
> these feelings in intimate, personal, emotional terms,
> *subjective* terms: I feel wonderful, it's great to be alive . .
> . . Each level also transcends and include its predecessor,
> each follows the . . . *interior depth* that is *consciousness*
> itself. (p. 76)

Given these preliminary observations, therefore, interior psychological
constructs are usually non-verbalizable hierarchical levels or aspects of

the human psychological urges grounded in the physiology of the person. An internal psychological construct is the physiological experience of a feeling, a mood, a longing, a want, repulsion, a passion, or a discomfort. These wants may fall out on a continuum of the most primitive aspects of survival to the most transcendent experiences of unitary oneness. The list may involve endless nuances.

Wilber (1996) not only delineates his hierarchy of interior psychological awarenesses, he (1986) also provides a psychological multi-stage chronology of human development noting each stage, e.g. infancy, practicing, rapprochement, oedipal and so forth, with optimal qualities of successful stage negotiation, and the psychological pathologies of the miss-navigation of the specific stages. Wilber (1981) describes the stages of human growth and development, both optimal and pathological, and the internal individual awareness that results as his "spectrum of consciousness" (p. 8). It is not until a person is fairly well developed that the "total organism" level of consciousness (p. 8), or what Wilber characterized as the "centaur" level of consciousness, is realized. A centaur is a horse with the head and shoulders of a man. Prior to the centaur level the human psyche is presented as a rider on the back of a horse, i.e. an experience of a person with a quasi mind-body split. Such a one's head is the horseman and the body is the horse, two separate entities, often characterized as being physiologically somatized, unattuned to the body, disconnected from the body, and having no sense of affect and no words for feelings.

Ichazo (1991) elaborates on this phenomenon when he posits that the human anatomy, rather than cognitive conceptual descriptions, e.g. ego and so forth, is the template, the holding environment of life experiences. He noted that in his "conservation" (p. 95) stage the infant's earliest traumas manifest as gastrointestinal emotional lesions or pain. Later the father relationship comes to play in the child's life, described in Ichazo's "relations" (p. 95) stage as being represented by cardiovascular health or weakness. Ichazo's final stage, the "adaptation instinct" (p. 96) or the brain-mind-body union, is reflected in the central nervous system connection. It is the physiological experience often beyond the descriptive awareness of many men that is fundamental to this understanding. This pre-centaur level is central to the theory and therapeutic work of many theorists (Diamond, 1979; Grof & Grof, 1989; Grof, 1990; Ichazo, 1991; Keleman, 1975; Lowen, 1958, 1967, 1975; 1977; Masterson, 1976, 1981, 1988, 1989; Reich, 1949).

This leads to a significant impasse. If there is a masculine consciousness characterized earlier by Levant's (1997) "restricted emotions" (p. 6) or limited emotional illiteracy; Pollack's (1998) loss of "emotional expressiveness" (p. 11); Kindlon & Thompson's (1999) "emotional withdrawal" (p. xiv); Gurian's (1999) "emotional masking" (p. 270); and Levant's (1995) "Alexithymia" — no words for feelings (p. 50), where does that leave many men? Unable to talk about feelings, they are stuck and frustrated.

The answer to this significant impasse, this dilemma, may come from Polanyi (1958, 1966), who presents the issue and then a solution. Polanyi (1966) summarizes the issue in his famous phrase: "We know more than we can tell" (p. 4). He then explores an epistemology that seeks to address what cannot be said. The tacit nature of knowledge is by definition inexpressible; "We know but cannot tell." That which can be described is explicit knowledge. The explicit dimensions of knowledge may be thought of as science. The task of making knowledge explicit has been developed extensively. It involves a branch of philosophy referred to as methodology and seeks to make ideas clear through logic, induction, deduction, analysis, synthesis, analogy, comparison, and the selecting and qualifying hypotheses. Language philosophy and semantics are also involved in the explication of knowledge. The attempt to talk about the tacit, the non-explicit, is examined from three vantage points in this study. How do many men in general communicate their inner world? How does a researcher get at this interior informational dimension? And, then, how does one communicate this non-explicit interior?

"Tacit" knowing by definition is non-explicit. Polanyi (1966) employs the concepts of "emergence"(p. 45), "indwelling" (p. 17), and the "focal/subsidiary" (1958, p. 55) as a means of communicating the non-explicit. The summation of Polanyi's methodology used here is to approach constructs indirectly through illustration, paradigm, metaphor, example, and their mirroring effect in the explicit. The discussion of internal psychological constructs now leads to the experiences of the six participants.

As I entered into the interiority of the six participants, several significant themes began to emerge. These themes gave clues to aspects of each man's interior self that the external events awakened. The subject matter of these themes marked out the consciousness of each person and prescribed the reality of his world. It is possible the internal constructs in some way created the events through contagion.

The first major theme has been labeled the ecstasy construct. The second major theme was the agony construct. The third major theme was the outcome of the agony construct, the unexpected experience of being arrested, going to jail, facing a judge, and being placed on probation and the organism-as-a-whole experience that event elicited. The fourth

175

major theme was the trigger point for the agony construct. The fifth major theme was also a sub-theme of the agony construct disillusionment, anger and acting-out. The sixth theme dealt with the psychological origins of the internal constructs. The seventh theme was the predictable patterns of internal constructs each person brought with him when entering into therapy.

Theme One: The Ecstasy Construct

The origin, nature, and outcomes of the ecstasy construct will now to be considered. Many terms are employed to designate these constructs: "goddesses . . . angels, Madonnas . . . Gypsy maidens, earth mothers" (Keen, 1991, p. 16). The term "ecstasy construct" was chosen here for the seeming impact it had on the men's lives. With regard to the origins of the ecstasy construct, the review of the literature noted the centuries-long development and nature of the masculinity stereotype. Humanness evolved with the realization of the father role in the family social group. The survival of the family group, tribe, society involved for centuries the male "going out," hunting, gathering, working in the field, later the factory, going to war, and returning to the hearth. At the hearth, the division of labor involving the nurturing of the young and so forth was embodied in the other significant part of the family social group — the mother. Centuries of behavioral conditioning, the development and perpetuation of mores, and the hardening of masculinity prescriptions shaped male consciousness and behaviors. Culturally sanctioned perspectives of male behavior perpetuated the socialization process in male development, assumptions about male behavior, and parenting styles for males.

These centuries of psychological conditioning resulted in a template of present human consciousness. Wilber et al. (1986) developed what he called (using the electromagnetic spectrum as a metaphor) the "full-spectrum model" of human growth and developmental psychology. It was developmental, structural, hierarchical, and system-oriented. It blended the findings of both East and West. It employed the concept of the Great Chain of Being, similar to a ladder of increasingly complex structures. It involved, first off, basic structures that, having once emerged in the human organism, remain in existence as relatively autonomous units that remain with the person and serve as operands for new and higher levels of development. Wilber employed the term "eros" (love/life) to designate the human developmental process of integration, consolidation, pulling together, preserving, and synthesizing.

Secondly, in the spectrum model, Wilber discussed the concept of transitional structures. These are phase-specific and phase-temporary structures. They are replaced by subsequent phases. He employed the term *thanatos* (death) to denote the process of these structures being differentiated, separated, negated, dissolved, and subsumed into permanent structures. Both *eros* (integrating) and *thanatos* (differentiating) serve phase-specific tasks. Mental health is the successful negotiation of these phase-specific transitions. Pathologies develop if either eros or thanatos is misnavigated and result in a developmental lesion — fixation, or psychopathology. Wilber stated, "Negotiating these structual developments is the self (or self-system), which is the locus of identification, volition, defense organization, and 'metabolism' ('digestion' of experience at each level of structural growth and development)" (p. 67). Wilber's synthesis provided an overview of the contemporary conclusions regarding the process of the developing stages, possibilities, and pathologies of human consciousness.

Still considering the origin of the ecstasy construct, little boys have a different developmental journey than little girls. Males have an experience no female has ever had. They spend the first nine months of their existence within the anatomy of a member of the other sex. From this other-sex parent they must negotiate a separation drama to become an individualized human being. In this separation journey, *al la* Wilber, every phase is significant; however, one phase stands out. It is the practicing phase — from the 12th to the 24th month. It is referred to as the age of narcissism, or the "junior toddler's oyster" during which "Narcissism is at its peak" (Mahler, 1975, p. 17). At this point this little boy is mobile, with abundant energy, and totally curious. He is not self-conscious. He can play in the yard with no clothes on and it doesn't matter to him. He has very limited ability to reflect upon himself. His moods change dramatically. This phase is the precursor to and the pathway into the next phase, the "psychological birth of the human infant" (p. 104).

The dominant pervasive cocoon is the mother. She feeds, clothes, guides, protects, bathes, wipes, holds, consoles — she is everything to this small child. This practicing phase remains eternal in the male psyche. As a gosling is imprinted by the mother goose, this little boy is imprinted by the all-encompassing mother. The little boy, plays in ecstasy, making small forays away from the mother only to return quickly for refueling, climbs on her, pulls on her, and trusts her as his whole world. Forever, she lives in his soul, and it is she through which he views his world and especially other women.

   With regard now to the nature of the ecstasy construct, the internal psychological female is an unlived, disowned, split off, psychological structure — a construct. It is Jung's (1959) archetype the anima: "She intensifies, exaggerates, falsifies, and mythologizes all emotional relationships with his work and with other people of both sexes" (p. 70). Keen (1991) stated it as follows:

> The secret men seldom tell, and often do not know (consciously) is the extent to which our lives circle around our relationships to WOMAN. It takes half a lifetime of struggle for us to win a separate identity. We are haunted by woman in her many manifestations. She is the center around which our lives circle. Woman is the mysterious ground of our being that we cannot penetrate. She is the audience before whom the dramas of our lives are played out. She is the judge who pronounces us guilty or innocent. She is the Garden of Eden from which we are exiled and the paradise for which our bodies long. She is the goddess who can grant us salvation and the frigid mother who denies us. She is at once terrifying and fascinating.

> One of the major tasks of manhood is to explore the unconscious feeling that surround our various images of WOMAN, to dispel false mystification, to dissolve the vague sense of threat and fear, and finally to learn to respect and love the strangeness of womankind [a specific woman]. It may be useful to think about the sexual-spiritual maturation — the journey of manhood — as the process of changing WOMAN into women into Jane (or one certain woman), of learning to see members of the opposite sex not as archetypes or members of a class but as individuals. It is the WOMAN in our heads, more than the women in our beds or boardrooms, who causes most of our problems. And these archetypical creatures — goddesses, bitches, angels, Madonnas, castrators, witches, Gypsy maidens, earth mothers — must be exorcised from our minds and hearts before we can learn to love women. So long as our house is haunted by the ghost of WOMAN we can never live gracefully with any woman. If we

continue to deny that she lives in the shadows she will
continue to have power over us. (pp. 15-16)

It is the practicing phase (12- 24 months) that infuses and imprints
the goddess/mother into the souls of men. It is this lens through which
a man may observe women, dream of women, be mystified by women,
and long for a woman. This internal psychological construct and energy
force field differs for all men, compelling on the one hand desperate
pursuits, and on the other gentle longings. She is always there. It is the
template for viewing, comparing, measuring, and assessing women, and
especially one's intimate partner. It takes "half a lifetime" (Keen, 1991 p.
15) to integrate her/it into a man's consciousness. For many men there is
a sense of terror connected with the anima. "The male resists closeness
and dependency on the female *because once the unconscious defense is*
penetrated by a woman he becomes profoundly attached to the point of
deep and almost total dependency" (Goldberg, 1976, p. 12).

With the discussion of the origin and nature of the ecstasy construct
as a background, the outcome of this construct as it found expression in
the participants' lives is explored. Each of the participants had his unique
way of describing the initial encounter with his significant other that led
to their intimate relationship.

A year after my first wife died of cancer I received the
manifestation of one of my prayers. I had prayed for a
Christian woman to come into my life. I met her at the
church for the first time. I realize now that when I prayed
for a Christian woman I didn't have a clue. I remember
she was wearing a woman's Navy blue dress jacket with
lieutenant bars. Since I more or less grew up in the
military my approach and the ensuing conversation with
her came rather easy. I was immediately attracted to her.
Her smile and laughter was fascinating. I was captivated
by her beauty, exuberance and charm. I could hardly take
my eyes off of her.

Our first meeting eventually led to our first date. I
was happily surprised when she agreed to go with me
after church for a sandwich and coffee before she went
home. This was a scary time for me. I was clumsy
and embarrassed and I felt guilty since she was the first
woman I had been out with in 42 years except my wife.
Her lovely smile and the easy conversation did finally

> bring us together on future dates. In July she accepted
> my engagement ring and in October we were married in
> our church. (Arvil Stimpson, Responsibility Letter)

Mr. Stimpson's encounter would seem to carry much greater implications than the average man meeting a woman. When one prays to God, and it seems God responds, this encounter is not a man meeting a woman: It is a divine event sanctioned by the Creator and Final Arbiter of the cosmic universe. The construct itself and the meeting itself is elevated to transcendent proportions.

> I dated quite a few women in high school and found
> myself doing everything I could to please them. I was
> always watching what I said when my girlfriend was
> around . . . . I held out a belief that this woman would
> love me unconditionally and see me as a god in a sense.
> I thought she would do anything for me. As much as I
> wanted to believe that there might be someone out there
> for me, I never thought I would find her. I found my wife
> and married her. (Art Yount, Responsibility Letter)

A clue might be derived from Mr. Yount's expectations as to the internal woman construct he carried with him. Mr. Yount's ecstasy construct also carried with it elements of the divine, "see me as a god in a sense." The nature and origin of this internal female construct carries with it a heat-seeking phenomenon that magnetizes one person to another.

> I did something I never thought I'd do. I got married to
> a woman. I was, basically what I saw was, I saw blonde
> hair, blue eyes, two-piece, G-string bikini walking up the
> dock. There was probably, I don't know, 100 yards of
> dock going out to the marina where I had a crew, three or
> four guys under me, trying to, you know, kept them busy
> and everything, rent out the rental boats, ran the gas dock.
> I'm looking around, you know, where in the hell's all my
> guys. I'm just swamped. I popped around the corner, and
> they're all standing there on this pontoon boat, looking at
> what's coming up the main walkway. So, I take a look,
> and it's this gal in a little, two-piece, G-string bikini, and
> I said, "You guys might as well go back to work 'cause
> I'm gonna marry that woman someday," and sure as shit,
> Herb, I did it. And she was just, holy smokes, Constance

Baker, or Connie for short. I married her. (Sid Belini,
taped interview)

This is an example of "love at first sight." It again gives a clue to the
male's inner female psychological construct. And "there she is": from
across a crowded room the trigger mechanism sets off a total physiological
response. On a continuum from genuine interest to the powerful pain of
"love at first sight," the male organism is not a passive viewer. Activation
of a significant physiological force field of energy takes place. If pursued
and acquired, the woman becomes the most significant bond in the man's
life.

This instant internal activation is reminiscent of MacLean's (1980) triune
brain research into the "primal mind, emotional mind, and a rational mind"
(p. 12) that suggests a nanosecond reptilian brain response. More recently
Aharon, Etcoff, Ariely, Chabrid, O'Connor, and Breiter (2001) conducted a
study that reveals that for many men the sight of a beautiful woman activates
a primal "reward circuitry activity" (p. 15) in a manner like that of cocaine
or food. It is a "primal mind" response — reptilian brain activation that is
a priori to neo-cortex activity, or a learned response. It is a force field of
varying degrees of psychic energy. The frontal lobe acts as an *a posteriori*
steering mechanism to pursue and acquire the object of interest.

> I was brought up with the conception that an intimate
> relationship could only be carried out with honesty and
> respect for your partner. In all my past relationships, I
> carried high expectations of my partners to not disrespect
> me around other men and to not lie to me.

> When I met you, I fell in love instantly and wanted to
> give you my best, my honest and my full commitment.
> My past relations with girlfriends have always been long
> term. I expected you to be my only love, and for me to
> never have to lie to you or you lie to me. I wanted you to
> put me in the place as your man and your one and only.

> Our relationship started out just about as wonderful as
> one can hope to wish for. I loved you more than I had
> loved any other human being before. I would tell you
> this, and I also stated that I believe you were my soul
> mate. You were very young at the time.

> When I met you, I was ready for you to give me your best. We were going to make this work, and perhaps marry each other. (Rondel De Marco, Responsibility Letter)

Again, whatever this internal psychological female is, she is a sublime, captivating being. The next two individuals had a slightly different experience. Circumstances led them together and love eventually resulted.

> I didn't really fall in love with her. I mean we got together and two weeks later, she got pregnant. I mean we had both just got off drugs. She was doing the same thing. You know and since I quit and I heard she quit then it been like two or three weeks since she quit, and I figured well if you need anybody to talk to, she can always call me, because I was dead set on ever doing it again. So, she'd, well give me a call. Well, we... she ended up coming over and watching a movie with me, and that was it. Then two... three weeks after that, that's when she got pregnant. I loved her, don't get me wrong, but it was a nightmare. I grew to love her after time. (Shane Sagen, taped interview)

> The first time I saw you was over 20 years ago. You and your family moved to the community. I thought then that you were very attractive. Over the next 10 years we were together often in group situations and became good friends. We came together naturally and eventually moved in together. (Robert Stemmes, Responsibility Letter)

Each participant made statements about the attitudes and beliefs they held about the women they hoped to find. The statements about the women in their lives reveal an idealistic expression of the ecstasy construct.

Mr. Stimpson wanted a "Christian woman." He stated: "I believe all of us from the time we are at puberty have a mental acceptance or belief about the one person we would consider spending the rest of our lives with. . . . When I met you, I was walking around looking at you through my expectations. I actually expected you to act and behave in a certain way."

> I dated quite a few women in high school and found myself doin' everything I could to please them. I was

always watching what I said when my girlfriend was around. (Art Yount, Responsibility Letter)

Glenda Eades was . . . pretty much larger than life. (Sid Belini, taped interview)

I was brought up with the conception that an intimate relationship could only be carried out with honesty and respect for your partner. In all my of past relationships I carried high expectations of my partners to not disrespect me around other men and to not lie to me. (Rondel De Marco Responsibility Letter)

Mr. Sagen didn't state clearly his expectations regarding women. He did state that there was a Connie, his first girlfriend: "I had been wanting to go out with her since like the fourth grade. I was like so in love with her. She was so cool." This would indicate some unexpressed ideal in Mr. Sagen that Connie awakened. However, he never stated in the interview any clear map-like expectation about his ideal woman.

Mr. Stemmes also did not clearly state or at least record his belief system regarding the nature and behavior patterns for his ideal woman. They are inferred by indirect reference as to what made him attracted to her and what made him angry about her behaviors.

What, then, is the nature and what are the roots of this "ecstasy" construct? What is this magnetic power of a woman over a man? It is a power that voids all risks! It is Ovid's Pyramus and Thisbe, the death-by-love bond, and the precursor to Romeo and Juliet. It is Cleopatra and Mark Antony. It is the love bond between Justinian and Theodora, the sailor and the hooker who built the Hagia Sophia, the church of Holy Wisdom in Constantinople; of Peter Abelard and Heloise; of Dulcinea, the unreachable love quest of Don Quixote; of Voltaire's Candide and Cunagonde. This magnetic attraction force is mysterious in its source and expression.

In sum, the ecstasy construct is an internal psychological phenomenon born of centuries of repetitive masculine behaviors ingrained in the developmental and socialization process of men's lives, perpetuated by current parenting styles and planted there in the boy before he knew what was happening. It is a resident goddess-like vacuum that may be triggered by the phenomenon of a woman passing though a male's field of vision that activates the long buried anima, unlocks powerful force flows of energy that often defy common sense or explication, and motivates the pursuit. The simple means by which the essence of this ecstasy construct is expressed compared to its profound origin and depth of its content may be captured with the phrase, "I love you." It is the mechanism and template some men use to evaluate all women, and especially the intimate partner. It is evident in the second half of the trite/profound saying, "You can't *live* with them and you *can't live* without them."

Theme Two: The Agony Construct

The origin, nature, and outcomes of the agony construct will now be considered. Other terms also have been used for this construct: "bitches . . . castrators, witches" (Keen, 1991, p. 16). Once again, the centuries of masculinity conditioning resulted in the following dicta: Avoid anything feminine, eschew expressions of emotion, be strong, stoic, and aggressive, be able to stand alone, be self-reliant, compete and pursue status, don't be tied to a woman, have nonrelational sex, and be homophobic (Levant, 1997). Male children did, early on, experience a greater degree of expression of emotion, lability, and sensitivity (Haviland & Malatesta, 1981). They were in the practicing phase (12-24 months), and became imprinted by a mother who mostly appropriately met the child's needs. The mother became the all-loving goddess and the children were set up with the expectation that the reality of the practicing phase would continue. However, that was lost through the "crossover" (Levant, 1995), and may be completely forgotten by most men. The next phase of the child's development, the rapprochement phase (24-36 months), set the stage for potential bitter conflict. The rapprochement phase is the time in the child's life when the individualization process becomes more acute. It is the earliest phase of psychological separation from the mother. It is the first phase of the significant psychological birth toward true individuality. It is seldom negotiated smoothly. It is fraught with temper tantrums, things being thrown, a pulling away, and a chorus of "Nos."

Additionally, with regard to the origin of the agony construct, not only is Junior experiencing the pulling away behavior, but also mother has now lost her cuddly, lovable little baby. He now is a rogue from Hell and mother reacts logically by employing discipline; she "pushes" the boy away, potentially causing a lifelong trauma (Dutton, 1995; Pollack, 1998). This mother is now the child's mortal enemy even though he can't survive without her. She blocks him from his desires; the struggle becomes a life or death experience, and she becomes the wicked witch. The great nurturer and protector of the practicing phase becomes the great destroyer and devourer in the rapprochement phase (Sullivan, 1953).

This begins the rocky separation drama from the mother. The trauma of maternal separation results in a post-traumatic stress syndrome and pervades the male's life (Dutton, 1995; Pollack, 1998). When human developmental phases are accompanied by abuse, humiliation, shame, and isolation, rather than weakening the parental attachment to the female parent, these childhood experiences intensify the attachment need. According to Dutton (1995), "These experiences are replete with feelings of yearning, frustration, and abandonment, with love, fear, and rage, and they inscribe themselves indelibly in the psyches of wife abusers" (p. 96).

The nature, then, of the agony construct finds many men who have not finished the separation drama with their mothers working with that unfinished situation with any woman who comes into their life. The objectification of women by men, mentioned earlier, becomes, it seems, the logical outcome of this person's serious experience of objectification at this age, "the terrible twos." He could only absorb the trauma physiologically, and does not have the cognitive managerial skills to process and mediate those experiences. The degree of stress, pain, conflict, abandonment, and anger in a child's home may determine the degree of psychological distance, polarity, and antithesis he later feels toward everyone in society, and especially his intimate partner. There is a significant sense of distance, loneliness, and powerlessness. His intimate partner mitigates these feelings. To lose her is impotence and death. Therefore, as Eric Fromm (1973) stated, "The passion to have absolute and unrestricted control over a living being is the transformation of impotence into omnipotence" (pp. 322-323).

The nature of this agony construct becomes evident in the lives of the six research participants. With the disillusionment of the ecstasy construct, unexpected but certain conflict entered each relationship. The following statements reveal the agony resultant from the significant fragility and vulnerability they experienced around the behavior of an intimate partner.

> This was a scary time for me [first dates with new woman after wife died]. I was clumsy and embarrassed and I felt guilty since you were the first woman I had been out with in 42 years except my wife.

> I became very jealous, suspicious, and angry, doubting almost everything you told me. I attempted to control your every move, stalking and accusing you of being with

other men. We fought and my language and accusations became unscrupulous, unreasonable, and excessive. We had no peace or joy. Strife from anger and rage became the order of the day.

It was a frightening time. The stress was almost unbearable. I had no appetite and I took nighttime sleep aids like they were candy. There was a lot of confusion and my thought process was a mess. I would call you but you either weren't there or didn't wish to speak with me. T.V. was out the question; so was reading. I just couldn't stay focused. (Arvil Stimpson, Responsibility Letter)

Every time a girlfriend would so much as raise her voice at me, the hair on the back of my neck would stand up and I would immediately lash out. In short, I had a "screw them" type attitude and felt that women needed to be "put in their place."

I then told her that if she didn't like it I was going to take our son and move the hell out. At that point that the statement had been made I couldn't see her standing there anymore. She hit me a couple of times in the face and before she had a chance to blink I hit her back, knocking her back a couple of feet. I was so engulfed with rage she was no longer my wife, much less a human being. I hit her twice in the face, picked her up, ran her down the hall, and put her through the wall in the entryway. As she lay there crying, I remember being numb, angry, and feeling detached from her as a person. I kicked her in the head and walked outside. (Art Yount, Responsibility Letter)

On the way, you started talking about our finances, and this upset me. I called you a stupid bitch and told you to shut the fuck up. When we reached the bar, you said that we should break up. This enraged me.

I asked for the car keys, and you said no. So I walked outside, got into the car and pulled the fuse box. I was so angry I punched the rearview mirror and broke the windshield. Some people said they were calling the police, so I started walking home. When I arrived, I started drinking heavily, hoping to feel better about the situation. I then started destroying the house to get back at you. (Sid Belini, taped interview)

Men often inflict pain and destroy things as an ineffective way of getting the intimate partner to grasp, feel, and recognize the pain they think the woman is causing. They have no words; they act it out because "I just want her to understand and feel how bad she hurts me."

I got so angry and hurt that you were lying to me that I threw the cold water that I was drinking in your face. You just sat there in awe and then smiled with disbelief. I remember I felt like an out-of-control freak.

My whole world went down the tubes, and I felt like getting so far away from you.

Because I still feel pain and humiliation, I felt like I could never refill that space. (Rondel De Marco, Responsibility Letter)

Unbelievable pain [when she declared the relationship over]. Oh, just like somebody let off a nuclear weapon in my stomach. It was bad. I was always shaking, couldn't eat. I was just on edge. Oh I was freakin.' Yeah, it was bad, 'cause my mom and grandma were the ones that raised me, and they both had died the previous two years, so I had no family, none, except Andrea and the kids. So it was like losing them was like losing your arms and legs. I lived in that for about three months. I had to stay over there all the time. Oh I was going crazy. There was no doubt about that. I was just jittering. Couldn't focus on nothing, nothing. I couldn't do shit. Work was just a joke. I couldn't even function there. That went on for seven or eight months. (Shane Sagen, taped interview)

When she yelled at me I became so terrified and so full of rage I couldn't speak, I just had to leave the house then one time I slapped her. (Robin Stemmes, Responsibility Letter)

The agony and the ecstasy constructs, it seems, are flip sides of the same coin. If the ecstasy that results from the early encounters is great in that pleasure is a significant addictive elixir, it seems reasonable that the agony of contention, loss, and separation would be somewhat related in intensity. Maybe if the initial encounters were nice but mellow, the separation would be not so nice but not so devastating. Maybe if the little boy could have stayed in the loving cocoon during the rapprochement phase and have been allowed to do his separation drama at his own pace, the schism would not be a life-long reality (Pollack, 1998).

Goldberg found in his 1976 research that for every one woman who commited suicide over the loss of a love relationship, four men did. The agony is so great the tragic potential falls out on one of two poles, sometimes both. Projection of the pain, if carried to its logical conclusion, results in homicide, and if the person retroflects (turns everything back on himself) this retroflection of the pain, carried to its logical conclusion, is suicide. It's the same agony expressed as two different tragic outcomes.

Many women in counseling with their male partners say, "He won't listen to me, he won't talk to me, and he won't look at me when I talk to him." Most men say, "I just want her to be happy." The inability of men to listen, attend, and respond to an intimate partner is pervasive. One of the participants made this insightful presentation of his struggle:

> Since I have been coming to this program I have been really trying to talk to my wife at a feeling level. I used to just brush her off, tell her she was too emotional, or if she didn't know what she was talking about to keep quiet. Now I really try to listen, and I also try to share back also. When I try to share with her what's really going on with me it takes a while of talking for me to get around to it and tentatively approach my real feelings. Oh I can talk really well about most things in my life, but not about me to her. It's like trying to push through an enormous wall. It takes many false starts. I begin to feel giddish, bashful, stupid, and foolish. I catch myself grinning and I laugh a lot to cover things up. I think if I really told what I really feel I might disintegrate and die. She has to be patient, and it takes me a while even if she is patient.
>
> Her presence is so powerful to me that I get overwhelmed if I look at her while I am talking. I'm afraid of her disapproval. So I don't look at her. I make believe a little off to the side there is a wall between us. I look at the wall and not at her. I have to wall her off, or I can't think about

what I am trying to say. If I look at her I can't talk. Oh,
I can yell at her, but not this kind of talking. Sometimes
I can talk to a friend at work better. But that is *about*
feelings, not face-to-face feelings. When we separated I
could do a whole lot better talking to her over the phone.
Then I wouldn't get overloaded by seeing her facial
expressions about what I said. If she asks, for example,
"A penny for your thoughts," or "What are you thinking
about," I freeze. I can't come up with a thing. Trying to
say more than, "I love you," or "I'm madder than hell," is
the hardest thing I ever did. (Shane Sagan, session notes)

The outcome of this conflict reveals a significant polarity between
men and women. They breathe, eat, and do most things like each other and
many think they are alike or very similar; however, misunderstandings,
misinterpretations, and assumptions made about the other party abound.
Each partner has his or her own internal perceptions of the marriage.
The hardest obstacle to overcome is the belief that when the other partner
is continuing an unpleasant behavior he or she is "doing it on purpose."
Consequently, the agony construct is characterized by these revealing "tip
of the iceberg" statements of the men: "a scary, frightening, unbreakable
time," "my life went down the tubes," "Unbelievable pain . . . a nuclear
weapon in my stomach," "I was going crazy."

Theme Three: The Trigger Point

The third theme that emerged from the stories of the participants
involved the behavior of the female partner that activated strong negative
feelings. Whenever one of the participants encountered a behavior out
of character for the goddess ideal, that behavior triggered a terror-then-
rage response. They related the following statements said about them by
their intimate partners: "You are not going with me on the trip" (Arvil
Stimpson), "You said I was stupid and a jerk" (Art Yount), "You said we
should break up" (Sid Belini), "You chose to lie and keep things from me"
(Rondel De Marco), "I met somebody else and I'm leaving ya," (Shane
Sagen), "She argued with me" (Robin Stemmes).

Confrontations become triggering mechanisms. Interviews and
scientific research with polygraph electrodes (Gottman, 1999, 2000;
Jacobson, & Gottman, 1998) revealed that when one is negatively
confronted by an intimate partner, significant physiological trauma
results. The heart rate accelerates and an adrenal rush follows. When the

trauma sets in it takes several minutes for the male to be able to listen to the female partner. The typical male response to this trauma is to 1) fight; explain, tell, persuade, if not push, shove and hit, and so on; 2) flee; "I'm out of here"; 3) freeze; be unable to talk, be silent, be stuck. The resultant experience is often one of two polarities. One minute he is all loving, the next he is calling names. She is the goddess and then she becomes the bitch. These two positions can flip back and forth quite quickly.

This is consistent with the narcissistic, acting-out borderline personality characteristics (Masterson, 1989). Unable to express the life-long internal trauma, i.e. the male wound, the male often deals with the problem via aggressive anger. Two totally different realities are being experienced here. The female partner experiences a fear producing, insensitive, aggressive, controlling individual, and he comes across like Dr. Jekyll/Mr. Hyde, for example. The male partner is experiencing a Post Traumatic Stress death seizure. He feels traumatized, threatened, and betrayed; he is experiencing the dissolution of his world, his personality, and his life. He is entering a death siege that gets projected outward onto the partner. This may explain why four women a day in the United States are murdered by their intimate partners (Bachman & Saltzman, 1995; Straus, Gelles, & Steinmetz, 1980).

Theme Four: The Response Factor

The fourth theme that emerged from the experiences of the research participants revealed their reactions to the statements of their intimate partners. The participants reveal a limited response pattern to their intimate partner's statements. Once again their intimate partner statements: "You are not going with me on the trip" (Arvil Stimpson), "You said I was stupid and a jerk" (Art Yount), "You said we should break up" (Sid Belini), "You chose to lie and keep things from me" (Rondel De Marco), "I met somebody else and I'm leaving ya," (Shane Sagen), "She argued with me" (Robin Stemmes) reveal disapproval, rejection, and anger of the partner toward the men.

The responses respectively were: "I kicked things, threw things, slammed doors, cussed, and pushed you around" (Arvil Stimpson); "I pushed you and grabbed you by the hair, I hit her, knocking her back a couple of feet. I hit you twice in the face and picked you up and ran you down the hall and put you through the wall in the entryway . . . I kicked you in the head and walked outside" (Art Yount); "I was so angry I punched the rearview mirror and broke the windshield; I then started destroying the house to get back at you" (Sid Belini); "I got so angry I threw the cold water that I was drinking in your face" (Rondel De Marco); "I pushed her, I ripped the phone out of the wall, I smashed the table in half" (Shane Sagen); "I slapped you" (Robin Stemmes).

These statements reveal a regression into the agony construct and serve as an indicator of the degree of success in negotiating the separation transition the individual made from the practicing phase to the rapprochement phase, i.e. the separation drama from the mother. Lost in the narcissistic and symbiotic unity once experienced with the mother, the rage of the two-year-old temper tantrum continues. What the two-year-old could not talk about he acted out. Since he had to stuff his terror and rage at two, the emotions wait to be acted out on the next significant women in his life. At whatever age when men have no words for feelings (alexithymia), the feelings get acted out on the intimate partner. The significant psychological reaction reveals unfinished hurts and wounds from the past and indicates potential options for therapeutic work. These statements reveal only a minute indication that every 13 seconds a woman is beaten in America, and again, about 4-plus women a day are murdered by their intimate partners (Bachman & Saltzman, 1995; Straus, Gelles, & Steinmetz, 1980). The seriousness of these response styles becomes alarming as they are repeated throughout untold homes.

Theme Five: An Awakening Life-changing Event

The fifth significant theme involves the consequences when the agony construct is not appropriately managed. When it gets acted out on an intimate partner, society now intervenes; the way society says it will not tolerate physical harm to an intimate partner is to deprive the abuser of some of his liberties. Each of the men in our study was arrested for intimate partner violence. Each individual's description of that event was one of inexpressible pain, humiliation, and agony. They said:

> Jail, for me, a successful member of society, was the most degrading, terrifying experience of my life. (Arvil Stimpson, Responsibility Letter)

> It is something that I will never forget. (Art Yount, Responsibility Letter)

> As I sat in jail, I felt ashamed and abandoned. (Sid Belini, taped interview)

> I went to jail and got very embarrassed when my name hit the paper. I feel all the court costs, days missed from work, counseling and emotional problems were not worth it [the behavior that brought it about]. Because I still feel pain and humiliation. (Rondel De Marco, Responsibility Letter)

> Going to jail was the most humiliating experience of my life and I vowed to never go back again. (Robin Stemmes, Responsibility Letter)

The societal sanction of putting people in jail is very effective. The severe trauma of going to jail results in such an adverse physiological experience in individuals that the time spent there is a time of great pain, humiliation, and self-reflection. The surge of the unleashed energy force field brought on by a conflict with an intimate partner is often uncontrollable. The interior psychological constructs contain powerful force fields in which suppressed energy is stored. When that construct is ignited and the force released, it is often difficult to manage with one's conscious mind. The conflict is an open gestalt clamoring for closure. It can be overwhelming and seemingly life threatening for the one experiencing the loss. The excessive pain of prison often out-traumatizes the traumatizing event that led the person to jail. One would do anything to have the original trauma back, just to avoid the present trauma of sitting in jail.

Theme Six: Psychological Origins of Violent Intimate Partner Construct

All of the participants talked extensively about their family-of-origin experiences. The early family life, which shaped their lives and provided their developmental and socialization experiences, was carried with them throughout their lives. This fact is the sixth theme that was revealed from their stories. Some men had confusion, conflicts, and wounds with regard to their mothers.

> One night she [mother] came home while my dad was working a second job in the war effort, and I watched her get out of a car I didn't recognize with a man I'd never seen before. They stood kissing and I had my first taste of jealousy and anger. (Arvil Simpson, Responsibility Letter)

She was always pushing me to get better grades, and screaming at me if I struck out or had an error during a baseball game. Nothing was ever good enough. (Art Yount, History of Hurts and Beliefs Letter)

My mother left when I was about two. My babysitter wanted custody of me and eventually won custody of me. (Sid Belini, taped interview)

Both my Moms whipped me when I needed it. (Rondel De Marco, History of Hurts and Beliefs Letter)

My [mother] couldn't really discipline me. Once I got to be about nine years old, there really wasn't nothing she could do. I mean I'd just do whatever I wanted. I did that until I was about 19. I just did whatever. (Shane Sagen, taped interview)

Further conflicts and wounds resulted from relationships with their fathers.

He always seemed to be upset about something. His rage and filthy language at these times were unbearable for my mother. He slapped my mother around. He divorced my mom. (Arvil Stimpson, History of Hurts and Beliefs Letter)

My dad and mom rarely spoke civilly and for three years were constantly at each other's throats. My father didn't work at all. I felt like I was a mediator between [them]. (Art Yount History of Hurts and Beliefs Letter)

At age three my father married my babysitter, and mom was pushed totally out of the picture. And my father died on his motorcycle on their honeymoon night. My dad? [Stepdad] I still call him my dad; he's the only guy I've really known. He was always a pretty neat guy; I'd watch out for him cause he's a good-sized guy and had a pretty bad temper. He was the disciplinarian. And he whipped me for teasing some animals. (Sid Belini, taped interview)

My dad fills my memory base with being a real hardass.
It was a living hell with him. My whole life he made me
feel scared to talk to him, be around him. I hated him
because he was always so mean and irritated. He kicked
my ass all the time. When I was in kindergarten, I still
remember him bashing me into the wall, and he broke the
sheetrock with my head. I hated him with all my heart.
(Rondel De Marco, History of Hurts and Beliefs Letter)

My dad and mother were divorced. I didn't see him much
anymore. When I was with him it was a good experience.
When he was angry it was pretty scary. Uh, he'd get right
up and inch in your face, and scream in your face, tell you
what you're dong wrong, and he's got those eyes that look
right through ya. Scares the shit out of ya. (Shane Sagen,
taped interview)

Sometimes he would not talk to mom or the kids for
days. So I did not have a very good relationship with
my father. There was no touching or show of affection
from my father. I am sure that made it very difficult
for me to show affection in later years for my wife and
kids. I sill have difficulty forming warm and meaningful
relationships with women. (Robin Stemmes, History of
Hurts and Beliefs Letter)

Consequently, the earliest experiences of the male socialization
process with both mother and father linger throughout life. They shape
the internal realities, become a viewing point from which to measure
relationship expectations, and reside internally as force fields of psychic
energy that leak out or erupt as projected anger on intimate partners.
Unless the internal wounds are ferreted out and healed, they live on as
seething internal storms waiting to erupt into gross marital conflict.

Theme Seven: The Entry Level Attitudes
of Men Regarding Women

Each of the participants made statements about the attitudes and
beliefs he held regarding women with whom he was about to enter into
a relationship. This seventh theme seems to be an idealistic mapping
process and it is related to the ecstasy construct discussed previously.

Mr. Stimpson wanted a "Christian woman." His internal vision of a Christian woman carried with it a set of visions regarding behaviors he expected to experience from his intimate partner. "When I met you," he stated, "I was walking around looking at you through my expectations. I actually expected you to act and behave in a certain way" (Arvil Stimpson, History of Hurts and Beliefs Letter).

> I dated quite a few women in high school and found myself doin' everything I could to please them. I was always watching what I said when my girlfriend was around. (Art Yount, Quotient of Pain Letter)

> Glenda Eades was . . . pretty much larger than life. (Sid Belini, taped interview)

> I was brought up with the conception that an intimate relationship could only be carried out with honesty and respect for your partner. In all my of past relationships I carried high expectations of my partners to not disrespect me around other men and to not lie to me. (Rondel De Marco, Quotient of Pain Letter)

Mr. Sagen didn't state clearly his expectations regarding women. He did state that there was a Connie, his first girlfriend; "I had been wanting to go out with her since like the fourth grade. I was like so in love with her. She was so cool" (History of Hurts and Beliefs Letter). This would indicate some unexpressed ideal in Mr. Sagen that Connie awakened. However, he never stated in the interview any clear map-like expectation about his ideal woman.

Mr. Stemmes also did not clearly state or at least record his belief system regarding the nature and behavior patterns for his ideal woman. They are somewhat assumed by indirect reference according to what made him angry about her behaviors.

This internal mapping system, from the perspective of this writer, is the result of the imprints from the practicing phase of male social development (12 – 24 months). These imprints are often highly idealized, excessive, unrealistic, and impossible for any woman to fulfill. The internal images of the Madonna from the practicing phase become high and unrealistic expectations that set men up for disappointment, pain, and conflict in relationships.

Theme Eight: Action Plan for Healing

The noble goal of bridging the chasm between the often mutually exclusive factions of the ecstasy and agony constructs, between the "goddesses, angels, Madonna's Gypsy maidens, and earth mothers" and the "britches, castrators, and witches" (Keen, 1991, p. 16), and bringing these unlived disowned aspects of the personality into conscious awareness has become in fact an imperative. It is the significant eighth and final theme that emerged from the research.

Levant (1997) and Gottman (1999) use the concept of emotional intelligence when addressing the problem of the lack of an emotional vocabulary in men. Levant (1997) videotaped a series of counseling sessions with a client in training to facilitate the ability to differentiate and expand the subtleties of a range of emotional potential. This very focus is also the key element of the training program attended by the six participants. One element of that training is to first of all cognitively plan out a specific course for bridging the two polarities, which is called "An action plan for healing." Accompanying that action plan is a programmatic educational design to promote experientially the acquisition of those bridging skills.

Each of the participants in the training program developed a responsibility plan, or, as we called it in our program, an action plan for healing. Their reports were as follows.

Mr. Arvil Stimpson reported, as he progressed through the group process, how grateful he was for the skills of "letting go of the rope" and the skills of being able to acknowledge his partner's life experience and particular feelings.

> I know that I must have hurt you, that what I've done is wrong, and I can never go back and change what has happened. I hope that by paying attention to your needs and wants, goals, and ambitions I can somehow gain back some of your trust. I enjoy my life with you and our son and will never jeopardize that safety net you said I had once created. I love you.

> Looking back at the beliefs I had as a young man, having a few enlightening experiences and this class as reference, I can see now that I had been misled. My parents are not to be blamed directly, but indirectly were responsible for their actions, which I believed, was the way things were meant to be. Women bitched, and

men either went out to the garage or told her flat out to shut the hell up. I know now that there are many more choices than these and that our "letting go of the rope statements" are a guide, not necessarily commandments. Women need us to listen to them, to show compassion, and to feel empathy as they might for us in their time of need.

My action plan will include some changes I feel I must make to ensure that my family feels safe when I'm around. For the last few years, looking back, it's obvious now that by intimidating my wife I never got the chance to know who she really was. I spent all my time controlling her and convincing her that her lazy ass needed to stay home and take care of our son. I will stop trying to control her by telling her to have a great time if she goes out with her friends, and possibly hand her some money to show her that I'm okay with it.

I will no longer spend every waking hour wondering where she's at and to make this easier I can occupy my time by doing something with my son. I've wasted a lot of valuable time, time that I could have used to focus on the relationship with my son so that he can grow to be a strong, understanding man one day. I'm determined to change to better my family, but most of all, for the chance to see my son break the abusive cycle and have a family of his own. (Arvil Stimpson, Action Plan for Healing)

I'm starting to see now just by listening to her and handling problems calmly and rationally that there is hope. (Art Yount, Action Plan for Healing)

I wanted you to understand my frustration but you didn't so I took it out on you. I blamed everything that had gone wrong on you, when in reality it was me that was out of control.

I can only imagine your terror when I destroyed our car and home and how hurt you must have felt. I just wanted my pain to stop.

I know what I did was wrong and I have taken certain steps to prevent this behavior in the future. Since then I have stopped drinking and doing drugs. I also attend a DV Perpetrator program. These things are to better get to know myself and to understand my destructive behavior. I want you to know that I am responsible for my own actions and that none of this was ever your fault. (Sid Belini, Action Plan for Healing)

What I have to offer you from this point on is my sincere apology for losing control. You may never see me in your eyes as you did when we first connected, but I will dedicate my life to trying. I want to be the spark in your eyes forever, and I don't want anything like this to hinder that possibility. If I can't ever refill that space of trust in your heart, then I have failed yet another relationship. I promise to seek treatment for my own self-assurance. I need to be able to know I will never lose control, and I need to change my ways of thinking you are my property or that it needs to be perfect or nothing.

I promise to give you space and benefit of the doubt. It was not your fault totally that the argument took place. I should have approached it in a different manner. You don't deserve to have water in your face, shoved, squeezed, thrown or to be called names that are vulgar. You are very special to me, your daughter, and to our new boy. I want you to see that we can get through this evil and disgusting chapter. It will just take my full dedication and realization that relationships need to be worked on everyday. I promise to try and be the person you fell for from day one. I promise to be there for you until you say you don't need me anymore. God forbid that ever happens. I *will* work on this, day by day. (Rondel De Marco, Action Plan for Healing)

I understand now that you needed your space and did not have to justify your leaving to me. You had every right to leave. What I did was wrong and not something I will never be able to make up to you. But I will try in the years to come when dealing with our children. (Shane Sagen, Action Plan for Healing)

I can only imagine how hurt you were to be slapped by me. I knew that I would be terribly angry if the situation were reversed.

I want you to know that whether or not we get back together, I am deeply sorry for what I did and that it will never happen again. I will try to listen to you and understand how frustrated you must be with our situation. My goals for the future are to control my anger; when arguments start to escalate – walk away and cool off. I will try to listen better when you want to talk, be patient and not try to offer solutions, but just listen. I will be mindful of my drinking. I plan to do things together instead of drinking, for instance play golf or card games. I want to give you more space and your private time. (Robin Stemmes, Action Plan for Healing)

In sum, the two underlying constructs (the ecstasy and the agony) and their outcomes exist as subterranean force fields of male energy. The ecstacy of the practicing phase of male social development (12 to 24 months) lives on in most men as an internal uplift, buoyancy, and excitement in the presence of the desirable object. The ecstacy turns to the agony of the rapprochment phase (24 to 36 months) when the idealized woman does not mirror back the fantasies of the toddler's reality. The ramifications of the misnavigation of these two conflicting force fields often are observed in the way men get triggered, the inappropriate response to that triggering mechanism, and if the response is excessive, the outcome of arrest and jail. The origins of these constructs began prior to self-consciousness and are carried in male subconsciousness as visions, maps, or templates through which women are viewed. The journey toward healing and recovery is arduous, requiring the development of appropriate negotiation skills to manage these internal currents of subterranean energy forces.

These forces are not all negative, and many aspects of them are positive. However, they are often aberrations, distortions, and delusions. They are incomplete and inaccurate viewpoints from which to view and apparaise many factors in relationships. They are incomplete in that they contain elements in which there is often a partial fit. "Sometimes she is just wonderful," they say, and then "everything goes straight to Hell." It is these internal states that emerge in the way men speak about women and often about life. It is these internal states that must be addressed if one is to understand the male psyche, and initate any attempt to work toward the integration of men's souls and heal the male wounds.

CHAPTER VI
THE HEURISTIC FACTOR

There she sits. She's 92 now, a diminutive figure. Her white-covered head is back and her mouth is drooped open, emitting sounds of heavy breathing as she sleeps in her favorite chair. She walks slowly, stumbles and tells me of times she almost fell down. Her most common utterance to me is, "What do you know for sure?"— a door opener longing for conversation. She has macular degeneration and can't read or write anymore. She watches her favorite TV programs, "Jeopardy" and "Wheel of Fortune." She has vivid memories of earlier days, such as when the ranch house burned down in 1915 when she was eight years old. She commingles all the twenty-five or so grandchildren's names. When I take her places she often says, "What's the name of this road we're crossing?" "What's the name of that building?" "Look at all those cars" as if trying to fit some things together in memory. I think she's seeking some connection with the long ago familiar Spokane Valley she knew. She says I wish this and I wish that and I try unconsciously to do what she asks. She complains of sitting alone all day and that "Nobody comes to see me." She stands a little above my waist and still exerts power over me.

She does well, I think. She gets up every morning about six, fixes my breakfast, usually a half of banana and a piece of raisin toast and coffee. She then hollers downstairs "Herb! Herb! Get up!" The tone of her voice still pierces me to the bone like a knife. A woman from Elder Care comes each morning for two or three hours and helps her. Another old friend takes her to lunch every Wednesday. Sunday morning and evening and Wednesday night she can't miss church. She keeps herself very well. Her hair is permed and neat. Her bed is made every morning. The washing machine is running early every Monday morning before I get up, just as it was sixty years ago.

Alberta Robinson, my mother, was born Alberta Sperber on October 18, 1908 sixty miles northwest of Dickinson, North Dakota in the Killdeer Mountains. "Alberta" is a contraction from her two grandmothers' names: Alvira Adams and Bertha Sperber. She was born the second child of Christian Charles Sperber and Marie Adams. William Fredrick Sperber, later a judge in Dun County North Dakota, with his family, including his son Christian Charles Sperber, migrated from Renville County, Minnesota to North Dakota in the 1870s to take advantage of the free land to be homesteaded. C. C. [Christian Charles] Sperber, as Alberta's father was called, owned a 200 acre ranch on which he built a log and sod house with a grainery and barns. Alberta's older brother, Howard Sperber was the son of Marie Adams and adopted by C. C. Sperber. Five other sons were born to the Sperber family. When father Sperber called the children to breakfast, it was "Howard, Sis, Bill, John, Jim and Chris, and Herb *get up!*"

The sixty-mile trip to Dickinson, North Dakota was made a few times a year with horse and wagon to purchase supplies and staples. Alberta got to take her first trip to Dickinson when she was five years old. The family would leave the ranch and go to Oakdale, North Dakota about ten miles away up the side of one of the Killdeer Mountains with a view of the broad valleys below. There was a store and a mail drop where the stagecoach left mails a couple of times a week. Extended family members owned the store. The family would stay all night at Oakdale and continue on to Dickinson in the morning. It was about a two-to-four day trip. On Alberta's first trip to Dickinson when she was five years old, in 1913, a man driving a car met them along the way. When they stopped to talk (everybody that passed on the road stopped to talk) he asked Chris Sperber to let mother Marie and the kids ride to Dickinson in the car with him. The kids all bailed out of the wagon and were jerked up short by Chris Sperber's "You kids get right back in this wagon." After some discussion Marie and the family did get to ride to Dickinson in the car and Chris Sperber took another day to arrive there by wagon.

When Marie and the kids arrived in Dickinson that evening at the hotel, a train had stopped in town, and Marie asked a man to take Alberta out to see the train. Alberta's sole conception of a train came from a glittering silver Christmas ornament that they hung on their Christmas tree. She stated that when she saw the huge, dirty, noisy, ugly train she was sorely disappointed. Chris Sperber bought his first car, a white Buick, on this trip. He hired a man to drive the team and wagon back to the ranch.

In 1915, when Alberta was eight years old, a gasoline lamp accidentally spurted a stream of gas that hit the cook stove, burst into flame, ignited the ranch house and it burned to the ground. Marie Sperber was badly burned on her hands, arms, and face. During this time Alberta, being next to the oldest, had to assume adult tasks and do the cooking and take care of the younger children. She had almost sole care of Jim and Chris, twins five years younger than Alberta.

In 1923, after five years of crop failure, the family and extended family members, some 19 in all, sold out and, with a truck and two touring cars, drove the dirt roads, set up tents, and camped along the way as they moved to Whidbey Island, Washington. In 1929 the family moved to Spokane valley and continued to farm a piece of land about eight miles east of Spokane in an area called Velox. Alberta graduated from Otis Orchards High School in 1929 and worked in the apple industry packing apples. One day while taking a break from packing apples on a loading dock on Kenny Road in the Spokane Valley, she observed a man walking by on the road. He was walking to his parents' home across the railroad tracks near the apple packing house. She exclaimed to a friend on break with her, "Who is that tramp walking down the road?" "Oh that's no tramp," exclaimed her friend "that's Henry Robinson, Mrs. Robinson's son. She's a nurse you know," to which Alberta abruptly responded, "Well, I'll probably marry that man." After some social dances in the Otis neighborhood, she did. On November 15, 1930 in Peshastin, Washington, Alberta Sperber married Herbert Henry Robinson.

After my birth as Herbert Henry Robinson III, May 31, 1933, and then my sister's arrival as Louise Lavern Robinson on October 9, 1934, my parents moved back to Otis Orchards, Spokane and lived there for the next eighteen years. After my sister and I left home in the 1950s, Alberta lived in the Spokane Valley with her husband Henry Robinson until he died on July 5, 1977. In 1990, Alberta moved in with me and has lived there ever since.

Sitting and looking at her across the room now, I find that she is far removed from the dynamic, powerful woman I knew as a child. As I look at her, I know I began my existence in her womb. I knew nothing then. My growing awareness of the world was from her. My subliminal and then conscious awareness of listening to her talk about family history events, right and wrong, life in general, and the beautiful places she had visited defined my world. I got in touch with some wonderful inner feelings looking through her eyes. The feelings are often like worship — worship of life, sunsets, history, mountains, cumulus clouds, children, birds, flowers, waterfalls, and rainbows — everything. That thrill of discovery must have come from her in my early years. I got a fairly good body from her with good genes. Many of the previous family members lived into their eighties. I'm grateful for that. I don't know where my insatiable quest for learning came from — maybe it came from the Sperber's Gnostic attitude toward subsistence living. The family culture of the Sperbers and Robinsons passed down through centuries was one of hard work. You get coal from the badlands, and pick wild asparagus and berries. You make sausage sheaves with scraped animal guts. There is a way to churn, to snip beans, to shell peas, to husk corn, to milk cows, to cultivate a straight rill, to slop pigs, and to scratch (feed) chickens. There is a right and wrong way for everything. They knew what was right. Things had to be done the right way.

We lived on a five-acre truck farm. No work, no garden, no food the rest of the year. We lived on the food in our dirt cellar under the house. During the Depression there was no money — my parents lost all their money when the banks closed in 1934. They lost $125.

My mother was a Spartan mother. She demonstrated her love by working "like a fool," in her words. She did everything: she planted, irrigated, hauled hay, cultivated with our horse, plowed, milked cows (their wedding gift from her dad was a milk cow), worked days without end incessantly; and as children we had to be right there also. For all of that, the significant work ethic, I have great respect for her. She fed, clothed, and cared for us completely. But there was another side: there was minimal affection or respect for children's uniqueness. At family reunions, half-humorous tales are still told by her brothers and the cousins of severe corporal punishment — "ass whippins"— they called them. Family get-to-gethers involved sharing stories of old times — hard times. Her focus in child rearing was "Do they behave?" "Do they do what they're told?" Children were to be seen and not heard. Children were primarily to do what they were told, obey, and do their chores. I felt like I was going crazy when I got whipped. Even now, when a newscast reports on some of the behaviors of today's youth, her response in disgust is, "They just need a good beatin' — they need their asses whipped and they would cut that stuff out." Her tone of voice still jars me. She got that from her dad, whose roots were from Germany. It rings of Alice Miller's (1984) *Thou Shall Not be Aware: Society's Betrayal of the Child* and her documentation of the concept of "poisonous pedagogy." A key statement of Chris Sperber's regarding children, since work, farming, and survival was always the focus, "One kid is a kid, two kids is a half of a kid, and three kids is no kid at all."

So my inner experience of her was one of mostly fear. She didn't ask why a thing was broken or why a chicken died because of me; once I was chasing a chicken pullet through tall clover and it stopped, I didn't, and I stepped on its head and killed it. (She rung it's neck and we had it for dinner.) Her focus was pure obedience. I was afraid of her. One time when I was about four years old, my sister Louise and I were doing something — "goofing off, playing, getting into mischief" — and she was working and with anger she sent us to bed in the middle of the day. We laid in bed crying. I rose up crying and said, "Don't you love us any more?" and she said, "No I don't, not when you act like that!" We put our heads down and cried even louder. I was devastated.

So throughout the years those experiences of structure, clear right and wrong, black and white, and "obey, just do what you are told" shaped my world and my interior construct regarding women. My external needs were taken care of very well. We had a small house and I had my place at the table with Daddy at one end and Mother at the other and Louise across from me. Those are wonderful memories; I felt secure. I remember, however, very little touching, hugging, or show of affection from my mother. My father, by contrast, seemed to show love for me and it was as if he was the only person on the planet who loved me. I don't think he said, "I love you," he didn't have to; I felt it. When he would spank me he would say, "Son, this is going to hurt me more than it will you." I believe it did. He came home to us from work every night. Getting to go places with him was a great delight. It happened too infrequently. The emotional drought left a deep longing inside of me.

Against the backdrop of my experience of a spartan emotionally deprived atmosphere at home another parallel experience began to emerge for me when I started the first grade in 1939 at Otis Orchards grade school. Early on I became aware of a girl who sat there in class with me in the first grade and for ten years thereafter. In my junior year my parents moved away and I left Otis Orchards. This girl seemed very shy. She was an "A" student and everybody liked her. She seemed to me to be very kind, pleasant, and appropriate. The teachers seemed to admire her, and she was a leader in our classes for those ten years. So, logically, with everyone else, it seems to me, I admired her too. Since she was quiet, I projected all of the unlived polar opposite side of my deprived emotional experience from mother toward her. Over the years she became a person upon whom I projected all of my warm feelings, longings for attention, and from the little I knew then — I thought — love. Because of my interest in her and wanting her attention I showed off in front of her and did a lot of crazy fool things. This became more intense as time passed, and my perception at this late date is that a kind of imprinting happened in me and this person's persona became a set of prescriptive viewing lenses through which I looked at and for a woman. In my sophomore year I had one date with her. Otherwise I was too afraid of rejection to risk asking her out. I longingly admired her from a distance.

The experiences with these two women impacted me greatly. On the one hand there was the external, foreboding, take charge, always present, observing, controlling, and structure-giving woman. On the other was the soft internal, seemingly delicate and fragile, illusive, unapproachable, angelic goddess. These two internalized aspects of my inner self were played out in my future relationships with women. I was always gravitating toward the structured, familiar, decisive, and take-charge woman and always missing and longing for the illusive "angelic goddess." To borrow the archetype describing term "anima" from Carl Jung, used to describe the internal psychological female in every man, I have lived with an internal schizophrenic anima all my life.

I finished high school and my first year of college with almost no dates and joined the Marine Corps to play first trombone with the San Diego Marine Band. One time Harry James and Betty Grable came to the Mission Beach Ball Room in Mission Beach, San Diego. A tuba player, Bill Elam, and I went to hear Harry James. While I stood listening to the music, a woman walked by in front of me and smiled. I followed her to her seat and asked her to dance, somehow remembered her phone number, called her, dated her, and four months later, on November 24, 1954 married her. Her name was Georgia Jones. She was about eight years older than I and had two children: a girl, seven, Cheri Dean Jones, and a boy, four, David Keith Jones. I became emotionally attached to Cheri and David. During our time of dating the children would say to their mother Georgia, "Is he going to be our new daddy?" They were a motivating factor in my relationship with and marriage to Georgia Jones. I adopted her children. We lived together for twenty years.

Marrying Georgia was an immense decision. I wrestled with it a great deal. One time lying on my bunk in the marine barracks, a stream of thoughts went through my mind. It went something like this: "I don't know who you are, or where I'll ever meet you, but I'm not going to be able to marry you, because I'm going to marry Georgia and give my life as a sacrifice to help her raise Cheri and David." I had this discussion with my internal imaginary anima — my internal female goddess. I later learned that the bargains we make with ourselves come back to visit us. Georgia and I married and took our honeymoon on Catalina Island. Later in the relationship we had three daughters: Peri Elizabeth, Tanda Rene, and Gaila Derie. Georgia was a gritty, motivated, take-charge, dependable, sometimes controlling woman. I soon projected all of my familiar experiences with my mother on her, and she fit neatly into some of my comfortable (uncomfortable) maternal images. One day I was a single, carefree Marine, and the next day I moved into a house with a wife, two children, and a mother-in-law. Georgia's mother lived with us most of the time. I joined an existing ongoing family social system.

The twenty years with Georgia were very "rocky." We would have peaceful times intermingled with some stormy conflicts. She often threatened divorce when conflicts came. After ten years when one of those threats happened, I said to her; "you might as well face the fact that we are not getting a divorce. We have three beautiful daughters, I married you for keeps, and you might as well get used to the fact that you are stuck with me and we are going to make the best of it." Things improved and our last several years together were the less conflicted.

I don't think I really married Georgia Jones. I really think I tried to marry my internal magical fantasy concept of the girl I admired in high school. After a few significant conflicts the goddess thing regarding Georgia was shattered. I began subconsciously looking for the fantasy woman I gave up to marry Georgia. I looked into hundreds of women's eyes to see whether she was the one.

I thought I found her some seven years into our marriage. I had finished seminary, and I had taken a ministerial internship in a large church in the Midwest. I wrote the Sunday school literature, directed a 60-voice choir; and directed the youth ministry. I was twenty-six years old, and in my youth group was an eighteen-year-old young woman. She was sort of my assistant, secretary, and helper with the activities in the youth program. My inner sense of self, my interiority, and my sense of women were very diffuse and very undifferentiated. How did I know I had feelings for this young woman? She was nice and very pleasant to be around — so were a lot of other women in the church. However, one time she was gone for some reason, and I expected her to be there. I looked for her and she wasn't there. I felt hollow, empty, and longed to see her. For months through the winter, after that, I sat in the warmth of a dirty furnace room in the big cold church where I read my Bible, prayed, and wrestled with my feelings for this young woman.

My stream of consciousness went something like this. "If I am to experience the fulfillment of my thoughts and feelings for this person, it would mean being able to spend time with her, talk to her, probably be affectionate with her." And just those thoughts conflicted me greatly and inflicted me with great guilt and pain. I was afraid of Georgia, just as I was my mother. I again thought, "If I did do those things it would, for it to be righteous, have to be in the absence of me having a wife. That would mean that Georgia, my wife, would have to die, I thought." So in essence I came to think that in some way I was wishing that my wife would die. Just the thought of wishing someone to die so I could get what I wanted was tormenting. I felt I was usurping what was only in the hands of God. I had to get away from this torment. I resigned my position and moved with my family to Spokane, Washington.

In 1961, I founded a church in my home with only my family in Spokane Valley. In thirteen years it grew to an attendance of some 1,600 people. Georgia was my support person, my assistant, an organist in the church, and filled an important aspect of my inner self as I functioned in a leadership role. The family, then, consisted of Georgia, my wife, her mother, Jewell Caple, Cheri Dean and David, my two adopted children, and Peri, Tanda, and Gaila, our three daughters. For ten years the church did not grow the way I wanted it to. I was attending college and I taught college (five philosophy courses, music history and art history) during that time. After I had been pastor of that church for about ten years, a woman in the church passed away and left the church quite a bit of money. We bought property, built buildings, promoted significant growth, and hired new staff, including a secretary.

The new secretary became my right arm in managing the ten full-time staff members, and we had a very professional working relationship for some thirteen months. Then this plain, sometimes-insecure associate gradually became over a period of time transfigured in my mind into this amazing, desirable, beautiful goddess with whom I longed desperately to talk to and be near her. She seemed to step into the image and assume the mantle of the young woman I cared for so in my early school years, the one I said good-by to in my bunk in the Marine Corps barracks, and the one whom I had to get away from at the church in Midwest. Here were these internal compulsive feelings I had walked away from before. Now she was my right-hand person in everything I did. She, her image, was right in my face every moment; I was compelled to see her and be with her. I was, it seemed to me, overtaken by a force field of driven compulsive energy I had no ability to manage cognitively. My guts, adrenal glands, and solar plexus said, "We're experiencing emotions you have no control over." My cognitive sense of propriety, right and wrong, and all my theological training stood on the sidelines aghast. On Sunday I would deliver my sermons. On one side of the auditorium was my wife, the mother of my children who I loved, and on the other side was this transfigured goddess whom I worshipped. The one I loved, my wife, with the familiar part of me, with my head and admiration, and the other, a kind of dreamworld projection, with god knows from where — it was a mystery. Over a period of eight months I become ambivalent and distraught; I became confused; I became disoriented; and eventually I was unable to function. I disintegrated into emotional disorientation. I thought I was going crazy. I had no theoretical information to understand what was happening to me. I was having an emotional breakdown. I left my life's work. I left my wife and my daughters, whom I loved intently. I went away with this young woman. Soon she could no longer deal with the weight of it all and terminated the relationship.

I had burned all my bridges, crashed and burned in the community where I had built a reputation, and became a homeless person living in my car, sleeping in county parks, and eating in rescue missions. I cried every day for over two years. My life as I knew it was over; I died. Reminiscent of the cryptic phrase "Man must die before he dies. Nothing can you have . . . until you die" (Rajneesh, 1976, p. 2). My life was a maze of meaningless wanderings, many false starts, skimpy survival in many meaningless jobs, pennilessness, years of recrimination and guilt, wearing out many a confidant, and a slow ten-year journey back to self-discovery and some sense of self. I began to study psychology in earnest in order to understand what had happened to me. This led, over the next thirty years, to my work as a counselor, over 3000 hours in face to face therapy, work on a doctorate, and a practice as a licensed mental health counselor.

Some twenty years after the relationship with the secretarial staff-member of the church I pastored ended, I received a letter from her. We met and spent a day together. Deep feelings still remained. We shared our separate journeys together. Some significant closure resulted. We wrote to each other for a time. Then the letters came back "unable to deliver, forwarding address unknown." I never heard from her again. She went on her way.

I later married another wonderful woman. It soon ended in divorce, however, the relationship has continued for over twenty-six years and even though divorced, we still celebrate our wedding anniversaries. She is a wonderful woman. She has traveled the world, taught school in the Orient and in Europe, and has higher education degrees. She also is structured, meticulous, clear thinking, proactive, orderly, and caring. She is all of that and also has a delightful, charming "little girl" inside that comes out to play. She has a wonderful heart. She has been a great support person to me. She is my greatest cheerleader.

As I sit with hundreds of men arrested for domestic violence and breaking restraining orders: I identify with them. When they sit in front of me shaking and crying over their lost love: I feel it. When they report a burning compulsion to see her so badly they ignore restraining orders and break the door down: I know the burning compulsion. When they drive by her house to see if someone else's car is in the driveway: I can understand that longing. When they talk of the terror and isolation of sitting in a jail cell: I can feel their terror. When they shake with fear of going back to court: I can grasp that fear. To do this work one must have a robust empathy for men. As I listen long to their sobs I remember back through the long years when I was going through my own death siege. At forty years old, when I was in the midst of my doldrums, I wanted to go back and get on my mother's lap and have her hold me and rock me. Beneath all the pain, wounds, hurt, anger, and rage without the ability to differentiate, we men, it seems, live with this deep longing: I want my mommy.

I have lived with my mother for the last ten years. In hundreds of ways I had to get in touch with the early years of frustration and pain, befuddlement and confusion, and love for her. Mentally I love her and respect her for all that she has done. Physiologically, if she gets too close to me, or wants to touch me, I still hurt.

Since I began writing this chapter my mother has fallen several times, resulting in several trips to the hospital, and now lives in a nursing home. I go to see her and sit and hold her hand. She seems afraid and in shock. At first she was dead set on getting out of there. She said, "Get me out of here, I've got to get to work and get going." She couldn't walk or roll over in bed.

All the way there, during the visits, and on the way back I relived, like a drowning man, the flashbacks of my whole life. "Let's see, she is now 93 years old. She was born in 1908 and in 1918 she was ten years old, in 1928 she was 20 years old — oh! In the 20s she turned 20; in the 30s she turned 30. In each decade she was the same many years old as the decade. Then in 1930 at 23 she married Henry Robinson, my dad. He loved her. Then three years later I was born. And in 1934 she took care of me in Otis Orchards. In 1944 she taught me to play the tonette, and in 1945 the milk cow died . . . "

As I look over the other residents at the nursing home, 10 to 1 women, white hair, wheelchairs, and needing someone to spoon the food into their mouths, I reflect back seventy to eighty years to the days when some man's heart, now long gone, rose with excitement and delight over the visage of this woman.

My mother's distress at not being home comes with a sigh. The struggle of working the farm and living in poverty resulted in her sighing a lot. She restates some of her lifelong sayings: "Sigh! I wish I was rich instead of so darned good looking," and, "Sigh! Such is life without a wife." I hold her hand and give her a kiss good-by. She says, "I wish you would bring me some tooth picks." I do. She still has a mysterious power over me.

My wife Georgia, to whom I was married for twenty years, passed away since I began this paper. She died two days after Christmas on December 27, 2001. I again flashed back over my life, to a tender time when my children were born and were growing up. I relived again the many years of our stressful journey together. I respected her a lot. I cried when I heard she died. She was a Christian, and wherever she went she taught a Bible class for girls and women. She had a saying, "Never let your forgiver get stuck." She demonstrated that to me in the most remarkable way. Even though I initiated the divorce and left her, she always included me in all my daughter's birthdays and family events. For several years on Christmas Eve I was invited to her house. So on Christmas Eve I would take my second ex-wife to my first ex-wife's to celebrate Christmas with my family, Georgia and her husband of 25 years. Two days before she died, at my daughter's Christmas Eve gathering, my second ex-wife and my first ex-wife, I noticed, were sitting on the sofa chatting. I will be forever grateful for her kindness and lack of bitterness toward me. On the one hand there is the deepest warmth and gratitude for my daughters and the giggles and joy they shared with me, and on the other is deep regret and the pathos I feel that I couldn't have been more present and tender with them.

I feel like there are worlds happening around me and I can't take them in. I think I should feel more deeply. I should be more empathic. Then I think if I ever got into such a place I could never stop crying. Life seems so mysterious I can't fathom it all. Swirling and commingling in my mind are the currents of these female imprints. They are the lifelong themes that visit me in wistful moments. I'm reminded of Willie Nelson singing his song: "Of all the girls I loved before who wandered in and out my door." It sounds like deep respect for each of them. I think, in my case, each one gave me something very wonderful. They gave me more confidence, helped my low sense of self, helped me like myself a little better (if a wonderful person likes me maybe I'm okay); they helped me heal.

What I say here may be meaningless. My diffuse and undifferentiated urges and hints may disguise more than they reveal about my interior world of musings and remembrances. When I hear men talk about women I think that they are only taking about themselves and their inner perceptions. I don't think they even come close to the real person they think they are describing. There is no descriptor for the wonderful women who have graced my life.

Nevertheless, what I have discovered is that I live with two distinct aspects of my inner female self. One is the order-giving, powerful, maybe fear-inducing mother that captures the love of my admiring intellect. I always gravitate, as in the case of my two marriages, toward this familiar secure essence. Coupled with that is the illusive, out-of-reach, longed for, delicate, fragile, goddess force-field that eludes my managerial intellect and blasts past to the unidentifiable, inexpressible, diffuse, undifferentiated

211

surge of unmanageable love force. For me it is the scarier of the two. These two hold me juxtaposed between powerful forces.

In sum, I know little or nothing actually about the feminine gender; I can only guess — human beings are conceived and grow in their bodies — they are most mysterious. I only know some things about my inner experience of them. What I know and what I have written often seems more like the insignificance of someone attempting to understand.

The heuristic aspect of qualitative research involves the researcher. The factors of heuristic research, noted above, emphasized the connection and the immersion of the researcher in the discovery experience. It helps focus attention to the subtle realities of the interview subject, and employs the researcher's intuition, and tacit knowing of the experience. It tends to focus on the person as a whole, posits the researcher as his or her instrument in the inquiry process and is less oriented toward pure scientific objectivity. Consequently, this chapter is included in that it sets forth the filtering realities of this writer. One can only see from where they have been. The totality of one's experience become the viewing point, the biasis, the predjucies, the scotomas that open wide a viewing point or narrow the viewing point.

It is the experiences of my life that become the viewing point through which I join the inner world of my clients and reside there with them. I can join them in their agony, their lost soul experience, their sadness, and feel the terrifying abandonment they experience. The experiences of my life become the connecting point through which I joined with them.

CHAPTER VII
DISCUSSION, CONCLUSIONS, AND RECOMMENDATIONS

This study was initiated to enrich the theory base regarding intimate partner violence. I wanted to test, compare, refine, and amplify my theory base. As a counselor treating couples in conflict in private practice for over thirty years, and as a program supervisor treating court-mandated perpetrators of intimate partner violence, I wanted to pursue a more in-depth examination of the nature, origins, and possible prevention and treatment of intimate partner violence. I looked at men in general by tracing the 2500-year history of the masculinity stereotype. I examined the latest masculinity research, the socialization process of male children, and the way these factors contributed to the abuse of women. Sitting with some 2000 men for over fifteen years and listening to the way they speak about themselves and their intimate partners caused me to think that these statements concealed/revealed a deeper internal reality. I wanted to understand these internal realities.

The title of this study is "An Examination into the Internal Psychological Constructs of Men Who Perpetrate Intimate Partner Violence: A Qualitative, Phenomenological Study with a Heuristic Focus." It is the goal of this chapter to present the following: 1) general observations regarding men who present themselves for perpetrator treatment, 2) implications for treatment, and educational philosophy in progress, 3) an educational design for treating intimate partner perpetrators, and 4) conclusions and recommendations.

What I have discovered sitting with an interior view, looking with men from the depth of their wounds and vulnerabilities, is that many men get struck with an instantaneous hypnotic regression to the years of being little boys, wounded little boys, traumatized little boys (Pollack, 1998). A summarization of the participants' experience may be described as powerful slugs in the gut, rapid heart rates, inability to breathe, and crawling skin. This terror turns to survival-level rage, and is accompanied by no impulse control skills to manage the feelings. According to Farmer (1992),

> We are the walking wounded. All the disappointments,
> hurts, and losses throughout our lives that went ungrieved

213

and unacknowledged are wounds. And each unhealed wound keeps us from ourselves, keeps us from feeling our emotions fully, and pushes us further down the road to emptiness, aloneness, and addictive behavior. (p. 3)

Out of that emptiness and aloneness (many men I've heard say, "I can't stand to be alone"), men pick women to complete them; they marry their disowned and unlived self. And when this intimate partner expresses this disowned and unlived aspect of the male self, and precisely because he has disowned it, he can't hear and see and embrace it coming from her; hence the rage and violence. It is only with much training that men are able to develop a larger interior in which to process their partner's issues and be able to surround the pattern with their heart, absorb the attacks, and buffer the negative remarks. The initial reactivity demonstrated above may then be turned into appropriate responses.

Consequently, each participant carried an idealized internal mapping system, a construct, about what his intimate partner would be like. When the intimate partner does not measure up to the ideal, great frustration, conflict, and often anger ensues. They work effortlessly to get the woman back into the ideal state. Almost all men entering treatment minimize, deny, and blame their partners. Many men in treatment often state that their problems with women come from the fact that they haven't found the "right one" yet. Also when the woman doesn't meet their ideal, a broad system of male speak ensues regarding what women are like. Drawing from a broader sample to include statements of men in treatment, I enclose a list I call "Male Speak." The way men describe their partners reveals the emotional gulf between them and their partners and their inability to understand and empathize with them. These statements reveal that when men talk about their intimate partners, they are not talking about their intimate partners — they are taking about themselves, their perceptions, their expectations, and their internal constructs.

Speaking about their partner, they said:

She was snotty.	She's a control freak.
She was causing static.	She's bull headed.
She went off on me.	She whimpers and cries a lot.
She is a hot head.	She is grouchy.
She rambles on and on.	She's crabby.
She won't shut up.	She's pissy.

She was crabbin' out.

She nags and nags.

She was on the cranky side.

She was snippy.

She is uppity.

She freaks out.

She beats around the bush.

She's heartless.

She's totally selfish.

She is a snag.

She stovepiped on me.

She has a case of the jaws.

She is a P.M.S. wreck.

She knotted up on me.

She won't let up.

She keeps beating a dead horse.

She is irrational.

With regard to her intentions, they said:

She is doing this to provoke me.

She is doing it on purpose.

She is paying me back.

She is trying to push my buttons.

She is doing this deliberately.

She yanks me around.

With regard to the relationship, men have said:

The relationship is getting rocky.

The relationship went downhill.

The relationship fell apart.

The relationship is hard to deal with.

She puts up walls.

She is distancing herself.

She doesn't understand a thing about me.

She doesn't care about what I need.

She doesn't listen.

She's out to get me.

All she wants is my money.

You can't ever trust a woman.

She gets out of hand.

Men have to put up with a lot of anger.

She stresses me out.

She freaked out.

She moved out for no reason.

She ripped my guts out.

Don't ever bow down to a woman.

I didn't find the right one.

She wasn't the right one.

She knew what she was doing.

Consequently, it seems when men describe the misbehaviors of their intimate partners they use pejorative referents to describe them. The statements above reveal a great chasm between the man's perception of the woman and the actual intimate partner's state of being. If I asked some of these women, "Are you nagging, irrational, or heartless?" They would probably say, "No. I just want my partner to hear and understand what's bothering me."

These men, often frozen by the trauma of premature separation from the mother and similarly frozen and abusive fathers, were left with significant aspects of their potential personalities undeveloped. Without access to that undeveloped self, they sought a woman to express what to them is the inexpressible. Consequently, any unmanageable situation with an intimate activates fearful or terrifying feelings. As the men lack the ability to express these feelings, the negative emotions are often acted out as anger and rage. The window into the souls of the six participants revealed two illusionary perceptions. No woman is as exotic as the ecstasy construct, and no woman is as horrific as the agony construct. These women placed into categories by men speak only of the internal-viewing prism carried in the souls of these men. It is this great chasm a man can, through months of training, bridge in order to begin to build a participative team relationship with his partner.

Implications for Treatment: A Treatment Philosophy

An Education Philosophy, in Progress

The attempt to explore a method for treatment and prevention of intimate partner violence led to a reevaluation of my own views about education in general. A philosophy of education is a process of clarifying what one believes goes on in an educational endeavor. It becomes a theory base that influences what one does as an educator. I have drawn from and imitated my teachers, who have inspired the greatest passion for learning in me. Most of that is subliminal; however, I find that I am attracted to some ideas of several theoreticians in the field that help me formulate my philosophy of education. I shall mention some of them and try to formulate an eclectic statement. I shall then speak to implications for treatment of intimate partner perpetrators of violence in particular. When thinking of education, one may just point to the library and say, "It's all there — just go get it." However, we spend billions on schools teaching teachers learning techniques and philosophies about how to teach. The following is a brief overview of some thinkers about education with whom I am impressed. This may just be an incomplete list of my mentors.

John Dewey, according to Dworking (1959), came to "place his emphasis upon social purposes and political action that is inherent in what he came to term his 'experimentalism,' and, later, 'instrumentalism'" (p. 6). Education gets things done; it contributes to society and to social well-being. Alfred North Whitehead (1929) noted, "It can be stated briefly thus: The students are alive, and the purpose of education is to stimulate and guide their self-development. It follows as a corollary from this premise, that the teachers also should be alive with living thoughts" (p. 11). Education is the transmission of life from one living being to another. Paulo Freire (1996) opposed the banking concept of education, i.e. students are receptacles in which to deposit information. To impede two-way communication is to reduce men to the status of "things." He described teacher-centered education as cultural invasion, as opposed to cultural synthesis, wherein students are the center of the learning process.

> In cultural invasion, the actors draw the thematic content of their action from their own values and ideology, their starting point is their own world, from which they enter the world of those they invade. In cultural synthesis, the actors who come from "another world" to the world of the

> people do so not as invaders. They do not come to teach
> or to transmit or to give any thing, but rather to learn,
> with the people, about the people's world. (p. 181).

His goal was to help student participants in the learning process to find their own words and become a part of a learning community. Brown, Yeomans, and Grizzard (1975) emphasized his concepts of the "dead" and "alive" classroom.

> In the dead classroom learning is mechanistic, routine,
> over-ritualized, dull, and boring. The live classroom,
> on the other hand, is full of learning activities in which
> students are enthusiastically and authentically involved.
> The student takes on as much responsibility for their
> learning as their capacities allow. Each student is
> genuinely respected and treated as a human being by his
> teacher. (p. 1)

He emphasized the concept of "confluent education," i.e. putting feeling and thinking together in the learning process, whereby "the confluent teacher ...tends to be more sharing of himself" (p. ix). Parker Palmer (1993) stated, "Beneath the broken surface of our lives there remains — in the words of Thomas Merton — 'a hidden wholeness.' The hope of every wisdom tradition is to recall us to that wholeness in the midst of our torn world" (p. x).

> Authentic spirituality wants to open us to truth . . . (it)
> does not dictate where we must go, but trusts that any path
> walked with integrity will take us to a place of knowledge.
> Such spirituality encourages us to welcome diversity and
> conflict, to tolerate ambiguity, and to embrace paradox.
> By this understanding, the spirituality of education is not
> about dictating ends. It is about examining and clarifying
> the inner sources of teaching and learning, ridding us of
> the toxins that poison our hearts and minds . . . it addresses
> the fear that so often permeates and destroys teaching and
> learning. It will understand that fear, not ignorance, is the
> enemy of learning, and that fear is what gives ignorance
> its power. (p. xi).

Finally, J. Gordon Chamberlin (1964) may help us summarize our definition. His definition of education is as follows:

> Education is a consciously selected set of activities in which an individual or a group intentionally presents selected ideas or action to particular individuals in a particular setting by a controlled process that seeks the student's understanding and his conscious choice of response. (p. 157)

In sum, a philosophy of education involves an interactive process wherein thoughts and feelings commingle, enabling students to be enthusiastically and authentically involved (Brown et al., 1975). In this process these thoughts and feelings are transmitted by teachers alive with living thoughts to students who are also alive (engaged). The purpose of education is to stimulate and guide their self-development (Whitehead, 1929) in a way that helps student participants in the learning process to find their own words (Friere, 1963), to discover a hidden wholeness in order to welcome diversity and conflict, to tolerate ambiguity, and to embrace paradox (Palmer, 1993), and, according to Dewey, to improve themselves and society as a whole.

Education, therefore, is much more than the transmition of a concept from one frontal lobe to another. It involves the organism-as-a-whole. It involves the life-world experience the individual brings to the learning situation. It involves varying levels of existential fear. It involves one's attitudes regarding authority figures. The lifetime experience of the person is stored in the physiology of the person. It is the recapitulation of the womb, the crib, the terrible twos, Kindergarten, the ABCs, the times tables, recesses — everything — it's all there, sitting in my classroom.

Education, furthermore, is an enterprise that deals with a broad scope of reality that may require unique and varied approaches, depending upon the task and the student population (Armstrong, 1987; Gardner, 1993). In point, what is an appropriate educational approach to address the subliminal unlived constructs of the violent male interiority mentioned previously? Bear in mind that the populations here involved, regarding the information to be transmitted, according to many researchers, do not have a verbal repertoire adequate to address their interior constructs. What kind of an educational philosophy would be appropriate for a treatment program treating this population?

I have examined numerous program-training approaches; over my years as a therapist I have used many different treatment approaches. Most programs have a syllabus that delineates a great body of information regarding numerous aspects of the domestic violence problem. The treatment approach is similar to most educational endeavors. Information is transmitted via lectures, videos, discussions, handouts and workbooks. Mentally acquired information about appropriate behavior is important, and I believe there is a trickle-down phenomenon. However, I wonder whether there is a better way.

I have treated in counseling numerous professionals, all highly intelligent, motivated individuals; all, though capable of acquiring information, have difficulty in their interactions with female partners. I find the current information-giving approaches helpful for understanding the problem, but very limited as far as addressing internal psychological constructs.

What I am describing would be similar to a person's taking a ground-school training program to become an airplane pilot. Upon finishing the ground-school training, the instructor puts the person in an airplane and says, "Okay, now go fly this airplane" (treatment programs may serve as a "flight simulator"). Or, the situation could be compared to a person's taking a culinary arts course without ever seeing the inside of a kitchen, studying horsemanship without ever riding a horse, or studying automobile mechanics without ever seeing under a hood. What is a philosophy of education and training suitable for treating the internal constructs of the population we are describing?

An Educational Design for Treating Intimate Partner Perpetrators

I am drawing from several years of training in Gestalt Therapy theory. Gestalt Therapy is an existential, phenomenologically based orientation. Phenomenology deals with the content, the subject matter, the topic, in this case, the physiologically based stream of conscious awareness of the individual. Existentialism is stance that deals with the element of time. The time factor, in this case, is the now — here and now. The existential, phenomenologically based orientation involves attending to the stream of personal awarenesses and consciousness moment by momemt in the here and now. Its primary focus is upon facilitating experience rather than transmitting information. For the Gestalt therapist, information is an *a posteriori* cognitive learning process that comes as a result of an experiential learning environment that facilitates deep organism-as-a-whole experiences. The organism-as-whole realities of fear, defensiveness, or counterdependence modulate the potential for learning. Often after an experiential experiment in the program, I see a participant go to the rack of handouts in the group room and take a handout descriptor of the experiment that just took place. This kind of learning must be lived out physiologically. I shall illustrate. How would one present a lesson to access the preceding "ecstasy" section involving the interior goddess? Educational descriptions may be helpful, but may not access the construct. Consider the following exercise. The following exercise is typical, not necessarily universally absolute, and because I facilitate this exercise for a specific purpose, I direct the questions toward a teleological outcome.

A group of ten men are sitting in a circle. A chair is placed in front of the man who has volunteered or been selected. A statement is made to the person: "Let's make believe your ideal dream woman — not necessarily your intimate partner — your goddess, your Madonna is sitting on that chair. We all are going to interview you to find out what she is like." I call this the "meet the Goddess exercise." After a little confusion and clarification, the questions begin to flow and from the man in the chair answers begin to come freely. On the blackboard are recorded the growing personality profile factors of this dream woman. The questions and answers cover a broad array of factors: height, weight, size, color of hair, size of breasts, style of clothing. Does she wear jeans and cowboy boots, tailored suits, flowing scarves? What kind of car does she drive? What kind of house does she live in, what level of education does she have, and what kind of job does she have? After an hour or more a pretty clear profile is developed, and by this time the male participant is fairly well disassociated from the group setting and has become attuned to the inner goddess.

Then I say, "Let's all make believe that we are going outside and getting into a make-believe van. The woman lives here in town, and we are all going over to meet her." We drive over to her house. With the rest of men waiting in the van, the participant and I get out of the van and walk up the sidewalk to the house he described and knock on the door. By this time the participant is in obvious physical discomfort. His shirt is wet under the arms, his breathing is much more rapid, and he may be shaking. I have done this exercise dozens of times and the reactions are very similar. We may stop halfway up the sidewalk to query the participant about how he is doing. He is usually minimally hyperventilating. Finally, we knock on the door and we can hear her footsteps coming to the door. (Keep in mind we have just spent two hours fleshing out this dream woman and now he is going to meet her.) One response is rather typical. She comes to the door and I say to the man, "There she is." He has already ascribed a name to her. I say, "Crystal, I'd like to introduce you to Bill." I ask Bill what he would like to say to her. He says with a quivering voice, "I am going to shake her hand and say 'I'm glad to meet you.' And then I am going to turn around and run like hell and never stop" — terror of the goddess.

We then go back to the room and I place another chair beside the dream woman's chair. And I tell the man, this is your wife or girlfriend, and I invite the two imaginary women to have a conversation. That needs a little prompting. I ask the man to tell me the wife's response to the dream woman. He says his wife would like to claw her eyes out. I ask the man what the dream woman's response to the wife would be, and he says that she is very understanding of the wife and has great compassion for her.

Then I move the wife's chair around behind the dream woman's chair. There is a direct line of vision, with the male participant looking directly at the dream woman's chair with his wife's chair behind. And I ask him how much of the dream woman was present when he first met his wife. He says, "Oh, a lot." Then I move the wife's chair out from behind the dream woman's chair and make believe the wife is calling him a jerk, stupid, or wrong. I ask him what he feels when his wife disapproves of him and calls him a jerk. He says he feels crazy and wants her to get back in line of vision with the dream woman.

In this exercise the participant goes though all the real-life physiological experiences. Any learning from the experience is unique to the participant, and since it is physiological, it is much more relevant than just an intellectual explanation of the experiment. Gestalt therapy is experimental and experiential.

There is another experiment for the "agony" section mentioned above. I call it the "Getting in Your Face Exercise." Often I have women who are certified trainees participate in the men's group. This time I invite one of the women trainees to place her chair in front of a male participant. I tell the participant what to do and assign him his response. I tell the participant that no matter what she says he is to 1) thank her, 2) compliment her, and 3) let the angry words go over his shoulder and respond with a phrase that mirrors back to her the feelings she must be having. He is to formulate some simple phrases to let her know he understands how she feels experientially. She then confronts the male participant with one of several short scenarios. A couple of the scenarios are as follows:

> Bill! Whenever I get up in the morning I have to come out to a dirty kitchen. I have it all cleaned when I go to bed, and you come out here in the middle of the night and make yourself a peanut butter and jelly sandwich and leave crumbs, peanut butter and jelly, and milk all over the counter. I can't even make breakfast until I clean up your damn mess. If you want a maid *go get one!*

Or,

> Well! I see that *you* got to work on time! When I went out to get in my car to go to work I could see you had already left. I was dressed in my heels and lo and behold my battery was dead. Where were you? Gone! There I stood with jumper cables in hand, ten degrees above zero, trying to flag somebody down to give me a jump. (With intensity and volume) *You don't give a damn about anybody but yourself!*

(I saw a large man collapse into a fetal position on the floor when a petite woman with a shrill voice yelled at him in an experimental exercise). Now can these men follow instructions? No! They lapse right into their lifelong response patterns. At best, they begin to apologize with, "I'm sorry." We don't allow any statements of "I'm sorry," because that precludes an immediate expected response from the partner of "Oh that's okay" when it isn't. Usually they begin a long explanation. Explain! And tell! Explain! And tell! If only the woman could understand the man's point of view he would be relieved of tension, he would be okay, and homeostasis would return. Everything is attempted to get her to shift from confrontational to compliant. After considerable training, an appropriate response might sound something like this.

> Wow! Mary, that's awful. Thank you so much for being willing to talk to me about that. I just want to compliment you for coming and talking to me about this — you could have told your sisters, mother, and all your girl friends instead. I'll bet when you were standing out there with those jumper cables you must have felt really angry, abandoned, uncared for by me, and really humiliated. You had a right to feel like I didn't care about you and your car. That must have been awful!

Whatever suggestions are presented must be adapted to each individual's communication style. Some men can pick it up really soon, and others need a lot of practice, when a real woman is getting in their face, depending upon the degree of woundedness experienced by the person. The most common goal of many men is outcome oriented — to get her back to feeling happy again. It is difficult for a man to see from her perspective, take her at face value, and take her concerns seriously when his physiological defenses are activated.

One interaction stands out. A bright woman observer from a local university women's studies program confronted a banker in the group, using one of the typical scenarios. (Our program is a contracted training site for interns in a Masters of Social Work program at a local university.) The banker's immediate response as he clapped his hands together was, "That's settled, I'll take care of that right away. Now let's you and I go out for dinner." This woman's slow pointed response was, "You – take — your — god — damned — dinner — and — shove — it — up — your — ass. You — are — not — going — to — buy — me — off — and — not — talk — about — my — feelings — with — a — god — damned — dinner." This was one woman's insistence that external ploys were not going to substitute for interpersonal empathy.

I have developed numerous experiential training exercises designed to activate the organism-as-a-whole where the physiological lifelong construct data is stored. The main goal is training in empathy, attunement, and listening. Some men are very effective; some aren't.

In sum, traditional educational information transmission, lectures, handouts, logs, videos, talking, sharing experiences, describing the abuse, domestic violence theory and information (the cycle of violence, the Duluth Wheels, continua of domestic violence progressive severity, etc.), and victim theory may be helpful information to share; but they may make little impact on the internal psychological male wounds from childhood without the experiential exercises, e.g. the "flight simulator." Short, or even yearlong information-oriented educational courses, it seems to me, are less effective.

A lot of the treatment work for perpetrators is extrinsic. It addresses the cognitive intellect. However, what is being presented here is intrinsic work. It is work from the inside out. Women have served as trigger points of, activators of, and recipients of the activity of these internal constructs. In a program dealing with these internal shadows, it seems to me that, heuristically speaking, someone who has traversed these interior landscapes must help the client visit these terror places, activate them, elucidate them, dialogue with them, embrace them, and bring them into conscious awareness. It is interior work. It is emergent, and it requires a milieu of safety and self-motivation.

A metaphor that has been helpful is that of a minefield. I as the therapist move to be with and join this man in the minefield of conflicted internal psychological constructs. I join him. I enter into his world. I look out through his eyes, and seek to help him discover for himself the internal currents and nuances of fear, rage, dumbfoundedness, frozenness, and stuckness in the face of an angry intimate partner. Then we attempt to weave our way through the mines without getting blown up — that is, blowing up. Conflict management is always, in my view, first of all self-management.

The internal dimension of the perpetrator's world must be addressed. Quantities of research developed by therapists who have focused on the organism as a whole have attended to the intimate relationship between behavior and underlying emotions (Leventhal, & Scherer, 1987; Tompkins, 1982). These affect theorists explored the relationship between cognition and emotions. They built upon the earlier work of Reich (1949), Perls, (1951), and Lowen (1958) and have their focus upon undoing the psychological, behavioral, and physical defenses against emotional experience and emotional expression. Though we pride outselves on being logial thinkers, cognition is an insecure craft floating on a sea of emotions (Nathanson, 1992). The problem in treating perpetrators is the belief that giving them information about how to manage anger will make a difference. Treatment of perpetrators must move beyond information giving. "The problem in therapy is always how to move from an ineffectual intellectual appreciation of a truth about oneself to some emotional experience of it. It is only when therapy enlists deep emotions that it becomes a powerful force for change" (Sheikh & Yalome, 1996). Psycho-education falls short when it comes to addressing the life-long deposits of male wounds. "The aim of every moment in every [therepy] session is to put the patient in touch with as much of his true feelings as he can bear" (Malan, 1995).

The totality of the participant must be enlisted and motivated to explore and confront the deeper structures. Therefore, this work can't be done on ourselves or with other men because of some outside, extrinsic mandate — the courts, wives and partners, or the women's movement. We have to break out of the century's prescriptions of what it means to be a man and follow our intrinsic moral mandate that as men we need to "do what needs to be done" to be responsible to our internal journey. We must confront internally our limitations and our inapproprate responses to conflict that hurt others by confronting the deamons within ourselves. We need to work on ourselves toward our potential fulfillment as integrated human beings.

In experiential training programs men are helped to attune to a greater range of physiological nuances and to identify the activity in their bodies with words — for example, a knot in the gut, rapid breathing, skin crawling, and muscle tenseness. Many men have great difficulty talking about their physiological experiences. They are helped to differentiate affect.

An example of differentiating affect, finding words for inner realities, is as follows. During a check-in at a group meeting, a man said that he'd had a "shitty" week. When describing the intimate partner, one man said, "I have a piss-poor old lady." Some programs dismiss these men for "victim blaming." If a program atmosphere is a safe place for men to talk, their underlying resentments come out. It is at this point that the treatment process begins, not expulsion from the group. A rigorous interview process helps the client to describe the events or behaviors that brought him discomfort.

Secondly, it takes additional work to help him verbalize his physiological experiential feelings regarding those events and people. Thirdly, it takes much more interviewing and some suggestions to help this person to get into the shoes of the person (e.g. the "piss-poor old lady") that caused his discomfort, with a therapeutic eye, to understand, identify, and be able to value the other person's reality. Fourthly, the client is prompted to make a summarizing restatement of the event, a description of his experience, and an empathic statement of understanding about the derided event or person — a great improvement over "shitty." The goal is to develop a vocabulary for internal realities beyond clichés. If a man can't evoke and describe his internal physiological (feeling) realities, it is very difficult for him to identify and join another person, especially an intimate partner, in her internal affective reality. The goal is to find new techniques for treating normative male alexithymia, the inability of men to put their feelings into words, due to traditional gender role socialization (Levant, 1997).

Conclusions

I greatly benefited from the work of Karr-Morse and Wiley (1997). Based upon new technologies of observing experiences of the fetus within the anatomy of a female, it became clear that that experience had an impact upon the remainder of a human's life. As I contemplated the fetus and its context in the woman, my mind drifted back to origins and the centuries of the gene flow that was resident there in that womb.

Consequently, looking far back, I was impressed with the work of Habermas (1979) and his view of the awakening consciousness of the role of being a father as a significant member in the social group. Then, as I plunged into the views of what men were thought to be throughout the cultural epochs of history — in the classical period, the heroic male; in the medieval years, the otherworldly male and the knightly male; the Renaissance man, the bourgeois male, and in the United States, the aristocrat and his family, the common man and the suffragette, the he-man and his compatriots, to partners at last — I began to feel experientially this unconscious, internal masculinity programming.

The messages survived the centuries: Don't be afraid, never let them see you sweat, avoid anything feminine, keep a stiff upper lip, no sissy stuff around here, never become pussy whipped, don't be a crybaby, and never give up, to name a few. These are not just words, or landscapes; they are force fields of psychic energy that drive some men.

I was impressed with researchers such as Joseph Pleck, who began the task of destructuring the rules of manhood, who traced the development of masculinity research during the twentieth century to explore greater potential for men.

I greatly enjoyed the research on the distinctions between the way male and female children are raised and how many are socially conditioned to perpetuate the Male Sex Role Identity (Pleck, 1995). It was also helpful to update myself on the current theory of perpetrators and domestic violence.

In sum, ringing in my ears are the roles the male assumed as the provider for the survival of the family social group and how the hunting and gathering societies set the tone for maleness. Males went out and brought in. Females nurtured the young. This division of labor seemed to focus attention and activities toward one part of the male/female dichotomy and shaped the potential of both genders. Those characteristics for survival became mores, prescribed roles, and life patterns. They became a historically formed base and beliefs about maleness.

Small male children absorb their family cultures as if hypnotized. When a child receives adequate support, he blossoms and may become his own unique person. When the early growing environment is not conducive or is adverse to his growth, the child is overwhelmed with trauma or empty, lacking support, and longs and longs for that unmet need. The unfinished situation lingers in the consciousness, forever awaiting fulfillment. A single traumatic event repeated numerous times becomes a lifelong pattern of behavior. And that life-long pattern forms the lifelong view of the world. This unlived, split off, disowned aspect of the male psyche causes most men to seek a women to stand in that shadow and fulfill it. Much work is being done to help both men and women to embrace greater aspects of each other's polarity. Men who abuse their intimate partners are often acting out the experiences and programming they received. Whether a person is two years old or fifty years old, what that individual is not in touch with internally, what he cannot verbalize is likely to be acted out on the interpersonal environmental field. Those nonverbalizable constructs show up in our world, in our faces, to bug us until we finish the unfinished task. Intimate partner violence is an inappropriate response based on the limitations of human development, ranging from discomfort to disgust

227

with and/or vengeance upon an intimate partner when expectations are not met. The main impact this study had on me was to clarify and make definite the notion that children, beginning in the womb, must be parented appropriately throughout their developmental stages. It is the task of adult men to face and take responsibility for this national tragedy, to work toward its eradication, and to parent their children appropriately.

In sum, historical masculinity, while positing many wonderful masculine traits, leaves men with great personal qualities yet to be realized. Greater understanding and modification of current parenting styles may help males realize these missing personal qualities. In the meantime, damaged men who scare and hurt others must be healed. It seems that a loving healer addressing the roots and history of these fears and hurts best accomplishes this healing process.

Recommendations

As I worked through these pages I could not avoid reflecting on the internal constructs of women. I wondered what centuries of subordination to men did to women's psyches. I wondered what the realities of their internal psychological constructs are that is evident in their sacrificing for their families. I wondered what internal force fields their fathers created in them. I wondered what internal realities, beneath the commonly stated reasons, keep women in battering relationships. I think it is important to keep looking behind the surface statements for these deepseated realities in women.

Specific needs for future research involve longitudinal studies to attempt to discover patterns for the escalation and cessation of female abuse. Additional research is needed with regard to ethnic minority communities and alternative lifestyle communities to discover similarities and differences in behavioral patterns in order to formulate appropriate treatment. Research is needed to discover community resource systems and to formulate protocols that may be applied among other communities.

When we are dealing with human lives, it seems that prevention of the problem might be given greater thought. Is it too idealistic to conclude that there is a problem with adolescents, of whatever age, bringing human beings into the world when it takes more thought, study, and training to obtain a driver's license than it does to produce a human being? Much is needed to insure adequate maturity, parenting and child development training, and an extended family support to insure adequate financial care. Human beings are cast aside for the rest of society to assume their care. Thousands are now being born for whom others, who never made the choice to bring these children into the world, will have to assume their care, in many cases resulting in great lifelong damage to the child. Prevention of this national tragedy is a dominant need.

REFERENCE LIST

Adams, D. (1994). *Historical timeline of institutional responses to battered women*. Cambridge, MA: Emerge.

Adams, D., Bancroft, L., German, T., & Sousa, C. (1992). *First-stage groups for men who batter*. Cambridge, MA: Emerge.

Adler, G., Fordham, M., & Read, J. (Eds.). (1953-1971). The collected works of C.G. Jung. Princeton: Princeton University Press.

Aharon, I., Ariely, D., Breiter, H., Chabris, C.E.N., Etcoff, N., & O'Connor, E. (2001). Beautiful faces have variable reward value: FMRI and behavioral evidence. *Neuron, 32* (November), 537-551.

Albert, D., Walsh, M., & Jonick, R. (1993). Aggression in humans: What is its biological foundation? *Neuroscience and Bio-Behavioral Reviews, 17*, 405-425.

Aldarondo, E., & Sugarman, D. (1996). Risk maker analysis of the cessation and persistence of wife assault. *Journal of Consulting and Clinical Psychology, 5*, 1010-1019.

Amanpour, C. (1997). Tyranny of the Taliban. *Time, 150*, 60.

Anderson, K. (1981). *Wartime women: Sex roles, family relations, and the status of women during World War II*. Westport, CT: Greenwood Press.

Anonymous. (1999). A painful tradition: Sabiny women of Uganda endure female genital mutilation. *Newsweek, 134*, 323.

Ansari, M. (1997). Sati, the blessing and the curse. *Journal of Folklore Research, 34* (May/August), 161-164.

Archer, J. (1991). The influence of testosterone on human aggression. *British Journal of Psychology, 82*, 1-28.

Archer, J., & Lloyd, B. (1985). *Sex and gender.* Cambridge: Cambridge University Press.

Arieti, S. (1967). *The intrapsychic self.* New York: Basic Books.

Armstrong, T. (1987). *In their own way*. New York: Jeremy P. Tarcher, Inc.

Babbie, E. (1995). *The practice of social research*. New York: Wadsworth Publishing Company.

Babcock, J., Waltz, J., Jacobson, N., & Gottman, J. (1993). Power and violence: The relation between communication patterns, power discrepancies, and domestic violence. *Journal of Consulting and Clinical Psychology, 61*(1), 40-50.

Bachman, R., & Saltzman, L. E. (1995). *Violence against women: Estimated from the redesigned survey.* Washington D.C.: U.S. Department of Justice, Bureau of Justice Statistics.

Banerjee, P. (1999). Burning questions: Widows, witches, and early modern European travel narratives of India. *Journal of Medieval and Early Modern Studies, 29*(3), 529-61.

Barker-Benfield, G. (1976). *The horrors of the half known life: Male attitudes toward women and sexuality in nineteenth-century America.* New York: Harper & Row.

Barnhouse, T. (1974). Forward. In R. A. Johnson, *He: Understanding masculine psychology*. New York: Harpers.

Barns, F. (1999). *The war on boys*. The National Desk Season II (Producer)PBS Television.

Barrett, W. (1962). *Irrational man*. Garden City, NY: Doubleday Anchor Books.

Becker, E. (1975). *Escape from evil*. New York: Free Press.

Belcher, R.W., & Pollack, W.S. (1993). *In a time of fallen heroes: The re-creation of masculinity*. New York: Atheneum.

Berger, P. (1973). *Invitation to sociology: A humanistic perspective*. Woodstock, NY: Overlook Press.

Berne, E. (1961). *Transactional analysis in psychotherapy*. New York: Grove Press.

Berry, D. (2001). *The domestic violence sourcebook*. Chicago: Contemporary: St. Albens: Verulam.

Blanck, G., & Blanck, R. (1974). *Ego psychology: Theory and practice.* New York: Columbia University Press.

Blocker, K. (2001 July). Court handles large caseload. *The Spokesman-Review*, B1.

Bloland, P. (1992). Qualitative research in student affairs. *ERIC Document Reproduction Services No. ED 347 487.* Ann Arbor, MI.

Bodnarchuk, M., Kropp, R., Ogloff, J., Hart, S., & Dutton, D. (1995). *Predicting cessation of intimate assaultiveness after group treatment.* Ottawa, Heath Canada: Family Violence Prevention Division (No. 4887-10-91-106) .

Boehm, F. (1932). The feminity-complex in men. *International Journal of Psychoanalysis, 11,* 444-469.

Borg, W., & Gall, M. (1989). *Educational research: An introduction.* White Plains, NY: Longman.

Boss, M. (1963). *Psychoanalysis and daseinanalysis.* New York: Basic Books.

Boszormenyi-Nagy, I., & Ulrich, D. (1981). Contextual family therapy. In A S. Gurman & D.P. Kniskern (Eds.), *Handbook of family therapy.* New York: Brunner/Mazel.

Bowlby, J. (1969). *Attachment and loss: Attachment (Vol. I).* New York: Basic Books, Inc.

Bowlby, J. (1973). *Attachment and loss: Separation (Vol. II).* New York: Basic Books, Inc.

Bowlby, J. (1980). *Attachment and loss: Loss (Vol. III).* New York: Basic Books, Inc.

Brody, L., & Hall, J. (1993). Gender and emotions. In M. Lewis & J. J. Haviland (Eds.), *Handbook of Emotions.* New York: Guilford.

Brooks, J., & Lewis, M. (1974). Attachment behavior in thirteen-month-old, opposite-sex twins. *Child Development, 45,* 243-247.

Brown, G., Yeomans, T., Grizzard, L. (1975). *The live classroom: Innovation through confluent education and Gestalt.* New York: The Viking Press.

Brown, N. (1959). *Life against death*. Middletown, Conn: Wesleyan University Press.

Brownlee, S., & Seter, J. (1994, February 7). In the name of ritual. *U.S. News and World Report, 116*, 56-58.

Buber, M. (1958). *I and thou*. New York: Charles Scribners Sons.

Buck, R. (1984). *The communication of emotion*. New York: Guilford.

Buckley, J. (1986). *Female fault and fulfillment in Gnosticism*. Chapel Hill, N.C.: University of North Carolina Press.

Butterfield, L., Friedlander, M., & Kline, M. (1975). *The book of Abigail and John: Selected letters of the Adams family, 1762-1784*. Cambridge: Harvard University Press.

Buzawa, E., & Buzawa, C. (1996). *Domestic violence: The criminal justice response*. Thousand Oaks, CA: Sage.

Cahoone, L. (1996). *From modernism to postmodernism: An anthology*. Maden, Massachusetts: Blackwell Publishers Inc.

Callahan. (1960). *An introduction to education in America*. New York: Knopf.

Campbell, A. (1993). *Men, women and aggression*. New York: Basic Books.

Campbell, J. (1959). *The masks of God (Vol. 1, Primitive mythology)*. New York: Viking Press.

Cantarella, E. (1987). *Pandora's daughters: The role and status of women in Greek and Roman antiquity*. Baltimore: Johns Hopkins University Press.

Chamberlin, J. (1964). *Toward a phenomenology of education*. Philadelphia: The Westminster Press.

Chaucer, G. (1952). The nun's priest's tale. In Neville Coghill (translator), *Canterbury Tales*. Baltimore: Penguin Books.

Chavetz, J. (1984). *Sex and advantage*. Totowa, NJ: Rowan & Alanheld.

Cheakalos, C. (1998, November 2). Mercy mission; W. Dirie speaks out against female genital mutilation. *People Weekly, 50*, (16) 149-150.

Chodorow, N. (1978). *The reproduction of mothering: Psychoanalysis and the sociology of gender.* Berkeley: University of California Press.

Clark, S., Burt, M., Schulte, M., & Maguire, K. (1996). *Coordinated community responses to domestic violence in six communities: Beyond the justice system.* Newbury Park, CA: Sage.

Coleman, D., & Straus, M. (1990). Marital power, conflict, and violence in a nationally representative sample of American couples. In M. Straus & R. Gelles (Eds.), *Physical violence in American families: Risk factors and adaptations to violence in 8,145 families* (pp. 287-304). New Brunswick, NJ: Transaction.

Collingwood, R. G. (1965). *Essays in the philosophy of history.* New York: McGraw-Hill Company.

Common Purpose. (1996). *Common purpose training.* Boston: Author.

Corey, G. (1986). *Theory and practice of counseling and psychotherapy.* Pacific Grove: California: Brooks/Cole Publishing Company.

Cott, N. (1977). *The bonds of womanhood.* New Haven: Yale University Press.

Cousin, M. (1997). State certified domestic violence treatment issues. In A. Ganley (contributor), *Domestic violence in civil court cases: A national model for judicial education.* Spokane, WA: Spokane Domestic Violence Consortium.

Crary, D. (2000, January). Activists say intimate murder often preventable. *Spokesman-Review,* B1.

Curwen, E. (1953). *Plough and pasture: The early history of farming.* New York: Henry Schuman.

D'Andrea, M. (2000). Postmodernism, constructivism, and multiculturalism: Three forces reshaping and expanding our thoughts about counseling. *Journal of Mental Health Counseling, 22* (1), 1-16.

Davis, E. (1972). *The first sex.* New York: Penguin.

Davis R., & Taylor, B. (1999). Does batterer treatment reduce violence? A synthesis of the literature. In L. Feder (Ed.), *Women and domestic violence: An interdisciplinary approach.* New York: The Haworth Press, Inc.

235

Decker, D. (1999). *Stopping the violence*. New York: The Haworth Press, Inc.

Degler, C. (1980). *At odds: Women in the family in America from the revolution to the present*. New York: Oxford University Press.

Delk, J., Madden, B., Livingston, M., & Ryan, T. (1986). Adult perception of the infant as a function of gender labeling and observer gender. *Sex Roles, 15*, 527-534.

DePuy, J. (1995). *Power, control, and abuse against women in Swiss families*. Durham, NH: Paper presented at the Fourth International Family Violence Research Conference.

Diamond, J. (1979). *Your body doesn't lie*. New York: Warner Books.

Dillenberger, J. (1985). *The Magdalen: Reflections on the image of the saint and sinner in Christian era*. Albany: State University of New York Press.

Dobash, R. P., & Dobash, R. E. (1979). *Violence against wives*. New York: The Free Press.

Dobash, R. P., Dobash, R. E., Wilson, M., & Daly, M. (1992). The myth of sexual symmetry in marital violence. *Social Problems, 39* (1), 71-91.

Donavan, J. (1985). *Feminist theory: the intellectual traditions of American feminism*. New York, NY: A Fredrick Unger Book: Continuum.

Donegan, J. (1985). *Women & men midwives: Medicine, morality and misogyny in early America*. Westport, CT: Greenwood Press.

Douglas, A. (1977). *The feminization of American culture*. New York: Knopf.

Douglas, H. (1991). Assessing violent couples. *Families in Society,* 525-535.

Doyle, J. (1983). *The male experience*. Dubuque: William C. Brown Publishers.

Dubbert, J. (1974). Progressivism and the masculinity crisis. *Psychoanalytic Review, 61,* 433-455.

Dunn, J., Bretherton, I., & Munn, P. (1987). Conversations about feeling states between mothers and their children. *Developmental Psychology, 27,* 132-9.

Dutton, D. (1995). *The batterer: A psychological profile.* New York: Basic Books.

Dutton, D., & Starzomski, A. (1993). Borderline personality in perpetrator of psychological and physical abuse. *Violence and Victims, 63*(4), 614-622.

Dworkin, A. (1974). *Woman hating.* New York: E.P. Dutton.

Dworking, M. (1959). *Dewey on education.* New York: Bureau of Publications Teachers College, Columbia University.

Edleson, J., & Tolman, R. (1992). *Intervention for men who batter.* Newbury Park, CA: Sage.

Eisenberg, N., & Lennon, R. (1983). Sex differences in empathy and related capacities. *Psychological Bulletin, 94*(1), 100-31.

Eisler, R. (1987). *The chalice & the blade: Our history, our future.* New York: Harper & Row, Perennial Library.

Eisler, R., & Skidmore, J. (1987). Masculine gender role stress. *Behavior Modification, 11,* 13-36.

Ells, A. (1990). *One-way relationships: When you love them more than they love you.* Nashville: Thomas Nelson Publishers.

Erikson, E. (1963). *Childhood and society.* New York: Norton.

Fagan, J., & Browne, Q. (1994). Violence between spouses and intimates: Physical aggressions between women and men in intimate relationships. A. Reiss & J. Roth (Eds.), *Understanding and preventing violence* (Vol. 3 pp. 115-292). Washington D.C.: National Research Council, National Academy of Sciences.

Fagot, B. (1985). A cautionary note: Parents' socialization of boys and girls. *Sex Roles, 12,* 141-146.

Fall, K., Howard, S., & Ford, J. (1999). *Alternatives to domestic violence: A homework manual for battering intervention groups.* Philadelphia, PA: Accelerated Development.

Farber, M. (1966). *The aims of phenomenology: The motives, methods, and impact of Husserl's thought*. New York: Harper & Row, Harper Torchbooks.

Farmer, S. (1992). *The wounded male*. New York: Ballantine Books.

Feder, L. (1999). *Women and domestic violence: An interdisciplinary approach*. New York: Harworth Press.

Felson, R., & Russo, N. (1988). Parental punishment and sibling aggression. *Social Psychology Quarterly, 51*, 11-18.

Fenichel, O. (1945). *The psychoanalytic theory of neurosis*. New York: Norton.

Ferrante, J. (1980). The education of women in the Middle Ages in theory, fact, and fantasy. In P. Labalme (Ed.), *Beyond their sex: Learned women of the European past* (pp.9-42). New York: New York University Press.

Field, S., & Straus, M. (1990). Escalation and desistance from wife assault in marriage. In M. A. Straus & R. J. Gelles (Eds.), *Physical violence in American families: Risk factors and adaptations to violence in 8,145 families* (pp.489-505). New Brunswick, NJ: Transaction.

Filene, P. (1986). *Him/her/self: Sex roles in modern America (2nd ed.)*. Baltimore: John Hopkins University Press.

Finkelhorr, D. (1984). *Child sexual abuse: New theory and research*. New York: Free Press.

Finn, J. (1987). Men's domestic violence treatment: The court referral component. *Journal of Interpersonal Violence, 2*(2), 154-165.

Fivush, R. (1989). Exploring sex differences in the emotional content of mother-child conversations about the past. *Sex Roles, 20*, 675-91.

Flannery, D., & Huff, R. (1998). *Youth violence: Prevention, intervention, and social policy*. Washington, D.C.: American Psychiatric Press.

Flexner, E. (1959). *Century of struggle*. Cambridge: Harvard University Press.

Florisha, B. (1978). *Sex roles and personal awareness*. Morristown, NJ: General Learning Press.

Flowers, R. (2000). *Domestic crime, family violence and child abuse: A study of contemporary American society.* New York: McFarland & Company, Inc.

Freire, P. (1996). *Pedagogy of the oppressed.* New York: Continuum.

Frey, S., & Morton, M. (1986). *New world, new roles: A documentary history of women in pre-industrial America.* Westport, CT: Greenwood Press.

Fried, M. (1967). *The evolution of political society.* New York: Random House.

Fromm, E. (1973). *The anatomy of human destructiveness.* New York: Fawcett.

Fuchs, D., & Thelen, M. (1988). Children's expected interpersonal consequences of communicating their affective state and reported likelihood of expression. *Child Development, 59,* 1314-1322.

Fulghum, R. (1989). *All I need to know I learned in kindergarten.* Berkeley: Celestial Arts.

Understanding domestic violence, improving the health care response to domestic violence: a resource manual for heath care providers. (1995). Reading, PA: Family Violence Prevention Fund in collaboration with the Pennsylvania Coalition Against Domestic Violence.

Ganley, A., Warshaw, C., & Salber, R. (1995). *Improving the health care response to domestic violence: A resource manual for health care providers.* Reading, PA: Family Violence Prevention Fund in Collaboration with the Pennsylvania Coalition Against Domestic Violence.

Gardner, H. (1993). *Multiple intelligences.* New York: Basic Books.

Gardner, J. (1986). *Women in Roman law and society.* Bloomington: Indiana University Press.

Garrison, D. (1974). The tender technicians: The feminization of public librarianship 1876-1905. In M. Hartman & L. Banner (Eds.), *Clio's consciousness raided: New perspectives on the history of women* (pp.158-178). New York: Harper & Row.

Gebser, J. (1985). *The ever-present origin.* Athens: Ohio University Press.

Geertz, C. (1973). *The interpretation of cultures: Selected essays.* New York: Basic Books.

Gelles, R. (1993). Through a sociological lens: Social structure, and family violence. In R. Gelles & D. Loseke (Eds.), *Current controversies on family violence* (pp. 31-46). New York: Sage.

Gelles, R., & Loseke, E. (1993). *Current controversies on family violence.* Newbury Park, CA: Sage Publications.

Gendlin, E. (1978). *Focusing.* New York: Bantam New Age Books.

George, M. (1997). Into the eyes of Medusa: Beyond testosterone, men, and violence. *The Journal of Men's Studies, 5*(4), 295.

Gibb, J. (1978). *Trust: A new vision of human relationships for business, education, family, and personal living.* North Hollywood: Newcastle Publishing Co., Inc.

Gilligan, C. (1982). *In a different voice: Psychological theory and women's development.* Cambridge, MA: Harvard University Press.

Gilmore, D. (1990). *Manhood in the making: Cultural concepts of masculinity.* New Haven: Yale University Press.

Gimbutas, M. (1973). The beginning of the bronze age in Europe and the Indo-Europeans: 3500-2500 B.C. *Journal of Indo-European Studies, 1,* 166.

Gimbutas, M. (1991). *The civilization of the goddess.* San Francisco: Harper Collins.

Glasser, W. (1970). *Mental health or mental illness?* New York: Harper & Row, Publishers.

Gleason, J., & Greif, E. (1983). Men's speech to young children. In B. Thorne, C. Kamarae, & N. Henley (Eds.), *Language, gender and society* (pp. 140-150). London: Newberry House.

Goble, F. (1970). *The third force: The psychology of Abraham Maslow.* New York: Pocket Books, Gulf & Western.

Gold, P. (1985). *The lady and the virgin: Image, attitude, and experience in twelfth-century France*. Chicago: University of Chicago Press.

Goldberg, H. (1976). *The hazards of being male: surviving the myth of masculine privilege*. New York: Signet Books.

Goldberg, S., & Lewis, M. (1969). Play behavior in the year-old infant: Early sex differences. *Child Development, 40*, 21-31.

Gondolf, E. (1987). Evaluating programs for men who batter: Problems and prospects. *Journal of Family Violence, 2*(1).

Gondolf, E. (1990). An exploratory survey of court-mandated batterer programs. *Response to Victimization of Women and Children, 13*(3), 7-11.

Good, H. G. (1964). *A history of American education (2nd ed.)*. New York: Macmillian.

Gordon, M. (1980). The ideal husband as depicted in the nineteenth-century marriage manual. In E. Pleck & J. Pleck (Eds.), *The American Man* (pp. 145-157). Englewood Cliffs, NJ: Prentice-Hall.

Gottman, J. (1994). *Why marriages succeed or fail*. New York: Simon & Schuster.

Gould, R. (1978). *Transformations: Growth and change in adult life*. New York: Simon & Schuster.

Gray, J. (1996). *Men are from Mars, women are from Venus*. I. Genesis Media Group (Producer).

Gray, W., & Arbuthnot, M. (1940). *Fun with Dick and Jane*. Toronto: W. J. Gage & Co.

Greenwald, M. (1980). *Women, war and work: the impact of World War I on women workers in the United States*. Westport, CT: Greenwood Press.

Greer, G. (1979). *The obstacle race: The fortunes of women painters and their work*. New York: Farrar Straus Ciroux.

Groetsch, M. (1997). *He promised he'd stop: Helping women find safe passage from abusive relationships*. Brookfield, WI: CPI Publishing.

Grof, S. (1990). *The stormy search for the self.* Los Angeles: Jeremy P. Tarcher, Inc.

Grof, S., & Grof, C. (1989). *Spiritual emergency: When personal transformation becomes a crisis.* Los Angeles: Jeremy P. Tarcher, Inc.

Gurian, M. (1999a). *The good son.* New York: Tarcher/Putnam Books.

Gurian, M. (1999b). *The war on boys.* In The National Desk Series II (Producer) Fred Barns, PBS Television.

Habermas, J. (1979). *Communication and the evolution of society.* Boston: Beacon Press.

Hall, J. (1978). Gender effects in decoding nonverbal cues. *Psychological Bulletin, 85(*40), 845-57.

Halpert, H. (1999). *Washington State governor's domestic violence action group report.*

Hamberger, L., & Hastings J. (1986). Personality correlates of men who abuse their partners: A cross-validation study. *Journal of Family Violence, 1,* 37-49.

Hamberger, L. K., Saunders, D. G., & Hovey, M. (1992). The prevalence of domestic violence in community practice and rate of physician inquiry. *Family Medicine, 24*(4), 283-287.

Hamby, S. (1998). Partner violence: Prevention and intervention. In J. Janinski & L. M. Williams (Eds.). *Partner violence: A comprehensive review of 20 years of research.* Thousand Oaks: CA: Sage.

Hammer, J., & Itzin, C. (2001). *Home truths about domestic violence: Feminist influences on policy and practice.* New York: Rutledge.

Hammer, J, & Maynard, M. (1987). *Women, violence, and social control.* Atlantic Highlands, NJ: Humanities.

Hanson, S., & Bozett, F. (1985). *Dimensions of fatherhood.* Beverly Hills, CA: Sage.

Hardgrove, A. (1999). Sati worship and Marwari public identity in India. *The Journal of Asian Studies, 58* (3 August), 723-52.

Hart, B. (1992). *Accountability: Program standards for batterer intervention services*. Reading, PA: Pennsylvania Coalition Against Domestic Violence.

Hartley, R. (1974). Sex role pressures and the socialization of the male child. In J. Pleck & J. Sawyer (Eds.), *Men and masculinity* (pp. 7-13). Englewood Cliffs, NJ: Prentice Hall, Spectrum Books.

Haviland, J., & Malatesta, C. (1981). The development of sex differences in nonverbal signals: Fallacies, facts, and fantasies. In C. Mayo & N. M. Henly (Eds.), *Gender and non-verbal behavior.* New York: Springer-Verlag.

Hawka, S. (1985). *The experience of feeling unconditionally loved.* Ann Arbor: University Microfilms International.

Herman, J. (2001). *Trauma and recovery: The aftermath of violence — from domestic abuse to political terror.* London: Pandora.

Herzberger, S., & Tennen, H. (1985). Snips and snails and puppy dog tails: Gender of agent recipient, and observer as determinants of perception of discipline. *Sex Roles, 12* 853-865.

Hines, M. (1982). Prenatal gonadal hormones and sex differences in human behavior. *Psychological Bulletin, 92,* 56-80.

Hole, J., & Levine, E. (1984). The first feminists. In J. Freeman (Ed.), *Women: A feminist perspective* (pp. 533-542). Palo Alto: Mayfield.

Holmes, R. (1986). *Acts of war: The behavior of men in battle.* New York: Free Press.

Honey, M. (1984). *Creating Rosy the Riveter: Class, gender, and propaganda during World War II.* Amherst: University of Massachusetts Press.

Horney, K. (1932). The dread of women. *International Journal of Psychoanalysis, 13,* 348-360.

Houston, J. (1982). *The possible human.* Los Angles: J. P. Tarcher, Inc.

Hunt, E. K. (1990). *Property and prophets.* New York: Harper & Row.

Ichazo, O. (1991). *The Arican: International journal of Arica institute.* New York: Arica Inc.

Jacklin, C., Maccoby, E., & Dick, A. (1973). Barrier behavior and toy preference: Sex differences (and their absence) in the year old child. *Child Development, 44,* 196-200.

Jacobson, N., & Gottman, J. (1998). *When men batter women: New insights into ending abusive relationships.* New York: Simon & Schuster.

Jaggar, A. (1988). *Feminist politics and human nature.* New Jersey: Rowman & Littlefield.

Janus, L. (1997). *Echoes from the womb.* New York: Jason Aronson.

Jasinski, J., & Williams, K. (1998). *Partner violence: A comprehensive review of 20 years of research.* Thousand Oaks, CA: Sage Publications.

Jaspers, K. (1966). *The great philosophers.* New York: Harcourt.

Jaynes, J. (1976). *The origin of consciousness in the breakdown of the bicameral mind.* Boston: Houghton Mifflin.

Jenkins, P., & Davidson, B. (2001). *Stopping domestic violence: How a community can prevent spousal abuse.* New York: Kluwer Academic/ Plenum Publishers.

Jensen, J. (1986). *Loosening the bonds: Mid-Atlantic farm women, 1750-1850.* New Haven: Yale University Press.

Johnson, E. (2000). *Assessment of violent and potentially violent youth in the schools.* Portland, OR: Oregon Forensic Institute.

Johnson, M. (1995). Patriarchal terrorism and common couple violence: Two forms of violence against women. *Journal of Marriage and the Family, 57,* 283-294.

Johnson, R. (1974). *He: Understanding masculine psychology.* New York: Harper and Row.

Johnson, R. (1991). *Transformation.* New York: HarperCollins Publishers.

Jones, A. (1981). *Women who kill.* New York: Fawcett Columbine.

Jones, R. (1961). *Ancients and moderns: A study of the rise of the scientific movement in seventeenth century England.* Los Angeles: University of California Press.

Jordan, J., Kaplan, A., Miller, J., Stiver, I., & Surrey, J. (1991). *Women's growth in connection.* New York: Guilford Press.

Jourard, S. (1971). *Self-disclosure: An experimental analysis of the transparent self.* New York: Wiley-Interscience.

Kakar, S. (2002). *Domestic Abuse.* San Francisco: Austin & Winfield.

Kant, I. (1962). Lectures on ethics. In W. Jones, F. Sontag, M. Becker & R. Foglin (Eds.), *Approaches to Ethics* (pp. 280-301). New York, NY: McGraw-Hill Book Company.

Kaplan, L. (1978). *Oneness and separateness: From infant to individual.* New York: Simon and Schuster.

Karr-Morse, R., & Wiley, M. (1997). *Ghosts from the nursery: Tracing the roots of violence.* New York: Atlantic Monthly Press.

Katsoff, L. (1953). *Elements of philosophy.* New York: Roland Press.

Katz, P. (1986). Gender identity: Development and consequences. In R. Ashmore & F. Del Boca (Eds.), *The social psychology of female/male relations: A critical analysis of central concepts* (pp. 21-67). Orlando, FL: Academic Press.

Kaufman, G., Jasinski, J., & Aldarondo, E. (1994). Socio-cultural status and incidence of marital violence in Hispanic families. *Violence and Victims, 9*(3), 207-222.

Keen, S. (1991). *Fire in the belly: On being a man.* New York: Bantam Books.

Keleman, S. (1975). *Your body speaks its mind.* New York: Pocket Books.

Kellerman, A. L., & Mercy, J. A. (1992). Men, women, and murder: gender-specific differences in rates of fatal violence and victimization. *Journal of Trauma, 33*(1), 105.

Kelly-Gadol, J. (1976). The social relation of the sexes: Methodological implication of women's history. *Signs: Journal of Women in Culture and Society, 1*(4), 809-823.

Keltikangas-Jarvinen, L. (1982). Alexithymia in violent offenders. *Journal of Personality Assessment, 46,* 462-467.

Kerber, L. (1974). Daughters of Columbia: Education women of the Republic. In S. Elkin & E. McKitrich (Eds.), *The Hofstadter Aegis: A memorial* (pp. 36-59). New York: Knopf.

Kessler, R., & McRae, J. (1981). Trends in the relationship between sex and attempted suicide. *Journal of Health and Social Behavior, 24,* 98-110.

Keyes, K. (1975). *Handbook to higher consciousness.* Coos Bay, Oregon: Ken Keyes Publications.

Kimmel, M. (1987). *Changing men: New directions in research on men and masculinity.* Newbury Park, CA: Sage.

Kindlon, D., & Thompson, M. (1999). *Raising Cain: Protecting the emotional life of boys.* New York: Ballantine.

Kipnis, A. (1994). Men, movies and monsters: Heroic masculinity as a crucible of male violence. *Psychological Perspectives, 29,* 38-51.

Kline, M. (1975). *The psychoanalysis of children.* New York: Delacorte.

Kohut, H. (1971). *The analysis of the self.* New York: International Universities Press.

Kohut, H. (1977). *The restoration of the self.* New York: International Universities Press.

Kohut, W., & Wolf, E. (1978). The disorders of the self and their treatment. *International Journal of Psychoanalysis, 59,* 413-425.

Komarovsky, M. (1940). *The unemployed man and his family.* New York: Dryden Press.

Kort, C., & Friedland, R. (1986). *The fathers' book.* Boston: G.K. Hall.

Kristeva, J. (1981). Women's Time. *Signs: Journal of Women in Culture and Society, 7,* 13-35.

Krystal, H. (1982). Alexithymia and the effectiveness of psychoanalytic treatment. *International Journal of Psychoanalytic Psychotherapy, 9,* 353-378.

Kuhn, T. (1970). *The structure of scientific revolutions.* Chicago: University of Chicago Press.

Labalme, P. (1980). Introduction. In P. Labalme (Ed.), *Beyond their sex: Learned women of the European past* (pp. 1-8). New York: New York University Press.

Laeuchli, S. (1972). *Power and sexuality: The emergence of canon law at the synod of Elvira.* Philadelphia: Temple University Press.

Lamb, M. (1981). *The role of the father in child development.* New York: Wiley.

Lamb, M. (1986). *The father's role: applied perspectives.* New York: Wiley.

Langlois, J., & Downs, A. (1980). Mothers, fathers, and peers as socialization agents of sex-type play behaviors in young children. *The Children Development, 51,* 1217-1247.

Large, P. (1994). The micro revolution revisited. In Price Pritchett, *New work habits for a radically changing world* (p. 5). Dallas: Pritchett and Associates Inc.

Larsen, U., & Yan, S. (2000). Does female circumcision affect infertility and fertility? A study of the Central African Republic, Cote d'Ivoire, and Tanzania. *Demography, 37*(3 August), 313-21.

Laszlo, E. (1987). *Evolution: the grand synthesis.* Boston: Shambala.

Lee, C. (1993). *Talking tough, the fight for masculinity.* London: Arrow Books.

Lenski, G. (1970). *Human societies.* New York: McGraw Hill.

Levant, R. (1992). Toward the reconstruction of masculinity. *Journal of Family Psychology, 5* (3/4), 379-402.

Levant, R. (1995). *Masculinity reconstructed: Changing the rules of manhood at work, in relationships and in family life.* New York: Dutton.

Levant, R. (1997). *Men and emotions, a psycho-educational approach.* New York: Newbridge Professional Programs.

Levant, R., & Pollack, W. (1995). *A new psychology of men.* New York: Basic Books.

Leventhal, H. & Scherer K. (1987). The relationship of emotion to cognition: A functional approach to a semantic controversy. *Cognition and Emotions.* 1(1), 3-28.

Levinas, E. (1973). *The theory of intuition in Husserl's phenomenology.* Evanston, IL: Northwestern University Press.

Levinson, D. (1978). *The seasons of a man's life.* New York: Ballantine.

Levinson, D. (1989). *Family violence in cross-cultural perspective.* Newbury Park, CA: Sage.

Levy, H. (1966). *Chinese footbinding: The history of a curious erotic custom.* New York: W. Rawls.

Lewis, C. (1986). *Becoming a father.* Philadelphia: Open University Press.

Lincoln, Y., & Guba, E. (1985). *Naturalistic inquiry.* Beverly Hills: Sage Publications.

Long, D. (1987). Working with men who batter. In M. Scher (Ed.), *Handbook of counseling and psychotherapy with men.* Newbury Park, CA: Sage.

Loseke, D. (1993). Introduction. R. Gelles & D. Loeske. (Eds.), *Current controversies on family violence.* New York: Sage.

Loste, B. (2000). *Life stories of artist Corita Kent (1918-1986): Her spirit, her art, the women within.* Unpublished doctoral dissertation, Gonzaga University, Spokane, WA.

Lovinger, J. (1976). *Ego development.* San Francisco: Jossey-Bass.

Lowen, A. (1958). *The language of the body.* New York: Collier Books.

Maccoby, E., & Jacklin, C. (1974). *The psychology of sex differences.* Stanford, CA: Stanford University Press.

MacLean, P. (1980). Dromenon. *A Meeting of Minds, III* (1 Fall-Winter), 12-20.

Mahler, M. (1975). *The psychological birth of the human infant.* New York: Basic Books Inc. Pub.

Maina, J., & Oyaro, K. (2000). The fear of becoming an outcast: Female circumcision among the Masai in Kenya. *Wold Press Review, 47*(4), 41-42.

Martin, D. (1976). *Battered wives.* New York: Pocket Books.

Martin, M., & Voorhies, B. (1975). *Female of the species.* New York: Columbia University Press.

Maslow, A. (1971). *The farther reaches of human nature.* New York: Viking.

Maslow, A. (1978). *Toward a psychology of being.* New York: D. VanNostrand Company.

Masterson, J. (1976). *Psychotherapy of the borderline adult.* New York: Brunner/Mazel, Inc.

Masterson, J. (1981). *The narcissistic and borderline disorders: An integrated developmental approach.* New York: Brunner/Mazel Inc.

Masterson, J. (1988). *The search for the real self: Unmasking the personality disorders of our age.* New York: The Free Press.

Masterson, J. (1989). *Psychotherapy of the disorder of the self.* New York: Brunner/Mazel Inc.

McCarthy, T. (1978). *The critical theory of Jergan Habermas.* Cambridge: MIT Press.

McNeill, W. (1963). *The rise of the west: A history of the human community.* Chicago: University of Chicago Press.

Mickunas, A. (1973). Civilization as structures of consciousness. *Main Currents, 29*(5).

Miles, R. (1992). *The rites of man: Love, death and sex in the making of man.* London: Grafton Books.

Milkman, R. (1987). *Gender at work: the dynamics of job segregation by sex during World War II.* Champaign, IL: University of Illinois Press.

Miller, A. (1980). *For your own good: Hidden cruelty in child-rearing and the roots of violence.* Toronto: Collins Publishers.

Miller, A. (1984). *Thou shalt not be aware: Society's betrayal of the child.* New York: A Meridian Book: New American Library.

Miskimin, H. (1969). *The economy of early Renaissance Europe.* Englewood Cliffs, NJ: Prentice-Hall.

Model, A. (1976). The "holding environment" and the therapeutic action of psychoanalysis. *The Journal of the American Psychoanalytic Association, 24,* 285-308.

Money, J., & Tucker, P. (1975). *Sexual signatures.* Boston: Little, Brown.

Montague, A. (1974). *The natural superiority of women.* New York: Collier.

Mosse, G. (1996). *The image of man.* New York: Oxford University Press.

Moustakas, C. (1990). *Heuristic research.* Newbury Park, CA: Sage Publications.

Muraskin, R., & Alleman, T. (1993). *It's a crime: Women and jusice.* Englewood Cliffs, NJ: Regents/Prentice Hall.

Murphy, C., Meyer, S., & O'Leary, K. (1992). Emotional vulnerability, psychopathology, and family of origin violence in men who assault female partners.

Nathanson, D. (1992). Shame and pride: Affect, sex, and the birth of the self. New York: W.W. Norton & Company, Inc.

Neilson, J. (1990). *Sex and gender in society.* Prospect Heights, IL: Waveland Press.

Neumann, E. (1973). *The origins and history of consciousness.* Princeton: Princeton University Press.

Nielsen, J. M. (Ed.). (1990). *Feminist research methods: Exemplary reading in the social sciences.* San Francisco: Westview Press.

Nochlin, L. (1988). *Women, art, and power and other essays.* New York: Harper & Row, Publishers.

O'Brien, J. (1971). Violence in divorce-prone families. *Journal of Marriage and the Family, 33,* 692-698.

O'Leary, K. (1993). Through a psychological lens: Personality traits, personality disorders, and levels of violence. In R. Gelles & D. Loseke (Eds.), *Current controversies on family violence* (pp. 7-30). New York: Sage.

O'Leary, K., & Maiuro, R. (2001). *Psychological abuse in violent domestic relations.* New York: Springer Publishing, Inc.

O'Leary, K., Malone, J., & Tyree, A. (1992). *Physical aggression in early marriage: Relationship and pre-relationship efforts.* Stoney Brook: State University of New York.

O'Neil, M., Good, G., & Holms, S. (1995). Fifteen years of theory and research of men's gender role conflict: New paradigms for empirical research. In R. Levant & W. Pollock (Eds.), *A New Psychology of Men* (pp. 164-207. New York: Basic Books.

Oakley, A. (1981). Interviewing women: A contradiction in terms. *Doing feminist research* London: Routledge & Kegan Paul.

Ornish, D. (1990). *Dr. Dean Ornish's program for reversing heart disease.* New York: Random House.

Osborne, J. (1993). Some similarities and differences among phenomenological and other methods of psychological qualitative research. S. Ferch (Ed.), *Foundation Articles* (pp. 167-189).

Pagels, E. (1979). *The Gnostic gospels.* New York: Vintage Books.

Palkovitz, R. (1985). Fathers birth attendance, early contact, and extended contact with their newborns: A critical review. *Child Development, 56,* 392-406.

Palmer, P. (1993). *To know as we are known.* New York: Harper Collins Publishers.

Patton, M. Q. (1990). *Qualitative evaluation and research methods.* Newbury Park, CA: Sage Publications.

Paymar, M. (1993). *Violent no more: Helping men end domestic abuse.* Alameda, CA: Hunter House Inc., Publishers.

Peers, E. (1961). *Interior Castles: St. Teresa of Avila.* New York: Image Books: Doubleday & Company, Inc.

Pence, E. (1985). *Coordinated community response to domestic assault cases: A guide for policy development.* Duluth, MN: City of Duluth Word Processing Center.

Pence E. (1996). *Coordinated community response to domestic assault cases: A guide for policy development.* Duluth, MN: City of Duluth Word Processing Center.

Pence, E., & Paymar, M. (1986). *Power and control: Tactics of men who batter.* Duluth, MN: Minnesota Program Development, Inc.

Pence, E., & Paymar, M. (1993). *Education groups for men who batter: The Duluth Model.* New York: Springer Publishing Company Inc.

Perls, F. (1969). *Gestalt therapy verbatim.* New York: Bantam Books.

Perls, F., Hefferline, R., & Goodman, P. (1951). *Gestalt therapy: Excitement and growth in the human personality.* New York: Dell Publishing Co.

Perry, B. (1997). Incubated in terror: Neurodevelopmental factors in the cycle of violence. J. D. Osofsky (Ed.), *Children in a Violent Society.* New York: Guilford Press.

Piaget, J. (1977). The essential Piaget. In H. Gruber & J. Voneche (Eds.), *The essential Piaget.* New York: Basic Books.

Pizzey, E. (1974). *Scream quietly or the neighbors will hear.* Short Hill, NJ: Ridley Enslow.

Pleck, E., & Pleck, J. (1980). *The American man.* Englewood Cliffs, NJ: Prentice-Hall (Spectrum Books).

Pleck, J. (1981). *The myth of masculinity.* Cambridge, MA: MIT Press.

Pleck, J. (1985). *Working wives/working husbands.* New Berry Park, CA: Sage Publications.

Pleck, J. (1995). The gender role strain paradigm: An update. In R. Levant & W. Pollack (Eds.), *A New Psychology of Men.* New York: Basic Books.

Poirier, F. (1974). *In search of ourselves: An introduction to physical anthroplogy.* Minneapolis, MN: Burgess Publishing Company.

Polanyi, M. (1958). *Personal knowledge.* Chicago: University of Chicago Press.

Polanyi, M. (1966). *Tacit dimension of knowing.* New York: Doubleday & Co.

Polkinghorne, D. (1989). Phenomenological research methods. In R. S. Valle & S. Halling (Eds.), *Existential-phenomenological perspective in psychology* (pp. 41-60). New York: Plenum Press.

Pollack, W. (1990). Men's development and psychotherapy: A psychoanalytic perspective. *Psychotherapy, 27,* 316-21.

Pollack, W. (Presenter). (1992). Boys will be boys: Developmental traumas of masculinity — psychoanalytical perspectives.

Pollack, W. (1998). *Real boys.* New York: Henry Holt & Company.

Pollack, W. (1999). *The war on boys.* The Nation Desk Session II (Producer): Fred Barns PBS Video NDSK 924.

Pope, K., & Singer, J. (1978). *The stream of consciousness.* New York: Plenum.

Powel, J. (1969). *Why am I afraid to tell you who I am?* Niles, Illinois: Argus Communications.

Pritchett, P. (1994). *The employee handbook of new work habits for a radically changing world.* Dallas: Prichett & Associates, Inc.

Prusak, B. (1974). Women: Seductive siren and source of sin? In R. Ruether (Ed.), *Religion and sexism* (pp. 89-16). New York: Simon & Schuster.

Rabinow, D., & Schmidt, P. (1996). Androgens, brain, and behavior. *American Journal of Psychiatry, 153,* 974-984.

Rabinow, P. (Ed.). (1984). *The Foucault reader.* New York: Pantheon Books.

Rajneesh, B. (1976). *Journey toward the heart: Discourses on the Sufi way.* San Francisco: Harper & Row, Publishers.

Ramirez, A. (1994). *Men and domestic violence.* Lightbridge Productions Video (Producer) Evanston, Ill: Altschul Group Corporation.

Reich, W. (1949). *Character Analysis.* New York: Noonday.

Roberts, A. (2002). *Handbook of intervention strategies with domestic violence: Policies, programs, legal remedies.* Oxford: Oxford University Press.

Robinson, M. (1959). *The power of sexual surrender.* New York: Doubleday.

Rogers, C. (1961). *On becoming a person.* Boston, Mass.: Houghton Mifflin Company.

Roleff, T. (2000). *Domestic Violence: Opposing viewpoints.* San Diego, CA: Greenhaven Press.

Rosenfeld, B. (1992). Court-ordered treatment of spousal abuse. *Clinical Psychology Review, 12*(2), 205-226.

Rotundo, E. (1993). *American manhood: Transformations in the masculinity from the Revolution to the modern era.* New York: Basic Books.

Rubin, J., Provenzano, F., & Lauria, Z. (1974). The eye of the beholder: Parents' view on sex of newborns. *American Journal of Orthopsychiatry, 44,* 512-519.

Russell, D. (1983). Introduction. In D. Martin, *Battered Wives* (pp. vi-viii). New York: Pocket Books by Simon & Schuster.

Said, A. (2001). *A man's guide to the ten most effective methods of preventing domestic violence.* New York: Vantage Press.

Salmon, M. (1986). *Women and the law of property in early America.* Chapel Hill, NC: University of North Carolina Press.

Samad, A. (1996). Cultural aspects of female circumcision in Africa. *Natural History, 105* (August 1996), 52-53.

Sanday, P. (1981). *Female power and male dominance.* Cambridge: Cambridge University Press.

Sanford, F. (1961). *Psychology: A scientific study of man.* Belmont, California: Wadsworth Publishing Company, Inc.

Saunders, D. (1984). Helping husbands who batter. *Journal of Contemporary Social Work.*

Saunders, D. (1992). A typology of men who batter: Three types derived from cluster analysis. *American Journal of Orthopsychiatry, 62*(2), 264-275.

Schaef, A. (1981). *Women's reality: An emerging female system in a white male society.* Minneapolis: Winston Press.

Schell, A., & Gleason, J. B. (1989). *Gender differences in the acquisition of the vocabulary of emotions.* Paper presented at the annual meeting of the American Association of Applied Linguistics, Washington, D.C.

Schmidt, R. (1967). Phenomenology. In P. Edwards (Ed.), *The encyclopedia of philosophy* (1972, Vol. 5, pp. 135-151). New York: Macmillan Publishing Co. & The Free Press.

Searles, H. (1968). *Logic and scientific methods.* New York: Ronald Press Company .

Selman, R. (1980). *The growth of interpersonal understanding: Developmental and clinical analyses.* New York: Academic Press.

Sesonske, A., & Fleming, N. (1965). *Plato's Meno: Text and criticism.* Belmont, California: Wadsworth Publishing Company, Inc.

Shahar, S. (1983). *Fourth estate: A history of women in the middle ages.* New York: Methuen.

Shane, M. (1973). *Some men are more perfect than others.* New York: Bantam Books.

Sheehy, G. (1976). *Passages: Predictable crises of adult life*. New York: E.P. Dutton and Co. Inc.

Sheikh, J., & Yalom, I. (1996). *Treating the elderly*. San Francisco Josey-Bass Publishers.

Shephard, M. (1992). Predicting batterer recidivism five years after intervention. *Journal of Family Violence, 7*(3), 167-178.

Sidorowicz, L., & Lunney, G. (1980). Baby X revisited. *Sex Roles, 6,* 67-73.

Sifneos, P. (1967). Clinical observations on some patients suffering from a variety of psychosomatic diseases. *Proceedings of the Seventh European Conference on Psychosomatic Research*, Basel, Switzterland: Kargel.

Silverman, D. (1987). What are little girls made of? *Psychoanalytic Psychology, 4,* 315-334.

Smith, H. (1980). The mountain man as Western hero: Kit Carson. In E. Pleck & J. Pleck (Eds.), *The American man* (pp. 159-172). Englewood Cliffs, NJ: Prentice-Hall.

Soler, E. (1987). Domestic violence is a crime: A case study: San Francisco family violence project. In D. Sonkin (Ed.), *Domestic violence on trial*. New York: Springer.

Sommers, C. (2000). *The war against boys*. New York: Simon and Schuster.

Sonkin, D., Martin, D., & Walker, L. (1985). *The male batterer: A treatment approach*. New York: Singer Publishing Company.

Spitz, R. (1965). *The first year of life: A psychoanalytic study of normal and deviant development of object relations*. New York: International Universities Press.

Sprague, E. (1961). *What is philosophy?* New York: Oxford University Press.

Starr, B. (1983). *Helping the abuser: Intervening effectively in family violence*. New York: Family Service Association of American.

Stets, J. E., & Straus, M. A. (1990). Gender differences in reporting of marital violence and its medical and psychological consequences. In M. A. Straus & R. J. Gelles (Eds.), *Physical violence in American families: Risk factors and adaptations to violence in 8,145 families* (pp. 151-165). New Brunswick, NJ: Transaction.

Stewart, A., Winter, D., & Jones, A. (1975). Coding categories for the study of children from historical sources. *Journal of Interdisciplinary History, Spring,* 687-701.

Stoltenberg, J. (1993). *The end of manhood.* New York: Dutton: Penguin Group.

Stouffer, S., Suchman, E., DeVinney, L., Starr, S., & Williams, R. (1949). *The American soldier: Adjustment during army life.* Princeton: Princeton University Press.

Straus, M. (1992). Sociological research and social policy: The case of family violence. *Sociological Forum, 7*(2), 211-237.

Straus, M. (1998). Forward. In J. Jasinski & L. Williams (Eds.), *Partner Violence.* Thousand Oaks, CA: Sage Publications.

Straus, M., & Gelles, R. (1990). *Physical violence in American families: Risk factors and adaptations to violence in 8,145 families.* New Brunswick, NJ: Transaction.

Straus, M., Gelles, R., & Steinmetz, S. (1980). *Behind closed doors: Violence in the American family.* Garden City, NJ: Anchor.

Stroll, A. (1971). *Introduction to philosophy.* New York: Holt, Rinehart, and Winston, Inc .

Sullivan, H. (1953). *The interpersonal theory of psychiatry.* New York: Norton.

Tannen, D. (1990). *You just don't understand: Men and women in conversation.* New York: Marrow.

Tart, C. (1983). *Transpersonal Psychologies.* El Cerrito, California: Psychological Processes, Incorporated.

Taylor, B. (1983). *Eve and the new Jerusalem: Socialism and feminism in the nineteenth century.* New York: Pantheon Books.

Taylor, G. (1994). The Alexithymia construct: Conceptualization, validation, and relationship with basic dimensions of personality. *New Trends in Experimental and Clinical Psychiatry, 10,* 61-74.

Thilly, F., & Wood, L. (1957). *A history of philosophy.* New York: Holt, Rinehart and Winston.

Tift, L. (1993). *Battering of women.* Boulder, CO: Westview Press.

Tiger, L. (1999). *The decline of males.* New York: Golden Books.

Toffler, A. (1994). *Creating a new civilization.* Atlanta: Turner Publishing, Inc.

Toleman, R., & Edleson, J. (1995). Intervention for men who batter: A review of research. In S. Stets & M. Straus (Eds), *Understanding partner violence: Prevalence, causes, consequences and solutions.* Minneapolis, MN: National Council on Family Relations.

Tolman, R., & Bennett L. (1990). A review of quantitative research on men who batter. *Journal of Interpersonal Violence, 5*(1), 87-118.

Tompkins, S. (1982). Affect theory. In P. Ekman (Ed.), *Emotion in the human face* (second edition) (pp. 353-395). New York: Cambridge University Press.

Travis, C., & Wade, C. (1984). *The longest war: Sex differences in perspective.* Orlando, Florida: Harcourt, Brace, Jovanovich.

Verny, M. (1981). *The secret life of the unborn child.* New York: Summit Books.

Vincent, J., & Jouriles, E. E. (2000). *Domestic Violence: Guidelines for research-informed practice.* Philadelphia, PA: Jessica Kingsley Publishers.

Vine, W. (1940). *An expository dictionary of New Testament words.* Old Tappan, NJ: Fleming H. Revell Company.

Walker, L. (2000a). *The battered woman syndrome.* New York: Springer Publishing Company Inc.

Walker, L. (2000b). The battered woman syndrome study. In D. Finkelhor, R.J. Gelles, G. Hotaling, & M. Straus (Eds.), *The dark side of families: Current family violence research.* Beverley Hills: Sage Publications.

Warbasse, E. (1987). *The changing legal rights of married women, 1800-1861*. New York: Garland.

Wasserman, G., & Lewis, M. (1985). Infant sex differences: Ecological effects. *Sex Roles, 12*, 665-675.

Weinberg, M. (1992). *Sex differences in 6-month-old infants' affect and behavior: Impact on maternal caregiving*. University of Massachusetts: Doctoral Dissertation.

Weiss, E. (2000). *Surviving domestic violence: Voices of women who broke free*. Sandy, UT.: Agreka Books.

Weitzman, L., Eifler, E., & Ross, C. (1984). Sex role socialization in picture books for preschool children. *American Journal of Sociology ,77* (1125-1150), 173 .

Wells, H. (1920). *The outline of history*. Garden City, New York: Garden City Books.

Welter, B. (1966). The cult of true womanhood: 1820-1860. *American Quarterly, Summer*, 151-174.

Werner, H. (1940). *Comparative psychology of mental development*. New York: International University Press.

Wexler, D. (2000). *Domestic violence 2000: An integrated skills program for men: Group leader's manual with cassettes*. New York: W.W. Norton.

White, L. (1962). *Medieval technology and social change*. Oxford: Clarendon.

Whitehead, A. (1929). *The aims of education*. New York: Mentor Books.

Whitehead, A. (1966). *Modes of thought*. New York: Macmillan.

Whyte, Jr. W. (1957). *The organization man*. Garden City, NY: Doubleday/ Anchor Books.

Widdowson, F. (1984). *Going up into the next class: Women and elementary teacher training, 1840-1914*. Dover, NH: Longwood Publishing.

Wilber, K. (1981). *Up from Eden*. Boulder: Shambala.

Wilber, K. (1983). *Eye to eye: The quest for a new paradigm.* New York: Anchor Books.

Wilber, K. (1996). *A brief history of everything.* Boston: Shambala.

Wilber, K., Engler, J., & Brown, D. (1986). *Transformations of consciousness: Conventional and contemplative perspectives on development.* Boston: Shambala.

Will, J., Self, P., & Datab, N. (1976). Maternal behavior and perceived sex of infant. *American Journal of Orthopsychiatry, 46,* 135-139.

Winston, S. (1932). Birth control and the sex ratio at birth. *American Journal of Sociology, 38,* 225-231.

Wirz, P. (1925). *Die marind-anim von Hollandisch Sud-Neu-Guinea.* Vol. II 40-44, Hamburg, Germany: L. Freidrichsen and Company.

Witherington, I. B. (1984). *Women in the ministry of Jesus.* Cambridge: Cambridge University Press.

Worley, S. (2000). *Personal Communication.*

Wurman, R. S. (1994). *Information anxiety.* In Price Pritchett, *New work habits for a radically changing world.* Dallas: Pritchett & Associates Inc.

Yllo, K. (1993). Through a feminist lens: Gender, power, and violence. In R. Gelles & D. Loseke (Eds.), *Current controversies on family violence* (pp. 47-62). New York: Sage.

Yllo, K., & Bofrad, M. (1988). *Feminist perspectives on wife abuse.* Newbury Park, CA: Sage.

Yllo, K., & Straus, M. (1990). Patriarchy and violence against wives: The impact of structural and normative factors. In M. Straus & R. Gelles (Eds.), *Physical violence in American families: Risk factors and adaptations to violence in 8,145 families.* New Brunswick, NJ: Transaction.

Zilbergeld, B. (1992). *The new male sexuality.* New York: Bantam.

APPENDIX A
RELEASE OF INFORMATION

I hereby grant the privilege and agree to participate in ongoing research regarding intimate partner issues. I am participating voluntarily and consent to the study. I agree to the use of case history records & notes (written, audio, and video) for the purpose of academic research, written preparation and presentation of academic papers, doctoral dissertation, manuscripts to further the academic pursuit in the field, and any further publication.

Confidentiality: I understand that the real names of participants, identifying institutions, demographic information that might identify me will not be used.

Researcher: _____ Date: _____

Signature: _____ Date: _____

APPENDIX B
DIAGNOSTIC CRITERIA FOR 309.81: POSTTRAUMATIC STRESS DISORDER

A. The person has been exposed to a traumatic event in which both of the following were present:

    (1) The person experienced, witnessed, or was confronted with an event or events that involved actual or threatened death or serious integrity, or a threat to the physical injury of self or others

    (2) The person's response involved intense fear, helplessness, or horror.

B. The traumatic event is persistently re-experienced in one (or more) of the following ways:

    (1) Recurrent and intrusive distressing recollections of the event, including images, thoughts, or perceptions

    (2) Recurrent distressing dreams of the event

    (3) Acting or feeling as if the traumatic event were recurring (includes a sense of reliving the experience, illusions, hallucinations, and dissociative flashback episodes, including those that occur on awakening or when intoxicated)

    (4) Intense psychological distress at exposure to internal or external cues that symbolize or resemble an aspect of the traumatic event

    (5) Physiological reactivity on exposure to internal or external cues that symbolize or resemble an aspect of the traumatic event

C. Persistent avoidance of stimuli associated with the trauma and numbing of general responsiveness (not present before the trauma), as indicated by three (or more) of the following:

    (1) Efforts to avoid thoughts, feelings, or conversations associated with the trauma

(2) Efforts to avoid activities, places, or people that arouse recollections of the trauma
(3) Inability to recall an important aspect of the trauma
(4) Markedly diminished interest or participation in significant activities
(5) Feeling of detachment or estrangement from others
(6) Restricted range of affect (e.g., unable to have loving feelings)
(7) Sense of a foreshortened future (e.g., does not expect to have a career, marriage, children, or a normal life span)

D. Persistent symptoms of increased arousal (not present before the trauma) as indicated by two (or more) of the following:
(1) Difficulty falling or staying asleep
(2) Irritability or outbursts of anger
(3) Difficulty concentrating
(4) Hypervigilance
(5) Exaggerated startle response

E. Duration of the disturbance (symptoms in Criteria B, C, and D) is more than one month.

F. The disturbance causes clinically significant distress or impairment in social, occupational, or other important areas of functioning.

PTSD is distinguishable from:
1) Acute Stress Disorder (ASD) by the onset and duration of the symptom pattern
2) Obsessive-Compulsive Disorder (OCD) because the recurrent intrusive thoughts are inappropriate and not related to a traumatic event.

Note:
   According to several researchers (Dutton, 1995; Karr-Morse & Wiley, 1997; Kindlon, 1999; Levant, 1997; and Pollack, 1998) a great many men have been traumatized during their early years, and the Post Traumatic Stress Syndrome literature and the Masculinity Stereotype literature both point out the consequences as a common male experience.

   Upon reviewing this list with me in couples counseling, a male client said, "Someone has been stalking and spying on me. Every line on this sheet applies to me."

APPENDIX C
AFFECT THERAPY THEORY*

"Despite our view of ourselves as thinking beings, cognition is but a frail craft floating on a sea of emotion." Donald Nathanson

"The problem in therapy is always how to move from an ineffectual intellectual appreciation of a truth about oneself to some emotional experience of it. It is only when therapy enlists deep emotions that it becomes a powerful force for change." Irvin Yalom

"The aim of every moment in every session is to put the patient in touch with as much of his true feelings as he can bear." David Malan

"Therapy" is derived from the Greek *therapia*. It carries the idea of healing, wholeness, or health. Healing what? Affect Therapy Theory presumes that humans are organismically or physiologically based. Whatever is going on with a person is rooted in the physiology of the person. In the development of individuals, numerous transitional phases or hurdles must be traversed. Most did not negotiate those stages artfully, and the result is developmental stage specific wounds. Psychotherapy seeks to heal early wounds. Consequently, Affect Therapists place much emphasis on the physical organism and the emotional nuances that are manifested therein. Human development is marked with wounds as follows:

A. The Wounds from the Womb

1. Long before we are born, we are experiencing. Our early brain is hard at work recording sensual input, beginning with the five senses.
2. Dr. David Chamberlain wrote in an article published in the *British Journal of Psychotherapy* in 1987:

> There is mounting evidence for a theory of "cellular" memory, which reaches back into the prenatal period. These memories are called cellular because they are usually behavioral

rather than verbal memories and because specific parts of the body seem to hold and express these memory patterns.

3. Numerous prenatal factors carry life-long implications, including: a) Alcohol/Nicotine; b) Lead; c) Cocaine; d) Marijuana; e) Heroin; f) Prescription Drugs; g) Maternal Illness; h) Malnutrition; i) Genetic Factors; and j) Parental Attitudes and Mental States (joy excitement/dread) of the Mother (Karr-Morse & Wiley, 1997).

B. Childhood Wounds

1. *Development of Armoring (Lowen, 1975; Reich, 1949).*
    a. *When that which is natural to living is met in the environment by either attack or absence of contact, the organism retreats in protection.*
    b. *This retreat is experienced as anxiety.*
    c. *The organism defends against the anxiety by inhibiting the bioenergetic expressions, that evoked it — Binding Bioenergy*
    d. *These chronic defenses coalesce into what Reich termed " body armor."*
2. *Concept of Armoring*
    a. *Armor develops during the course of one's lifetime in response to hurtful or non-nurturing environments and the need to defend oneself from painful emotions.*
    b. *Armoring is expressed in one's beliefs, attitudes, and interpersonal behavior; and in one's posture, breathing style, and pattern of muscular tensions.*
    c. *Armoring restricts the movement of energy and gives rise to painful emotions such as shame, anxiety, guilt, defensive anger and unresolved grief.*
    d. *Armoring diminishes one's capacity to experience healthy aggression, intimacy, and sexual excitation and pleasure.*

C. The Outcome in Relationships
2. *Contact Boundary Disturbances (Perls, 1951). Contact takes place at the place where the organism and environment meet. Interruptions or distortions of contact are termed "contact boundary disturbances."*
   a. *Confluence: the condition of no contact. Instead of an "I" and a "You" there is a "we" or a vague, unclear experience of him/herself, i.e. "codependency."*
   b. *Introjection: the individual experiences something as him/herself when in fact it belongs to the environment (false identification), i.e. "swallowing hook, line, and sinker."*
   c. *Projection: the individual experiences something as being in the environment when in fact it belongs to him/her (false alienation), i.e. "laying one's garbage on someone else."*
   d. *Retroflection: the individual holds back a response intended for the environment and substitutes it with a response for him/herself i.e. "turning everything back on one's self."*
   e. *Deflection: Turning aside, throwing it back, and rebutting, thus avoiding healthy contact.*

D. *Maximization of Human Organismic Functioning*
   1. *Bioenergetic perspective (Lowen, 1975; Reich, 1949) — energetic pulsation*
      a. *Bioenergetic pulsation: (expansion and contraction)*
      Pulsation = Tension -- Charge – Discharge – Relaxation
      b. *Energetic flow and emotions*
      c. *Energetic immobility leads to deadness and contactlessness — decreased awareness and contact*
   2. *Figural formation and destruction (Perls, 1951)*
      a. *Cycle of creation and destruction of the figure*
      b. *Emergence in the foreground of the figure, as contrasted against its background*

  c. *A natural spontaneous flow between figure*
   formation and destruction (grace)
 3. *Organismic Self-Regulation*
  a. *Organisms are ordered, intrinsically self-*
   regulating wholes
  b. *Organisms naturally seek growth towards*
   maturity
  c. *Organismic behavior is purposive and goal-*
   seeking, not random.
 4. *Existence of core emotions*
   "Pleasure, longing, anxiety, rage, sadness, in
   approximately the order given here, are the basic
   emotions of the living" (Reich, 1949)

E. Affect as the Primary Motivational System
  I view affect as the primary innate biological
  motivating mechanism, more urgent than drive
  deprivation and pleasure, and more urgent even than
  physical pain . . . . The drive must be assisted by
  affect as an amplifier if it is to work at all . . . . The
  affect system is, therefore, the primary motivational
  system because without its amplification, nothing
  else matters, and with its amplification, anything else
  matters. It lends its power to memory, to perception,
  to thought, and to action no less than to the drives.
  (Tomkins, 1982, pp. 354-356)

  Each affect is governed by an innate subcortical
  program, which involves correlated sets of responses,
  including facial, glandular, and muscular.

F. Emotionally Focused Psychotherapy
 1. *Role of emotions:*
  a. *Emotions organize us /or action*
  b. *Emotions are fundamentally adaptive*
  c. *Emotions are motivational*
  d. *Emotions inform us*
  e. *Emotion is communication (Greenberg, 1993,*
   1997)

2. *Types of Emotions*
   a. *Primary Emotions - fundamental emotional response to external stimuli*
   b. *Primary Adaptive*
   c. *Primary Maladaptive -primary emotional responses that have become dysfunctional based upon learning and embedded in emotional schemes*
   d. *Secondary Emotions - reactions to identifiable, more primary, internal, emotional, or cognitive processe*
   e. *Instrumental Emotions - emotions experienced and expressed because the person has learned (Greenberg, 1993, 1997)*

G. *Emotionally Focused Psychotherapy: Working With Emotions*
   1. *Acknowledgment and expression of feelings first step in change process.*
   2. *Safety and support crucial first step. The need to validate client's experience and help him/her restore rapport with feelings.*
   3. *Differential approach in working with painful primary emotions vs. painful secondary emotions.*
   4. *Importance of modifying defenses against emotional experience and expression. Promote awareness and mastery.*
   5. *Primary emotions need to be experienced, expressed, and symbolized in awareness — the "what" and "how" vs. the "why."*
   6. *Alternate emotionally based needs/goals and other internal resources' need to be accessed (Greenberg, 1993, 1997).*

H. *Therapeutic Practice - key processes*
   1. *Promotion of client's awareness of his/her bodily experience*
   2. *Promotion of client's awareness of emerging emotions and 'how' he/she defends against either its experience or expression*
   3. *Pressure upon defenses through concentrated awareness and intensification*

    b.   Use of enhanced respiration
    c.   Use of imagery or role playing
4. *Fostering of increased capacity to tolerate both emotional excitation and expression*
    a.   Use of controlled respiration
    b.   Use of in session experiments
5. *Use of therapeutic relationship to provide a safe and secure "holding environment" in which chronic patterns of emotional defense can be explored and challenged.*

*Credit and gratitude is expressed to Daniel Shiff, Ph.D., from whom I derived the above information, for his research. Dr. Shiff is a psychologist in private practice 6823 29th Ave. N. E., Seattle, Washington 98115, (206-522-9342). I came across the syllabus for his workshop that was offered at Eastern Washington University on May 17, 2002. The workshop was entitled *Reaching the Emotions in Psychotherapy: Lessons from Affect Theory and Body Psychotherapy.* While I have studied and written about Reich and Perls and Lowen, I was grateful to be introduced to some of the later works in Affect Theory. I have since read several of these sources. By chance I came across Leslie Greenberg's book *Empathy Reconsidered* (1997) and was impacted by his ideas. I did not use all of the information in Dr. Shiff's syllabus. The information I borrowed from Dr. Shiff's is in italics. I selected the information that I thought applied to my earlier contentions that pure academic cognitive psychoeducational applications do not address the intimate partner abuser syndrome.

The following is a record of Dr. Schiff's Reference List.

Greenberg, L.S., Paivio, S.C. (1997). *Working with emotions in psychotherapy.* New York: Guilford Press.

Greenberg, L.S., Rice, L.N., & Elliot, R. (1993). *Facilitating emotional change: The moment-by-moment process.* New York: Guilford Press.

Lazarus, R.S. (1991a). Cognition and motivation in emotion. *American Psychologist 46*(4), 352-367.

Lazarus, R.S. (1991b). Progress on a cognitive-motivational relational theory of emotion. *American Psychologist, 46*(8), 819-834.

Leventhal, H., & Scherer, K. (1987). The relationship of emotion to cognition: A functional approach to a semantic controversy. *Cognition and Emotion, 1*(1), 3-28.

Lowen, A. (1975). *Bioenergetics.* New York: Coward, McCann & Geoghegan, Inc.

Nathanson, D.L. (1992). *Shame and pride: Affect, sex, and the birth of the self.* New York: W.W. Norton & Company, Inc.

Perls, F., Hefferline, R., & Goodman, P. (1951). *Gestalt therapy.* New York: Dell Publishing Co., Inc.

Reich, W. (1949). *Character analysis* (3rd. ed.). New York: Farrar, Straus, & Giroux.

Reich, W. (1973). *The function of the orgasm.* New York: Farrar, Straus, & Giroux.

Tomkins, S.S. (1982). Affect theory. In P. Ekman (Ed.), *Emotion in the human face* (2nd edition) (pp. 353-395). New York: Cambridge University Press.

APPENDIX D
EMPATHY TRAINING AND THE HEALING OF INTERPERSONAL RELATIONSHIPS

Empathy has been defined as the "ability to share in another's emotions, thoughts, or feelings."[1] Empathy has been equated with emotional intelligence[2] [3] [4] and may be more important than IQ.[5] Carl Rogers popularized the concept in his non-directive therapy and stated that empathy was an ability to "perceive the internal frame of reference of another with accuracy and with the emotional components and meaning which pertain thereto as an ability as if one were the person."[6]

Carl Rogers launched the original interest in empathic therapy that was prominent during the 1960s and early 1970s. During this time there was a great deal of research activity regarding Carl Rogers' hypothesis that three therapeutic conditions — unconditional positive regard, empathy, and genuineness — were *necessary and sufficient causes* for therapeutic change. By the late 1970s, evidence accumulated by Charles Truax and his colleagues[7] suggested strong correlations between empathy and therapeutic outcomes. Research on empathy began to wane in the 1980s. However, at the same time, thanks largely to the development of psychoanalytic self-psychology, a renewed theoretical interest in empathy blossomed in the late 1980s. In addition, feminist self-in-relation theory stressed the fundamental importance of empathy.[8]

Empathy is seen as a significant predictor of success in the therapeutic [healing] relationship.[9] One of the key ingredients in fostering a healing relationship, not only in the therapeutic counseling setting, but also in all interpersonal relationships, the element of the empathic attitude is crucial. Empathy is believed to be a powerful curative agent in its own right. [10]

> First empathy includes the making of deep and sustained
> psychological contact with another in which one is highly
> attentive to, and aware of, the experience of the other as a
> unique other; in an empathic way of being, one appreciates
> the other's experience as it is, as an idiosyncratic

expression of the other in his or her difference. A genuine meeting of persons can occur. Second, empathic exploration includes deep sustained [attentive] inquiry or immersing of oneself in the experience of the other. This can lead to sensitive interpretations that help others access unconscious experiences.[11]

Empathy viewed from the perspective of intimate partner relationships, involves the attempt to sense into and reside quietly in another person's reality. Metaphorically it is like building a chair in the other person's heart, where one sits for a long time in silence absorbing the currents of thought, feelings, and beliefs of the beloved. First, it involves the goal of understanding, conceptualizing, and explicating the other's world. Second, it includes the ability to trace the currents of feeling in the other person. Third, empathy can involve action — the ability to mirror back to the other person his/her perceived reality. Fourth, empathy is a way of being together in relationship — breathing together — merely attending. Finally, empathy creates, by virtue of the universality of the human soul, commonness, a sense of oneness, and a glidepath toward fluidity in managing differences and leads to interpersonal confirmation and validation.

Empathy work with men in therapy is difficult and necessary. Most have suffered emotional fear and pain resulting in the posttraumatic stress syndrome that manifests as *normative male alexithymia* (the inability to express intrapersonal feelings). Empathy training transcends cognitive psychoeducation and contributes to the positive interpersonal outcomes. It is imperative in giving undivided attendtion when raising children. It is a powerful healing factor for maximizing intimate partner relationships. It manifests as pure willingness to understand and take the other at face value. It grants the other person permission to express their perceived world. Hundreds of women in relationship therapy voice a common theme, "He won't talk to me," "He won't listen to me," and "He won't look at me when I talk to him." Undivided empathic attention, often just by softly stating the other person's name, has been known to heal a broken heart.

---

[1]   Webster's New World Dictionary, Third College Edition, 1994.

[2]   Levant, R. (1995). Masculinity reconstructed: Changing the rules of manhood at work, in relationships and in family life. New York: Dutton.

272

[3]   Levant, R. (1997). *Men and emotions, a psycho-educational approach.* New York: Newbridge Professional Programs.

[4]   Levant, R., & Pollack, W. (1995). *A new psychology of men.* New York: Basic Books.

[5]   Goleman, (1995). *Emotional intelligence.* New York: Bantam

[6]   Rogers, C. (1959). A theory of therapy, personality and interpersonal relationships as developed in the client-centered framework. In S. Koch (Ed.), *Psychology: A study of a science* (Vol. 3, pp. 184-256). New York: McGraw-Hill. (p. 210).

[7]   Truax, C., & Carkhuff, R. (1967). *Toward effective counseling and psychotherapty.* Chicago: Aldine.

        Truax, C. & Mitchell, K. (1971) Research on certain therapist interpersonal skills in relation to process and outcome. In A. E. Bergin & S. L Garfield (Eds.), *Handbook of psychotherapy and behavior change* (1ˢᵗ ed., pp. 299-344). New York: Wiley.

[8]   Bohart, A. & Greenberg, L. (1997). Empathy and psychotherapy: An introductory overview. In. A. C. Bohart & L. S. Greenberg (Eds.), *Empathy reconsidered: New directions in psychotherapy.* Washington: American Psychological Association. (pp. 3-32)

[9]   Ibid. (p. 15).

[10]   Ibid. (p. 137).

[11]   Ibid. (p. 5).

APPENDIX E
A MAN IN SEARCH OF
HIS "OTHER HALF"

Aristophanes' love myth
from Plato's *Symposium*

By Herb Robinson

It was a sophisticated dinner party, a victory celebration for the tragic poet Agathon's first success at a poets' contest. Seven guests were invited to this dinner at the height of Greece's Periclean Age. After dinner, there was a unanimous decision that instead of drinking or flute playing they (letting the flute-girl "go and play by herself") would undertake a conversation on some subject. One of the party guests suggested that each one "make a speech in honor of love," no one, in his view, having ever praised it sufficiently. Plato (428-348 BC) presents the speeches in his *Symposium,* justly one of his most famous presentations (Violi, 1965).

Dinner guests in turn gave a talk on their definition, and in praise, of love. Aristophanes (the comic poet) in his light-hearted manner gave his usual humorous after-dinner speech. However, on closer reflection, it goes to the heart of men's dilemma over love and loss. Aristophanes began with his description of human prehistory — the "original man." Humankind existed as round roly-poly double creatures, a composite of both genders. Each had two faces, four hands and feet, two sets of genitals, male and female, and they fitted together perfectly. Men and women were merged together and enjoyed the greatest of pleasure. They could engage in all types of athletic feats with great success, and they fit the Greek ideal because their shape was that of perfection — a sphere. "He could walk upright as men do now, backwards or forwards as he desired, and he could roll over and over at a terrific rate, turning on his four hands and four feet like tumblers . . . spinning with his legs in the air; this was when he wanted to run fast" (Jowett, 1956).

Since they were so satisfied, perfect, powerful, and ambitious, in their pride, they brought down the wrath of the gods. To humble them, Zeus split them in two. Apollo was assigned the task of smoothing off the rough edges once they were divided in two. Their sense of oneness and wholeness was lost, leaving each as "but the indenture of a man . . . always looking for our *other half*" (emphasis added)

In Aristophanes' myth, each person is engaged in a search for lost "oneness" and yearns to find a mirror self, a complete self, within the connection to another — in order to be whole again. In finding the special other, one is truly finding oneself. And even more significant, it is not mere sexuality that drives us.

> When one of them finds his other half, the pair is lost in amazement of love and friendship and intimacy . . . . The intense yearning which each of them has toward the other does not appear to be in the desire of intercourse but of something else which the *soul desires and cannot tell, and of which she only has a dark and doubtful presentiment* (emphasis added). (Pollack, 1995)

This discovery is seen to be at the very heart of man's struggle, "so ancient is the desire for one another that is implanted in us, reuniting our original nature, making one of two and *healing the state of man.*"

> There is not a man among them [at that dinner party] when he heard this who would deny or would not acknowledge that this meeting and melting in one another's arms . . . this becoming one instead of two, was the very expression of his ancient need. *And the reason is that human nature was originally one and we were whole, and the desire and pursuit of that whole is called love* (emphasis added). (Pollack, 1995)

This myth of intimacy is indicative of man's search for a partner, his attempt to replace and/or repair his earlier lost love, and to regain a state of connection abruptly disrupted in his earlier developmental history. Unknowingly, men wish to merge with women precisely because of their "feminine" caring qualities, while they deny having any such yearnings. Men seek special women to love them with an exceptional blend of understanding, caring, and giving — qualities those men see as feminine and therefore unacceptable within their own selves. The internal male vacuum is so pervasive and powerful that when a man believes he has found completion in his other half, he may be overwhelmed with excitement and the electricity of her presence. Just the thought of losing such a love can be devastating and sometimes terminal. This man has found love — the experience and belief that he has at last found completion in his beloved — his other half.

1. Violi, U. (1965) *Greek and Roman classics*. New York: Monarch Press Inc. (pp. 388-392).

2. Jowett, B. (1956). *The Symposium of Plato*. New York: Tudor. (pp. 356, 357).

3. Pollack, W. (1995) No man is an island. In R. Levant & W. Pollack (Eds.), *A New Psychology of Men*. (p.36). New York: Basic Books.

APPENDIX F
X does not equal Y*

The "XXs" have it

1. We have already seen that there is good reason to believe that **the female enjoys, on the whole, a substantial biological advantage over the male.**

2. Does there exist some biological differentiating factor that may serve to explain or possibly throw some light upon the origin and meaning of these differences? The answer is "Yes." And I do not know that anyone has made anything of a key fact that lies at the base of practically all the differences between the sexes and the biological superiority of the female to the male. I refer to the chromosomal structure of the sexes, **the chromosomes being the small cellular bodies that carry the hereditary particles, or genes, which so substantially influence one's development and fate as an organism.**

3. **In the sex cells there are twenty-three chromosomes, but only one of these is a sex chromosome.**

   a. There are two kinds of sex chromosomes, X and Y, Half the sperm cells carry X- and half carry Y-chromosomes.

   b. **All the female ova in the female ovaries contain only X-chromosomes.**

   c. **When an X-bearing sperm fertilizes an ovum, the offspring is always female, XX.**

   d. **When a Y-bearing chromosome fertilizes an ovum, the offspring is always male, XY.**

   e. It is the initial difference between the sexes in a constitutionally decisive manner.

   f. This is not to say that the sex chromosomes are eventually entirely responsible for the development **of all the differences in sex characteristics**; it is to say that the chromosomes are decisive in determining whether an organism shall develop as a male or a female.

g. The sex chromosomes regulate the transformation of the fertilized ovum into an embryo that, **during the first few weeks of development, is sexually undifferentiated, though oriented toward femaleness**. Up to the end of the sixth week of embryonic development the appearance of the external genitalia is **identical in the two sexes**. If the embryo is a genetic male, masculinizing organizing substances will enlarge the phallus, extend the urethra along its length, and close the skin over the urogenital sinus to form the scrotum for the testes, which will later descend into it

h. If no masculinizing substance (i.e., testosterone, which is normally derived from the primitive gonad, the sexually indifferent organ that may develop either as an ovary or testis), the infant will develop as a female, even though a female organizing substance does not exist, This, as the distinguished experimental **endocrinologist Dr. Alfred Hoet and others have suggested, indicates that the basic surviving human form is female and that masculinity is something "additional."**

i. **Under normal conditions the sex rudiments are differentially affected toward maleness or femaleness depending upon whether the chromosomal constitution (the genotype) is XY or XX.** The genotype or chromosomal constitution therefore is decisive in initiating the direction of sexual development; thereafter it is a matter largely under the influence of the developing hormones secreted by the endocrine glands. The development of all bodily structures and their functions, in relation to the environment in which they develop, is set by the sex chromosomes at the time the sex rudiments and the gonads are sexually differentiated.

j. As Professor N. J. Berrill has written;

> . . , in any case, the status of the female is never in doubt. Whoever produces eggs is essential to the future, for eggs are reproductive cells, whatever else they may be. Sperm are not so in the primary sense

278

of the word. They serve two decidedly secondary ends—they serve to stimulate the other-wise comatose eggs to start developing, like the kiss that awakened the Sleeping Beauty, and they serve to introduce considerable variability derived from the male parent.

k. Eggs, of course, also contribute their variability to the offspring, but **eggs alone have the capacity, under certain conditions, to develop readily into grown organisms,** whereas sperms lack such a capacity altogether. In all sexual species the mature organism is the egg developed, with the extra touches added, usually but not always, only when a sperm is involved.

4. What is the difference between an XX and an XY cell?

a. **When one looks at a body cell containing a full complement of the forty-six chromosomes there will be no difficulty in recognizing the XX-sex-chromosomes because they belong with the group of quite large chromosomes.**

b. But if you pick up a body cell with the XY complement of the male, say at a magnification of two thousand diameters, **then it will be seen that the Y-chromosome is among the smallest of the forty-six chromosomes.**

c. **It may have the shape of a comma, the merest remnant; a wretched-looking runt compared with the well-upholstered other chromosomes!**

d. As we shall soon see, the **Y-chromosome really is a sad affair. In fact, its volume is only one-fifth that of an X-chromosome, and it is in that difference, and what it signifies, that there lies part of the answer to the question:** How do the sexes get that way?

5. Although it has long been known that **the Y-chromosome is virtually empty**, it has for long been believed that among the few genes it contained was the gene for inducing the secretion of the masculizing hormone testosterone, from the gonads,

a. It now appears that this gene is situated not on the Y-chromosome but upon the X-chromosome.

b. Dr. Susurno Ohno and his colleagues at the City of Hope Medical Center in Duarte, California, in 1971 brought forward convincing arguments to demonstrate that this was so. Their findings await further confirmation.

c. If, as seems to be lively, it is shown that femaleness is the non-induced state in the presence of two X-chromosomes, and maleness the induced state in the absence of one X-chromosome, the **wretched Y-chromosome will suffer its most ignominious demotion.**

6. The chromosomes, twenty-two in the haploid and forty-four in the diploid state which are neither X nor Y, are called "autosomes," There are twenty-two pairs of them in the body cells, and only twenty-two single ones in the sex cells. Each of the autosomes **contains factors that tend toward the production of femaleness**. Each of the X-chromosomes contains genes that tend toward the production of femaleness.

a. It used to be thought that the Y-chromosome carries factors that were male-determining, Hence, when a Y-carrying sperm fertilizes an ovum, the XY-chromosomes, in the presence of the twenty-two pairs of autosomes carrying genes directed toward femaleness, are insufficiently powerful to reduce their influence, and the result is the development of a male. On the other hand, the combination of two X-chromosomes is sufficient to overcome the influence of any possible male factors in the autosomes, and the result is a female.

b. The X-chromosomes together have quite a pull to them; **and the explanation of the biological superiority of the female lies in the male's having only one X-chromosome while the female has two. It is largely to the original X-chromosome deficiency of the male that almost all the troubles to which the male falls heir may be traced and to the presence of two well-appointed, well-furnished X-chromosomes that the female owes her biological superiority. As a consequence of the larger size of the X-chromosome the female's cells are about 4 percent greater in chromosome volume than**

the male's. As Drs. J. H. Tijo and T. T, Puck, who originally determined the difference in sex-chromosome size in 1958, have remarked, **the female has "a substantially richer genetic capacity than the male."**

c.   **The vital importance of the X-chromosome as compared with the Y-chromosome is evident because no fertilized cell can survive long unless it contains an X-chromosome. No matter how many Y-chromosomes a cell may contain, if it does not also contain an X-chromosome it dies. Males, therefore, survive only by grace of their having been endowed by their mothers with an X-chromosome.**

7.   In birds and some insects two X-chromosomes produce a male and an XY combination produces a female, but otherwise the conditions are precisely the same as in man, except that the autosomes contain the sex genes that are strongly organized toward femaleness, whereas the X-chromosomes are strongly, and in double dose, more powerfully organized toward maleness, That it is the X-chromosome that counts is borne out by the incidence of embryo deaths, which is much greater among the female birds than among the males.

8.   What the origin of the X- and Y-chromosomes may have been no one knows, but I find it amusing and helpful to **think of the Y-chromosome as an undeveloped X- chromosome or perhaps as a remnant of an X-chromosome. It is as if in the evolution of sex a fragment at one time broke away from an X-chromosome, carrying with it some rather unfortunate genes, and thereafter in relation to the other chromosomes was helpless to prevent them from expressing themselves in the form of an incomplete female the creature we call the male. This "just-so" story makes the male a sort of crippled female, a creature who by virtue of his having only one X- chromosome is not so well equipped biologically as the female.**

9.   **But that is not the whole story. That the male is endowed with a Y-chromosome seems to put him at a greater disadvantage than if he had no Y-chromosome at all, for while the Y-chromosome may carry a few genes of some value, it also occasionally carries some that are, to say the least, unfortunate.**

a. Thus far at least four conditions have been traced to genes which sometimes occur only in the Y-chromosome and hence can be transmitted only by fathers to their sons.

b. These are bark-like skin (ichthyosis hystrix gravior),

c. dense hairy growth on the ears (hypertrichosis),

d. non-painful hard lesions of the hands and feet (keratoma dissipatum),

e. and a form of webbing of the toes in which there is fusion of the skin between the second and third toes.

10. It is probable that the biological disadvantages accruing to the male are not so much **due to what is in the Y-chromosome as to what is not in it.** This is well exemplified by the manner in which the male inherits such a serious disorder as hemophilia (bleeder's disease). This is due to a mutant gene carried in the X-chromosome. A mutant gene is one in which a physio-chemical change of a heritable land occurs. It has been calculated that the normal gene for blood clotting mutates to the **defective hemophilia gene** in one out of every hundred thousand persons of European origin in each generation.

11. Since most hemophiliacs die before they can leave any offspring, the number of such unfortunate persons alive at any time is relatively small. **Hemophilia** is inherited as a single, sex-linked recessive gene, that is, a gene that is linked to the X-chromosome and that will not express itself in the presence of a normal gene on the opposite X chromosome. When, then, an X-chromosome that carries the hemophilia gene is transmitted to a female, it is highly improbable that it will encounter another X-chromosome carrying such a gene; it is for this reason that hemophilia is of the very greatest rarity in a female. Since the survival rate to reproductive age is very low, it is obvious why females are the most usual transmitters of the hemophilia gene, and it should also be clear why females practically never exhibit the condition. The males are affected because they don't have any properties in their Y-chromosome which are capable of suppressing the action of the hemophilia gene. Women could exhibit the condition only if they inherited a hemophilia gene from their mother and another hemophilia gene from their father, and this is extremely unlikely to occur. Whether she derived the defective X-chromosome from her father or her mother, the female would not suffer from hemophilia

because her normal X-chromosome would either compensate for, inhibit, or suppress the action of the hemophilia X-chromosome, and she would not become hemophiliac; but if she married a normal man and bore a number of children she would pass on the hemophiliac-bearing chromosome to about half her sons and half her daughters. The girl who inherits the defective gene will show no ill effects, but the males who have received the gene may show the effects even before they are born and die of hemoplulia ineutro, or they may fall victim to the disorder at any time from birth to adult life, but exhibit the condition they will, and in the greater number of instances they will die of its effects.

12. The mechanism of **color blindness (red-green, mostly)** and its explanation are precisely the same as for hemophilia. About 4 percent of American men BTC completely red-green color blind, while another 4 percent are color blind in varying degrees to red-green or other colors, whereas only half of 1 percent of American women are so affected.

13. More than thirty serious disorders 'occurring in the male are known to be due to genes present in the X-chromosomes; these conditions can occur in a woman only if her father was affected and her mother carried the gene. Below are listed some of the conditions occurring more frequently in males because of sex-linked genes.

14. Table II. Conditions Due Largely to Sex-Linked Genes---Found Mostly in Males

(1)   Absence of central incisor teeth

(2)   Albinism of eyes (depigmentation of eyes)

(3)   Aldrich syndrome (chronic eczema, middle ear disease)

(4)   Agammaglobuinemia (gamma globulin deficiency in blood)

(5)   Amelogemesis imperfecta (absence of enamel of teeth)

(6)   Angiokeratonia diffusum (lesions affecting many systems of body)

(7)   Anhidrotic ectodemal dysplasia (maldevelopment of sweat glands)

(8)   Borjeson syndrome (mental deficiency, epilepsy, endocrine disorders)

(9)   Cataract, total congenital

(10) Cataract, congenital with microcornea

(11) Cerebellar ataxia

(12) Cerebral sclerosis

(13) Choroideremia

(14) Coloboma iridis (congenital cleft of iris)

(15) Color blindness of the red-green type

(16) Day blindness

(17) Deafness, congenital

(18) Defective hair follicles

(19) Disticliasis (double eyelashes)

(20) Dystrophia bllosa (formation of swellings, absence of all hair, etc.)

(21) Dyskeratosis congenita. (malformation of nails, pigmentation)

(22) Epidermal cysts (skin. cysts)

(23) Glaucoma of juvenile type (Increase in fluids of eyeball)

(24) Glucose 6-phosphata dehydrogennase deficiency

(25) Hemophilia (bleeder's disease)

(26) Hurler syndrome {dwarf stature, generalized disease of bone)

(27) Hypochromic anemia

(28) Hydrocephalus

(29) Hyprophosphatemia

(30) Hypoparathyroidism

(31) Hypoplasia of iris with glaucoma

(32) Ichthyosis (scale-like skin)

(33) Keratosis fllicularis (thickening of skin, loss of hair)

(34) Macular dystrophy

(35) Megalocornea (enlargement of cornea of eyeball)

(36) Menkes syndrome (retarded growth and brain degeneration)

(37) Mental, deficiency

(38) Microcornea (diminution of cornea of eyeball)

(39) Microphthalmia

(40) Mitral stenosis (stricture of bicuspid valve of heart)

(41) Myopia (short-sightedness)

(42) Nephrogenic diabetes insipidus

(43) Neurohypophyseal diabete Insipidus

(44) Night blindness

(45) Nomadism

(46) Nystagnius (rhythmical oscillation of eyeballs)

(47) Ooulo-cerebral-renal syndrome of Lowe (cataract Mental retardation)

(48) Opkthalmoplegia and myopia (drooping, of eyelids, absent patellar reflexes)

(49) Optic atrophy (wasting of eye)

(50) Parkinsonism

(51) Peroneal atrophy (wasting of muscles of legs)

(52) Progressive bulbar paralysis

(53) Progressive deafness

(54) Pseudoglioma (membrane formation back of lens)

(55) Pseudo-hypertrophic muscular dystrophy (weakening of muscles with growth of connective tissue in them)

(56) Retinal detachment

(57) Retinitis pigmentosa

(58) Spinal ataxia

(59) Spondylo-epiphyseal dysplasia (short stature, severe hip disease)

(60) Thromboasthenia (defect in the thrombin, fibrin, and blood platelet formation of the blood)

(61) Van den Bosch syndrome (mental deficiency skeletal deformity, absence of sweat glands)

(62) White occipital lock of hair

15. So much, then, for the conditions directly traceable to genetic factors. It should by this time be quite clear that **to commence life as a male is to start off with a handicap**—a handicap that operates at every stage of life, from conception on.

16. Even though Male-determining sperms are produced in the same numbers as female-determining sperms, **between 180 and 150 males are conceived as compared with 100 females**. Why this should be so we do not know, but it is a fact.

   a. The ratio at birth for American whites **is 106 males to 100 females.** (The ratios vary for different human groups, depending largely upon their socio-economic or nutritional status.)

   b. **In India** the sex ratio of boys is 98·7 to 100 girls. In other words the poorer the nutritional conditions, the greater the

286

lethality of the males; even fetal females are stronger than fetal males.

c. The records uniformly show that from fertilization on, the mortality rates before birth are higher for the male than for the female fetus and that males after birth continue to have a **higher mortality rate** than females for every year of age.

d. **Within every age range, more males die than females**. For example, in 1946-48 three boy babies in the first year of life died for every two girl babies.

e. At about the age of twenty-one, for every female who dies almost two males die.

f. Thereafter, **at the age of thirty-five**, 1,400 men die for every 1,000 women;

g. **at fifty-five** 1,800 men die for every 1,000 women; after that the difference in death rate diminishes, though it always remains in favor of the female.

17. **Life expectancy at birth is higher for women than for men all over the world** (except certain parts of India), and this fact holds true for females as compared with males for the greater part of the animal kingdom.

18. In the **United States in 1965 life expectancy** at birth for a white female was 74.1 years, and for a white male 67.4 years; for a nonwhite female 66.3 years, and for a non white male 61.1 years.

19. These facts constitute further evidence that **the female is constitutionally stronger than the male.** There have been some who have argued that women live longer than men because they don't usually work so hard. Most men, it is urged, work harder, work longer hours, and usually under greater strain and tension than most women. These statements are open to question. I am under the impression that most housewives work at least as hard as their husbands, and under at least as great a strain.

a. Male fetuses do not work harder than female fetuses in the womb, yet they die more frequently before birth than female fetuses.

b. Newborn males do not work harder than newborn females, yet they die more frequently than newborn girls.

c. One-year-old boys do not work harder than one-year-old girls, but the boys die more frequently than the girls. And so one can go on for every age, with the difference in mortality in favor of the female.

20. In 1957. Francis C. Madigan, working at the University of North Carolina, published a study on the longevity of Catholic Sisters and Brothers who for many years had been living much the same lands of lives. The same sort of disparity in their mortality rates was found to obtain as among the rest of the general population.

a. The data were obtained on nearly **30,000 Sisters and more than 10,000 Brothers.** The expectation, of Life at the age of fifty-four was found to be an additional 34 years for the Sisters, but only 28 years more for the Brothers, a difference in favor of the Sisters of 5% years.

b. When we compare the longevity rates of bachelors with jobs with those of spinsters with jobs, we find that the advantage is again with the females.

c. Spinsters with jobs live longer than bachelors with jobs. In 1947 the age-adjusted death rate for single men was one and one- half times that for married men, whereas among single women the death rate was only 10 percent higher than that for the married. It is an interesting fact that both among men and among women, the married have lower death rates than the single, widowed, or divorced.

d. A 14-nation study of the working mother conducted under the auspices of UNESCO and published in 1967 showed that women in general work longer hours and have less leisure time than men.

e. As Professor Alexander Szalai, the project director, put it, "To summarize our "More precisely, both categories of women— the working and the non-working are at a disadvantage compared with men.

f. The working women because they are over- burdened with work.

g. The non-working women because their labors are underestimated and their existence is much more drab than that of the men.

h. **" Women are healthier than men—if by health one means the capacity to deal with germs and illness.** Statistics from the public health services of various countries, and especially the United States, show that while after the age of fifteen the sickness rate is higher among females than among males, females recover from illnesses much more frequently than males do.

i. Death from almost all causes are more frequent in males at all ages.

j. Almost the only disorders from which women die more frequently than men are those subserving the functional systems of reproduction; namely, the reproductive tract and the endocrine glandular system.

k. **Epilepsy** has about the same incidence in both sexes, but according to the vital statistics of the Bureau of the Census the death rate from epilepsy is about 30 percent higher for men than for women.

l. For every female **stutterer** there are five male stutterers. The "stutter-type personality," who is characterized by a certain jerkiness or "stutter" of movements, as well as of speech, occurs in the ratio of eight males to one female.

m. Word **deafness,** the inherited inability to understand the meaning of sounds, occurs very much more frequently in the male than in the female, and so do baldness, gout, and ulcers of the stomach. Need one go on?

21. The evidence is clear: From the constitutional standpoint woman is the stronger sex.

22. The explanation of **the greater constitutional strength of the female lies largely, if not entirely, in her possession of two complete X-chromosome** and the male's possession of only one.

23. This may not be the whole explanation of the physical constitutional superiority of the female, but it is certainly scientifically the most acceptable explanation and the one least open to question.

24. To the unbiased student of the facts there can no longer remain any doubt of the **constitutional superiority of the female.**

25. At the present time the insurance companies charge the same insurance rates for women as for men. This hardly seems fair to women. But then when has anyone ever been fair to women. The occasions have been the exceptions.

26. Man has projected his own weaknesses upon her and as the "muscle man" has maintained the myth of feminine weakness until the present day.

27. But it is not woman who is weak; it is man, and in more senses than one.

28. But the last thing on earth we want to do is to give the male a feeling of inferiority.

29. On the other hand, we consider it a wise thing for a man to be aware of his limitations and his weaknesses, for being aware of them; he may learn how to make himself strong.

30. The truth about the sexes will not only serve to set women free, it will also serve to set men free; for if women have been the slaves of men, men have been the slaves of their own prejudices concerning women, and this has worked no good to anyone.

---

*   Montagu, Ashley. (1952). *The Natural Superiority of Women.* New York: Collier Books (pp. 75-90).

INDEX

ABOUT THE AUTHOR

Herbert Henry Robinson III, Ph. D. (www.herb-robinson.com), a licensed psychotherapist, is the director of Tapio Counseling at Spokane, Washington, a National Board Certified Counselor, and a Certified Perpetrator Treatment Program Supervisor, a researcher, writer, lecturer, and consultant. He maintains general psychotherapy practice serving individuals, families, and court-mandated men arrested for domestic violence.

Printed in the United States
37710LVS00004BA/3